"Other Sheep I Have"

Father Paul Washington in the courtyard of the Church of the Advocate, June, 1980. (*Philadelphia Evening Bulletin*, Urban Archives, Temple University Libraries)

"Other Sheep I Have"
The Autobiography of
Father Paul M. Washington

with

David McI. Gracie

Afterword by

Barbara Harris

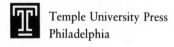
Temple University Press
Philadelphia

Temple University Press, Philadelphia 19122

The paper used in this publication meets the mimum requirements of American
National Standard for Information Sciences—Permanence of Paper for Printed
Library Materials, ANSI Z39.48-1984 ⊗

Library of Congress Cataloging-in-Publication Data
Washington, Paul M., 1921–
    "Other sheep I have" : the autobiography of Father Paul M.
Washington / with David McI. Gracie ; afterword by Barbara Harris.
        p. cm.
    Includes bibliographical references and index.
    ISBN 1–56639–177–6 (alk. paper). — ISBN 1–56639–178–4 (pbk.)
    1. Washington, Paul M., 1921–   . 2. Priests—Pennsylvania—
Philadelphia—Biography. 3. Episcopal Church—Pennsylvania—
Philadelphia—Biography. 4. Church of the Advocate (Philadelphia,
Pa.)—History—20th century. 5. Philadelphia (Pa.)—Church
history—20th century. 6. Pennsylvania—Church history—20th
century. 7. Race relations—Religious aspects—Episcopal Church.
8. Philadelphia (Pa.)—Race relations. I. Gracie, David McI.,
1932–   . II. Title.
BX5995.W3475A3 1994
283'.092—dc20
[B]   93–34730

Publication of this book has been assisted by a grant from The William Penn
Foundation.

And other sheep I have, which are not of this fold; them also I must bring, and they shall hear my voice; and there shall be one fold, and one shepherd. (John 10:16)

Contents

Preface

This is the story of Father Paul Washington and his twenty-five years as rector of the Episcopal Church of the Advocate in North Philadelphia. Many of Paul's friends have encouraged him to write about his role in the tempestuous times we have lived through together in Philadelphia, but I *required* him to do it. His story has personal significance for many Philadelphians, and historical significance for any who care about the future of our cities, and the role of the urban church in shaping that future.

During Paul's tenure, the Church of the Advocate became a gathering place and a place of shelter for the Black Power movement, the Black Panther Party, the Black Economic Development Conference, and numerous other groups that rose up in Philadelphia to challenge racial and social injustice. Paul saw himself—and to this day is regarded by many—as the shepherd of a very diverse flock of men and women who have struggled to convert themselves and our society from racism and sexism, taking action on the city streets, in the churches, and in the halls of government. Within the Episcopal Church, the Advocate gained both fame and notoriety as the site of the ordination of the first women priests in the United States; and it was from the Advocate congregation that an African American named Barbara Harris was called to become the first woman bishop in the history of the worldwide Anglican Communion.

The autobiography begins in Charleston, South Carolina, with Paul Washington's mother marking him for the ministry before his birth. It culminates with his sermon in Boston, Massachusetts, at the consecration of Bishop Barbara Harris, an event that he regarded as a new birth of ministry for the whole church. But the heart of the action is in North Philadelphia, at the corner of 18th and Diamond Streets, where for a quarter of a century Paul Washington labored to create a new understanding of what it means to be a church that serves the people of our cities.

When the Philadelphia Divinity School conferred upon Paul Washington the degree of doctor of divinity in 1970, they hailed him "disturbing prophet and healing priest." Like many other citizens of Philadelphia and members of the Episcopal Church throughout the country, I have felt that disturbing and healing power. It has been my privilege to know and work with Paul and Christine Washington, his wife, in the Episcopal Diocese of Pennsylvania since 1967. I was convinced that their story and the story of the Church of the Advocate needed to be told, as a matter of pride for the City of Philadelphia, and for the health of the whole church.

I salute Father Paul for his honesty about himself and his personal struggles, and his willingness to tell it like it is about the rest of us. Paul once said to me that he didn't know whether he loved God most or feared him most but he knew that he felt both fear *and* love toward him. "So if I have to offend *you* to please *God*, I'll do it," he added. "That is what kept me open—wanting to be on good terms with God."

As you read this autobiography, if you feel offended in any way, remember that it has been written with God's judgment, not yours or mine, in view.

David McI. Gracie
Philadelphia

Introduction | David McI. Gracie

To understand Fr. Washington, it is important to know something about the city in which he has carried out most of his active ministry. I offer my own early impressions of Philadelphia to provide a background for the reader, who should be aware that for the most part they are subjective impressions, although they allow me to identify some objectively real people and events.

From words about our city, I proceed to offer my own thoughts about the motivations and inner drive of the man whose story this is. I conclude with two real-life parables, which perhaps capture the flavor of the priest and his ministry better than my ruminations, however well founded they may be in the long years of our collaboration on many causes and in the production of this book.

City of Brotherly Love

In August, 1967, when I came with my family to live in Philadelphia, the smell of burning was still in the air of my hometown, Detroit, Michigan. We did not leave Detroit because of the racial uprising of that summer, but it marked our passage indelibly. St. Joseph's Episcopal Church, where I had been the pastor, was very close to the area where the disturbances began, so our parishioners and my young family had lived through the fear of those days of rioting in the streets, police repression, and military occupation. We went to bed at night choking on the smoke from the nearby neighborhoods that were aflame.

For those of us who thought in Biblical terms, the long, hot summers of the late 1960s spoke of God's judgment on us all for the years of racial discrimination and America's denial of hope to the poor. Coming to Philadelphia to work on the staff of Bishop Robert L. DeWitt, I believed the church had a role to play in interpreting these events and in mobilizing support for the civil rights movement, with its promise of a better day. I could not help but wonder in what form the judgment on Detroit might reappear, striking the city that was our new home. Would there be a similar shaking of the foundations here? The ingredients were all present, as I discovered in my first survey of civic life in Philadelphia. I found the familiar, unresolved tension between heightened demands for racial justice and "law and order" resistance to change: on the one side anger mixed with hope, on the other racism with fear. Yet this city would hold itself together as Detroit could not. What made the difference?

I had come too late to town to experience the period of governmental reform under Mayors Joseph Clark and Richardson Dilworth, a reform begun after World War II that had included passage of the Fair Employment Practices Ordinance, establishment of the Commission on Human Relations, the appointment of enlightened leaders in the police department, and forward strides in public health. I could see the physical transformation of the city that had taken place in those good government years. It was evident especially in downtown Philadelphia and in the renewed homes of Society Hill. This famed urban renewal had had its downside, however, in the displacement of many poor black families. No, all had not been golden in the golden era, which I was told had come to an end when Richardson Dilworth resigned as mayor to run unsuccessfully for governor of Pennsylvania in 1962.

I arrived only in time for the race for reelection of Mayor James H. J. Tate, Dilworth's successor and a politician in an older mold. Tate won the race by only 11,000 votes, against Republican candidate Arlen Specter (now U.S. senator from Pennsylvania). What made the difference for the incumbent mayor was the law and order reputation of his commissioner of police, Frank Rizzo. White voters were led to believe by the mayor and by Walter Annenberg's *Philadelphia Inquirer* that it was the firm and sometimes brutal hand of Rizzo that was saving the City of Brotherly Love from the looting and burning they saw on their TV screens in places like Watts and Detroit. Rizzo's tough cop image won reelection for Tate and would eventually lead "the cop who would be king" (the perceptive title of a Rizzo biography by Peter Binzen) to the mayoralty himself for two successive terms.

The reforming zeal of the earlier years lived on in citizen campaigns on issues like raising the piteously low state welfare grants, and organizing a citizens' review board to curb the notorious police brutality. Efforts to improve race relations and wipe out discriminatory practices were made by strong leaders of the Human Relations Commission and private institutions like The Fellowship Commission and Fellowship House. But what most caught my attention was the crusade for educational reform in the city schools.

The Philadelphia Board of Education was chaired by former mayor Richardson Dilworth, who was one of the most impressive civic leaders I have ever met. "D'Artagnan in long pants and a double-breasted suit," Dilworth's old friend Joe Clark called him. He and Clark, then a U.S. Congressman from Philadelphia, represented a breed I had known little of before—patricians dedicated to the well-being of their city. Dilworth's school board meetings were a welcome surprise. Televised by the local public TV station, they were run in a way that allowed citizens of Philadelphia to make themselves heard. There was more democracy at these meetings than in any meeting of the Philadelphia City Council that I attended. Dilworth and his superintendent of schools, Mark Shedd, were trying to build broad public support for curriculum reform, better pay for teachers, and more adequate budgets for a school system that had been allowed to decay.

On November 17, 1967, the two tendencies in Philadelphia civic life that were becoming so clear to me—one toward reform, the other toward repression—collided when Police Commissioner Rizzo ordered a police billy club charge against black high school students demonstrating in front of the offices of the Board of Education. This brutal attack sent out shock waves that would affect the politics of the city for years to come, adding greatly to racial polarization. And yet, the center held; the city did not erupt.

On April 4, 1968, when Dr. Martin Luther King, Jr., was assassinated, Washington, D.C., and other urban centers experienced riot and rebellion. In Philadelphia, where Dr. King had visited only recently to mobilize support for the Poor People's March on Washington, the pain of his loss was felt as deeply as anywhere else in the nation. Thousands marched and gathered for prayer and speech making, but people did not lash out at each other or tear at the fabric of their own communities. Singing gospel hymns in the overflowing balcony of a historic black church, I marveled that my adopted city was not in flames. I wondered at the patience, the endurance, and the hope of my new neighbors and fellow citizens. "Will the anchor hold in the storm of life?" asks an old Baptist hymn; I knew where the anchor was holding on that day. It was not in the law and order reaction of Mayor Tate and Commissioner Rizzo, banning gatherings of twelve or more on the streets of the city. This move, which in fact appeared unconstitutional, was simply ludicrous when seen against the background of the discipline of black Philadelphians.

Philadelphia has certainly known civil disturbances. Newspapers reported "race riots" during World War II, and as recently as the summer of 1964, $3 million worth of damage was done in North Philadelphia, where one life was lost and several were injured in the rioting and looting of stores following an arrest incident blown wildly out of proportion by rumors. Nor has the city been free from other manifestations of violence and rage. Far from it. Yet in the time that I have lived here, there has been a capacity to recover from the brink, to maintain some level of communication between different segments of society, to regroup and try once again, that has kept alive the vision of a city existing for all its residents.

In September, 1970, when Commissioner Rizzo staged armed raids on the Black Panther offices in Philadelphia following the killing of a Philadelphia park policeman, there was reason to fear the worst. A national convention sponsored by the Black Panther Party was about to take place in Philadelphia, and local Panther leaders, falsely accused and arrested, were being held in prison for extremely high bail. (News photos of young Black Panthers stripped of their clothes on the street at police gunpoint went around the world.) Yet black and white citizens of Philadelphia rallied to bail Panther leaders out of jail, to find adequate meeting space for the thousands who came to the convention, and to put legal restraints on further police raids.

In August, 1980, when a white policeman shot and killed a black Philadelphian named William Green, the conditions for riot once again heated up. In the tension on the city streets, fifteen people were injured in various incidents, but no one was killed and the peace was soon restored. Neal R. Peirce and Jerry Hagstrom, in *The Book of America*, found the reason to lie "in the strength and political importance of the black community and the mainstream black political leadership . . . who convinced young demonstrators not to turn the confrontation with the police into a riot."[1] The book notes that "the same week, racial tension in Miami resulted in 18 dead and 400 injured."

Citizenship is of the essence here. In my city of Detroit, which erupted in bloody rioting in 1943 and in 1967—the second time in ways from which the city will never fully recover—many of the inhabitants were people simply passing through. In Philadelphia, this "city of neighborhoods," many ethnic groups have long histories that bind them to a location. Neighborhood racial segregation is the rule, with poverty concentrated in large black sections like North Philadelphia and wealth in all-white Chestnut Hill and the white suburbs. But there are some lively exceptions, like the racially mixed Germantown and Mount Airy neighborhoods; and white flight to the suburbs was nothing like what I had known in Detroit—certainly nothing like the panicked exodus that followed the 1967 uprising.

Most important in such considerations is the long history and deep-rootedness of black neighborhoods and institutions in Philadelphia. Among those who have recounted the early history of black Philadelphia is W. E. B. Du Bois, who in 1899 gave us his classic sociological study, *The Philadelphia Negro*. Du Bois ended his book with an appeal to white and black Philadelphians to act so as to "realize what the great founder of the city meant when he named it the City of Brotherly Love."[2]

A new edition of Du Bois's book, published during my first year in Philadelphia, has remained one of my resources. Du Bois's account of earlier black religious institutions and self-help organizations prepares one to understand how a project like the Rev. Leon Sullivan's Opportunities Industrialization Council might be expected to flourish here. Alongside Rev. Sullivan, whose OIC became the best-known job training and placement program in the country in the 1960s, other black professionals were making their presence felt in civic life. The Rev. Henry Nichols was vice-chair of the activist school board, while Gratz High School principal Marcus Foster would win the Philadelphia Award in 1969 for his educational leadership in the inner city. Sadie Alexander was the dynamic leader of the Human Relations Commission. These and others in relatively high positions were using their status as a base from which to struggle for change and to keep the peace. Rev. Sullivan used his strong church base at Zion Baptist to organize black pastors to carry out effective consumer boycotts of companies that failed to hire or promote black workers. Attorney Raymond Pace Alexander applied his legal skills in winning the U.S. Supreme Court decision desegregating Girard College.

Grass-roots activism found expression in organizations like the Congress of Racial Equality, led by Bill Mathis, with both black and white participation in its direct action campaigns. Best known and most broadly represented in black neighborhoods when the cry for justice was heard was the National Association for the Advancement of Colored People (NAACP) and its charismatic leader, Cecil B. Moore. Moore led the protest marches against the exclusion of black children from Girard College, a school for orphaned white boys, situated in the heart of black North Philadelphia. The "CP" of NAACP was often translated "Cecil's People"—a sign of the esteem for this popular criminal lawyer, known for his white suits and big cigars, his profanity, and his neverending commitment to civil rights.

That some white Philadelphians shared William Penn's founding vision is worth noting in any calculus of what makes for peace in this town. In 1967, Dilworth openly condemned the action of the Philadelphia police in attacking the demonstrating school children, white church leaders also spoke out, and new organizations were formed to combat racism. In 1968, the racially integrated American Civil Liberties Union (ACLU) and the white antiracist group People for Human Rights challenged the "limited emergency proclamation" of Mayor Tate. In 1970, the Yearly Meeting of the Society of Friends put up property bail for the release of imprisoned Black Panther leaders. Robert Landis, chairman of the Philadelphia Bar Association, helped obtain use of the gymnasium at Temple University to house the events of the Black Panther convention, and federal judge John Fullam enjoined the Philadelphia police from actions that would further inflame the city. The legal action had been organized at an emergency meeting held at the headquarters of the Episcopal Diocese of Pennsylvania.

In this company of citizens who could agitate for justice while holding to brotherly love were the white bishop I had come to town to serve and the black priest in whom he placed his trust. Bishop DeWitt's strategy for urban ministry centered on the Church of the Advocate, so he wasted little time in introducing me, his new urban missioner, to Fr. Paul Washington. Only a few years earlier, the bishop himself had come from Detroit, where I had known him. He, too, was seeking a city with foundations. He had the good sense to recognize that the rector of the Church of the Advocate, that great gothic stone pile in the midst of North Philadelphia, had been a major force for unity, as he would continue to be in those divisive days.

Pastor to the Other Sheep

One ever feels his twoness—an American, a Negro; two souls, two thoughts, two unreconciled strivings; two warring ideals in one dark body, whose dogged strength alone keeps it from being torn asunder.[3]

Just as W. E. B. Du Bois helps me understand Paul Washington's city, I find that these words from his *The Souls of Black Folk* provide a key to understanding Fr. Washington himself. My own sense of loss because of the tearing asunder of the fabric of my hometown makes me value very highly those lives that can endure tension without splitting apart, and those people who have the dogged spiritual strength that can hold a community together.

Paul Washington is very frank about the "warring ideals in [his] one dark body." Black priest in a predominantly white denomination, he has directly challenged the prejudices and power imbalances of the Episcopal Church, U.S.A. For twenty-five years (from 1962 to 1987), that religious body relied upon him to carry out its ministry and mission in a poor, inner-city neighborhood, to be a sign that the Episcopal Church was capable of overcoming its race and class biases in serving as a church for all people. Yet how many in the Episcopal Church understood the nature of the man to whom they assigned this noble role?

Was this black priest what most white churchmen wanted him to be—a reconciler, a moderating influence on a community that seemed on the verge of revolt, and a trusted interpreter of the meaning of the social turbulence to members of the white establishment? Or was he himself an agent of revolt, adept at using the established Episcopal Church as a cover and a shelter for movements of black liberation that otherwise might be isolated and stifled? The truth is that he was both; and these two roles at times caused stress not only within the Episcopal Church but also within Paul Washington himself. However, the issue that brought him into the most direct confrontation with his church, and that carried the greatest threat (as he perceived it) to his own position in the church, had to do with women's demands for equal treatment.

It was at the Church of the Advocate in North Philadelphia that the first women were ordained priests, in a service opposed by the highest authorities in the Episcopal Church and watched by people around the world. The ordination took place on July 29, 1974—"that awful day," as Paul called it, "when we were disobedient to the church and obedient to God." Barbara Harris, a parishioner of the Advocate and protégé of Fr. Washington, carried the cross in leading the procession. She would later become the first woman bishop in the Episcopal Church and the worldwide Anglican Communion.

Preaching at the service in Boston where Barbara Harris was consecrated as bishop, on February 11, 1989, before a congregation of 8,000, Fr. Washington said: "We cannot and we must not overlook the fact that this woman who is being consecrated today is not just an American woman. She is a black woman. Called at one time Negro. Called at one time colored." He held her "twoness" before the congregation at the very moment when—if I, a white, may be so bold as to make this judgment—he broke through the boundary of twoness himself and achieved the goal Du Bois described in *The Souls of Black Folk:*

> The history of the American Negro is the history of this strife,— this longing to attain self-conscious manhood, to merge his double self into a better and truer self. In this merging he wishes neither of the older selves to be lost. He would not Africanize America, for America has too much to teach the world and Africa. He would not bleach his Negro soul in a flood of white Americanism, for he knows that Negro blood has a message for the world. He simply wishes to make it possible for a man to be both a Negro and an American, without being cursed and spit upon by his fellows, without having the doors of opportunity closed roughly in his face.[4]

When telling his own story, Paul Washington uses the "twoness" text from Du Bois to describe the warring ideals within his own body, not in the context of his ambivalent relationship with his church but in his relationship to the two tendencies within the black struggle for liberation, as represented by the lives and teachings of Martin Luther King, Jr., and Malcolm X. In 1970, Paul Washington had to decide whether, as a Christian minister who had preached and practiced Martin Luther King's ethic of nonviolence, he could invite the Black Panther Party into his church.

With their rhetoric of "Off the pig!" and their stated willingness to use guns in self-defense, were they not opposed to what he and King stood for? Typically—and in this regard he is very much an Anglican—Paul answered this question in a way that avoided an either/or.

"I felt in tune with Martin on the one hand, and with Malcolm and the Panthers on the other. For me it became not a matter of one or the other, but within my 'one dark body' the two represented what for me was wholeness."

Another dividing line of potentially warring ideals was class. Paul and Christine Washington, an educated, refined minister and his wife, had moved into North Philadelphia in 1962 to live next door to their church in a neighborhood that the then Philadelphia police commissioner called "the Jungle" because of its crime and gang activity. Paul lived and worked there but shuttled back and forth to the affluent suburbs of the Main Line and to Chestnut Hill, where he became a speaker much in demand, called upon to interpret inner-city conditions to suburban church members. He chastened them for their indifference, while accepting some as members of his own North Philadelphia flock, where well-to-do professional people from Bryn Mawr worshiped side by side with poor and middle-class blacks.

Related to the class divide, though not identical with it, was the line that separated the "establishment" from the "movement." Fr. Washington became a part of the establishment of the City of Philadelphia and of the Episcopal Church, serving on the Human Relations Commission of the city, as a member of the Executive Council of the Episcopal Church, U.S.A., and taking part in political campaigns that would eventually yield black elected leaders, even in the office of mayor. He tried at all times to put his acceptability to "insiders" to work on behalf of the outsiders—the grassroots movements for justice, to which he also belonged. "Father Washington was our legitimizer," said one community activist. Even so, on occasion he was regarded by both sides with suspicion.

And then the day came when Paul Washington, like all other

Philadelphians, could only watch helplessly the fatal clash between the members of the organization MOVE, who appeared to be the ultimate outsiders, and the City of Philadelphia, led for the first time by a mayor who was black and who had risen from poverty. When on May 13, 1985, the forces of law and order bombed and burned to death eleven men, women, and children in a residential neighborhood in West Philadelphia, even Fr. Washington, who is expected to bring the prophetic word to situations of community strife, could not find words. In the aftermath, reclaiming his role in bridging the political chasm between insider and outsider, he accepted Mayor Goode's appointment as a member of the commission to investigate the tragic events of May 13. At the same time, he became an advocate for the parole of Ramona Africa, the only adult survivor of the fire on Osage Avenue and (incredibly) the only person imprisoned as a result of the confrontation.

I believe that Paul Washington's life is an example of how from the "twoness" enforced upon black Americans there can come a creative drive toward unity that enriches us all. For the historic service of ordination of women to the priesthood at the Church of the Advocate, the women of the church prepared an altar frontal on which was sewn this paraphrase of St. Paul's words to the Galatians: "There is neither Jew nor Greek, black nor white, male nor female; we are one in Christ." The Episcopal Church and the City of Philadelphia have seen Father Paul and his ministry at the Advocate as a symbol of and a force for unity.

One who unifies must first see and feel the divisions within society. Paul has seen them and has felt their pain, entering easily into alliance with many of the groups of people who were separated from the mainstream. At an award night in 1985, at which it seemed the whole city had turned out to pay tribute to his love and pastoral care, Paul rather surprisingly spoke of the anger within himself, and of how—regarding this anger as a moral failing—he had asked God to take it away. God had told him, said Paul, that instead of removing it, he would show Paul how to use it for others by making him sensitive to the injustices they suffered.

From the time he arrived at the Advocate, Paul Washington reached the "other sheep," those outside the church and its assumed respectability, and those outside the political mainstream. Why was he so able to receive them, to "call them each by name"?—as St. John wrote about Jesus the Good Shepherd. It was because he as a black American was always one of the outsiders himself, and he knew that; but the anger occasioned by his own experiences of exclusion and rejection on the basis of race was transmuted—he would say, "by the grace of God"—into an ability to include many.

Tales from Two Cities

Fr. Paul Washington remains active in church and community to this day. There are more stories that could be told than appear in this book, but two certainly deserve the telling, because they are parables of the life and ministry about which I have tried to provide some hints. The first was told to me by Thomas Paine Cronin, president of AFSCME District Council 47, a union of Philadelphia municipal employees. Tom Cronin was a participant along with Paul in the demonstration for the homeless in the spring of 1990, which led to their arrest, as Cronin describes.

"Arrested for disorderly conduct, after sitting down on the pavement together at City Hall, we were piled into a police wagon to be taken to the 'Roundhouse' [police headquarters at 8th and Race] to be booked. It was a very hot day, and the first thing we noticed was that the ventilator on top of the wagon was not working. They kept piling people in until we were simply jammed up against each other. Some of us pounded on the side of the van. We gesticulated to the police through a plexiglass window. They were laughing at us. For half an hour we sat there and couldn't help the panic coming on. We worried most about one of our number who was ill—a person with AIDS. Father Washington looked frail, too; he was obviously struggling to breathe.

"Then the van started up with a great lurch. At every stop, the police driver slammed on the brakes, forcing us to bang against each other. We knew our destination and understood the arrest process, so when we arrived we expected to be let out immediately. That was not to be. It was another fifteen minutes in the van (about an hour, all told) before anyone opened the back doors. When they did, our friend with AIDS, who was jammed up against those doors, simply dropped out. A policeman stuck his head in the opening and said: 'We understand Father Paul Washington is in there. He can come out.' 'Not until everybody comes out,' said Paul. Then we were all released."[5]

The second story takes us from Philadelphia to Jerusalem—the key city in God's urban strategy. Jane Power, a participant with Paul in an interfaith peace demonstration in 1989, captures the essence of the man and his special ministry in a locale far from 18th and Diamond Streets. Inside the Old City of Jerusalem, she writes, tension mounted when the military authorities blocked passage through the Old City's gates.

"For the first time, I saw the Damascus Gate closed. Or nearly closed. A passage wide enough for one person remained, and in that passage stood a soldier, keeping most Palestinians in, letting some others leave, one by one. An old woman wanted to leave with her groceries. No. A father with small children hanging on to them. No.

"From our group, Rev. Paul Washington of Philadelphia stepped forward and with consummate dignity and a formidable baritone voice requested that his group be allowed to pass. The soldier gave way, allowing Rev. Washington to stand in the gateway like a shepherd, summoning his flock. Four among us were Palestinians; those who were not held hands, linked arms with them, and all of us came through."[6]

1. Offered to God

The key decision was made for me before I was born. My mother had made a bargain with God. She prayed, "If you will just give me a son, I will dedicate him to your service." My sister had been born in 1918, and while my mother and father were happy to have a healthy, beautiful daughter, they wanted a son, too. Six months went by in 1920, and my mother had still not conceived. It was then that she made her prayer.

When I was born in Charleston, South Carolina, on May 26, 1921, my course had already been carefully set for me by my mother. As I grew into awareness, I learned that I was to be a minister. I was expected to join the church and to be working at a part-time job by the age of ten. Then when I grew up, I was to go to college. My mother named me Paul because she so admired the courage and the eloquence of the Apostle Paul. She had dedicated me to God's service.

Even before I was ten years old, my mother got me a job with a friend of hers named Saxton Wilson, a printer. At about the same time, she took me to Memorial Baptist Church to the revival meeting and sat me down on the mourners' bench. There I found myself deeply moved, emotionally shaken by the preaching of an evangelist called Rev. Rickenbacker. I cried almost hysterically, and I remember people crowding around me and saying, "He's got the Spirit. He's been converted." When I regained my composure, I stood before the congregation and said, "Reverend White and members of Memorial Baptist Church, I feel that I am converted and I would like to be baptized and become a member of Memorial Baptist Church." That was my decision for Jesus.

For all my early experience in the Baptist Church, I could never see myself as a fiery preacher like Rev. Rickenbacker. It would not be until my college days at Lincoln University that I would enter the Episcopal Church, the church in which I felt that I could fulfill my mother's vow. I knew vaguely of the Episcopal Church in my growing up, but it did not seem to be a place for people like us, who lived "up d' road." Our family had class, but not the right kind to fit the image of Negro Episcopalians in Charleston.

An incident that illustrates the very real class structure among Charleston Negroes occurred in my high school years. The public high school taught classes only through the eleventh grade, so college-bound Negroes enrolled in either the Roman Catholic high school or Avery Institute (a combined high school and teacher's college). I enrolled at Avery, where I found that Mr. Cox, the principal, looked down upon me. One day when I was with Robert Morrison, a classmate and friend of mine, Mr. Cox approached us and said, "Morrison, you should not be playing with Washington. He is not our kind." To Robert's credit, he told the principal that he liked me and we were friends. At this, Mr. Cox turned to me and said, "Washington, you do not belong here at Avery. I don't want you in my school."

When I told my aunts, with whom I was then living, about the incident, they said I did not have to go to Avery and promptly enrolled me at Immaculate Conception High School. But a week later, Mr. Cox came by, telling my aunts that I had misunderstood him and that he wanted me back. I returned to Avery, which was by far the superior school. My aunts were schoolteachers themselves, and my mother a school librarian, but we were judged not to have the right family background, nor did we live in the right section of the Negro community.

The neighborhood where I grew up was, in fact, something of an anomaly. It was racially mixed—poor whites living alongside black working people. We got along well with our neighbors. Black and white youngsters played together. Our white playmates ate in our homes, and, although we were never invited to eat with them, we knew they did not eat as well as we did. Yet, in spite of these daily interactions, every Sunday evening on our block there would be a "race war."

The white boys at one end of First Street would gather bricks and stones, and at the other end of our little unpaved block, the colored boys would do the same—all in full view of each other. Then as the darkness descended, we would begin saturating the air above us with missiles directed toward each other. One evening one of their bricks landed squarely on the left side of my head, smashing into my skull and knocking me unconscious for about fifteen minutes. When I regained consciousness, my "soldiers" helped me to my feet to lead me home. Leon said, "Paul, your daddy is going to beat you when he comes home from church. Your head broke."

Part of my skull was visibly fractured, yet I felt no pain. We sat in the house waiting for Daddy to come home. He would be angry because I had been in a street fight. When he walked in, I showed him my skull. To my shock and to the relief of us all, he simply said, "Son, I'm going to have to take you to the hospital." We went there on the trolley, and I had neurosurgery the next morning. I will carry the stigma of that experience to the grave. But all these people were a part of the extended family to which I belonged. In Charleston, I knew whites as family just as I knew them as foe.

Certain lessons of class and race were taught early in life. In the South, Negro children had to learn early about white people. We learned that they had a need to believe they were superior to colored people. Regardless of what they said or did, we were always supposed to cause them to feel "white is right." When my friends Milton, Louise, and Johnnie stopped coming to our house and we could no longer go to theirs, I questioned my mother about this change. She answered matter of factly, "They are white, and white people think that they are better than colored people, and they are afraid that if they associate with us they will no longer be seen as being better." She did not elaborate any further.

What I find so interesting as I look back upon those years is that my mother never felt the need to assure me that, in spite of how much the white man tried to make us feel inferior, we had worth. But everything about her said that we were somebody. One day she made this very clear to a white insurance agent who regularly came to our home to collect the fifteen-cent premium. While sitting on the sofa in our living room, he made the mistake of putting his feet up on the coffee table.

My mother exploded: "Get your feet off my table, get out of my house, and never come here again!" I was petrified. But he quickly got up, closed his book, and left, without collecting the money. Mother said nothing to me about the incident, but I learned a few things from that dramatic event. I had seen a white man put in his place by a Negro woman. But I also learned that "freedom ain't free." From that day on, I had to go downtown to the insurance office to pay that fifteen-cent premium. And even as young as I was, I somehow knew that my father, a Negro man, would have paid dearly for insulting a white man.

Later in my younger years, I had experiences that would reveal a totally different attitude about race. My mother's oldest sister, Claudia, a schoolteacher, was part of a group of about a dozen who formed an ad hoc welfare agency to help people who were poor. This group was racially mixed. It included well-to-do whites and a Negro concert pianist, Mr. Johnnie Moore, who was the most sought-after piano teacher in Charleston. At this time, I was living with my two aunts and would occasionally have to visit some of the whites to pick up the donations they were providing. I remember helping the group at Christmas as they fed two or three hundred people at the Charleston Boys Club.

In this group, whites and colored met together periodically. I was somewhat disoriented to hear rich white people call colored men and women Miss or Mister. There in the Deep South, where racism had directly or indirectly infected us all, some people seemed to have matured and risen above race, color, and class, to that image wherein we are created. They related to others as living souls.

I never knew a grandmother, but right next door to us on First Street lived "Na," a woman in her sixties, who took the part of a grandmother for us and connected us to "the country," from which she had moved. Na always wore ankle-length dresses; she chewed tobacco, used snuff, and smoked a corncob pipe. She papered her walls every spring with the colorful "funny papers," and every fall she restuffed her mattress with dried "corn shucks."

Na had lived in an isolated, secluded area where people were still in touch with the beliefs, customs, and traditions of their African forebears. She was a gripping storyteller, telling me and my sister tales about the "root doctor," who could concoct medicines from various roots that were far more effective than anything the city doctors could prescribe. But he could do even more. With a single strand of hair from a person, he could make that person love you or he could cause that person to suffer harm.

Na's people could find out truths by "turning the Bible." A person would balance the Bible on a large brass key to find out who had stolen money, for instance. Everyone's name in the community would be called out, until the calling of the thief's name would cause the Bible to flip from the key. But one of the most tragic customs of the people from the country was that of "putting bad mouth" on a person who had maliciously done someone wrong. The custom was usually carried out by an elderly man or woman, who would say, "For the rest of your life, you will always be cursed." I knew a man who had been "badmouthed." He lived under that curse, and his life was indeed wretched.

Working as a domestic and a washerwoman, Na would do a week's wash for a family for seventy-five cents. I often went with her to deliver the laundry, holding one handle of the large, oval wicker basket while she held the other. When Na cooked for the "bukrah" (white folks), she always spat in "the bukrah widdis" (the white folks' victuals). (This memory came back to me when I saw Kizzi in the TV serial "Roots" spit into the dipper of water she brought to the white girl from whose grace she had fallen although they had been childhood playmates.)

Even though Na was older than my parents, she always addressed them as Mr. Tom and Miss Mayme. We loved her dearly and always looked forward to being allowed to sleep with her overnight on her corn shucks mattress. But Na lost her house when we finally got water and sewer lines on our street. She could not afford to pay the price of modernization and went back to the country.

My father, whom I deeply loved and respected, taught me many things. He showed me how to build things with my hands, letting me "work" alongside him as he added three rooms to our four-room house. He showed me how to walk through life befriending almost everyone, especially those "on the outside." But, inadvertently, he also taught me how to be tough and unyielding.

Daddy whipped me only twice in my life, and both times I thought I would die in the process—once after I stole something from the corner store, the other after I was impudent to my aunt in her class in school. Both times he spoke to me very quietly, showing absolutely no anger, but deep pain. He told me that "to sow an act is to reap a habit," and that he had to nip these acts in the bud.

During the whipping after the theft from the corner store, my father was determined to make me confess that I had done it. As he whipped me, he continued to ask, "Did you do it?" Each time I answered, "NO!" At one point, I was certain that I would die in misery, but at that point it was no longer a question of telling the truth; for me, it was something else. I was proving that there is no person nor any power that can change one's mind or will. These are inviolate and are broken only when one fears the worst, whatever the worst is. I proved that even the threat of death cannot in itself change one's will. I will say to anyone, "Don't tell me that you had to do it, or you had no choice." To such arguments, I answer, "You could choose to die."

In spite of these two severe beatings, I loved my father and greatly enjoyed his company. He was already forty years of age when I was born, but we had some great experiences together. Every Saturday he would take my hand to go to the colored theater to see cowboy pictures. Every year we went to the circus together. But what I enjoyed most was our visits to the city dump.

We each started with an empty bag, and as we waded through acres and acres of trash, he would retrieve the things that he wanted and I the things that I wanted. It was like going to a mammoth rummage sale. There I learned that "one man's trash is another man's treasure." (Incidentally, I still pick things out of other people's trash.)

My father was a hardworking man, a blacksmith, who worked with red-hot iron, a sledge hammer, and tongs for five and a half days a week. His hands were hard as leather, the palms cracked at the lines. Every Saturday he placed his paycheck on the bureau and my mother would dispense it, including his carfare. I remember how proud he was the day he first received a paycheck for $12.50 a week. Daddy was a superb cook and always cooked Sunday dinners—Christmas and Easter dinners, too. We were always pleased when he brought home a raccoon, a possum, or a rabbit that he then prepared for us. They were a delight to our palates.

He was a soft-spoken man, and friendly to everybody in our neighborhood, including those who spent their lives gambling, drinking, and hanging out on street corners. He deeply loved his family, and, furthermore, he believed it was a divine command that we respect everybody, both in the home and outside. He was not the American image of a typical man. He was too gentle for that. But of all the men in the world, I have wanted most to be like my daddy.

Even before my father administered a beating, at an earlier age I had dealt with my fear of death. I was eight or nine years old when I saw my first dead person. After church one Sunday, I had accompanied my mother to a wake. Miss Ella, a friend of the family, had died, and her body was laid out in her mother's home. Each friend or neighbor who entered the house went to the casket, looked down upon Miss Ella's remains, shook their heads sadly, and took a seat. My mother and I did the same. I looked down at Miss Ella; her face was more beautiful than ever, but she was not there. I do not recall any special feeling except the awareness that at some point down the road death awaits us all.

It was not until I went to bed that evening that I found I was deathly afraid of sleeping on my back. This sleeping position, with the hands substituting for fig leaves in covering the symbol of sin, certainly meant that I would die. Every night thereafter I would avoid sleeping on my back, except that during the night as you twist and turn during sleep it is inevitable that you end up on your back. Then something in me would immediately say: "Wake up. You are going to die." I would wake up almost petrified and would quickly turn over on my side or onto my stomach. I never screamed or cried out for my parents to come to comfort me.

After months of living through these frightful moments, one night I consciously told myself I could not go through the rest of my life being afraid to sleep on my back. That night I decided that I would destroy that enemy—or perhaps it would destroy me. I lay on my back with my hands exactly where they were supposed to be and prayed: "Now I lay me down to sleep; / I pray the Lord my soul to keep. / If I should die before I wake; / I pray the Lord my soul to take." I drifted into sleep, deliberately confronting death. The enemy was destroyed.

Another early test in dealing with fears was provided by the one very unhappy child in our big, happy extended neighborhood family. Jesse was filled with hostility, and he had the size to push us all around. Unfortunately for me, I became his favorite punching bag. I trembled every time I saw him, until eventually I reached a point where I had to overcome my fear.

I started going to the Charleston Boys Club gym. I lifted weights and wrestled. Paul, who studied and worked after school and spoke "proper English" at all times, had to learn to cope with all of life, and Jesse was life. I soon got to the point where I was ready to fight. He might bloody me, but I would not bow. The day for the showdown came.

Jesse saw me and called out, "Paul!" I stopped, turned to face him: "Yeah!" He saw no fear in my eyes. He saw a body language that said, Today we are going to tangle. He came up to me but didn't touch me. He said, "I ought to punch you in your nose," but he didn't. I said nothing. Then he added, "I'll let you go this time." He never challenged me again. Fears must be neutralized, then conquered; otherwise we will be cowards and victims for a lifetime.

At the age of seventeen I left our home in Charleston to go to Pennsylvania, where I attended Lincoln University. My mother's plans for me were indelibly programmed in my very soul, but I found myself very uncomfortable with the thought of becoming a minister. I had known only Baptist and Methodist ministers. They were what we called "black preachers," and I knew that I did not have that type of personality. I could not preach like Rev. Farmer, pastor of my father's Trinity African Methodist Episcopal Church. I could not preach like Rev. White, pastor of my mother's Memorial Baptist Church. I could not preach like Rev. Mitchell, pastor of Macedonia A.M.E. Church, where my mother was church organist; nor could I preach like Rev. Rickenbacker, who had preached me into conversion on the mourners' bench at Memorial Baptist.

What was even more disturbing to me was the fact that women, in particular, although faithful, devout, strong supporters of their various churches, were constantly engaged in fantasy about the hypocrisy of their ministers. They alleged that their ministers were womanizers, they took money from the church, they were liars, and some even drank. The women seemed to get what today I would call an inordinate sense of pleasure and satisfaction from such talk, but not one woman would even think of turning her back on her pastor. I eventually began to feel that if as a minister I too would become a hypocrite, that would be incompatible with what was within me. I decided before finishing high school that I wanted to be a doctor. But while in college, looking forward to preparing to become a doctor, I perceived myself to be on a collision course with my personal destiny. I would be preparing for a goal other than the one to which I had been committed even before I was born. Unable to live with this conflict, I surrendered. I would prepare for the ministry.

I would have to say that it was providential that the Rev. Matthew Davis, Episcopal chaplain at Lincoln University, knocked on my dormitory door wanting just to sit and chat with me. Fr. Davis had been rector of St. Mark's Episcopal Church in Charleston and knew my family. In fact, it was he who influenced my aunt, a lifelong Baptist, to join St. Mark's. For all of us in the family, this was indeed a radical happening. St. Mark's historically had been known as a congregation for "light skinned" Negroes of the "upper class." Our family was neither.

When Fr. Davis learned that I was planning to enter the ministry, he immediately talked to me about becoming an Episcopalian. For some reason, and again I would have to say it was providential, I agreed. I felt that temperamentally I was more like Fr. Davis than the other ministers I had known. He walked through the dormitory, knocking on doors, meeting students where they were, and they were not uncomfortable in relating to him, minister though he was.

Fr. Davis plotted out the road that would lead me to ordination. "I will get you ready for confirmation and take you to Bishop Oliver Hart. After the bishop has confirmed you, he will make you a postulant and next a candidate for holy orders; he will pick a divinity school for you, and probably give you financial help." It worked out as simply and directly as that.

After very brief preparation, I was confirmed by Bishop Hart in the chapel of the Episcopal Church House on Rittenhouse Square in downtown Philadelphia, on June 14 (Flag Day), 1943. The bishop himself had once been a rector of a church in Charleston, so his extra solicitude for me and the speed of the ordination process may have been due to the fact that I was a colored boy from the South, from a city where he had once served.

Bishop Hart sent me to the Philadelphia Divinity School, where I felt alternately welcomed and rejected, supported and suspect. The negative reception had to do with my race, as when Episcopal Hospital refused to take me along with my white classmates in its clinical pastoral training program—a requirement for graduation. Bishop Hart arranged for me to train at Bellevue Hospital in New York City instead. It turned out to be a superior program and led to more extensive clinical training than my classmates received. They realized this, giving me the nickname "Sigmund."

The positive reception of me at the divinity school had to do with race as well. Rectors of various white congregations invited me to visit so that their parishioners could meet this "different Negro," and checks from well-wishers regularly arrived for me in the mail. I was different, in that I was the first black seminarian to live in the seminary dorm. Previous black students had lived with black families in Philadelphia neighborhoods. A professor assured me that he had "prepared" the white students for my coming. Being a Negro in America, I had long since been prepared to live in a white world.

The Episcopal Church, on the other hand, did not seem quite prepared for me when I graduated. I wanted to serve overseas but was told by the director of the Episcopal Church's Overseas Department that there were no openings that a Negro priest could fill—not even in Liberia, where I had expressed a desire to go. The Bishop of Liberia, the Rt. Rev. Bravid Harris, thought otherwise, for he personally invited me to work as a priest and teacher in his country after I had served but a short time as a curate with Fr. Robert Tabb at the Church of the Crucifixion, a black congregation in South Philadelphia. After first saying no to the bishop, still feeling hurt because of the earlier rejection, I reconsidered when he pressed his case. I then wrote him a brief letter: "Dear Bishop Harris, I will come to Liberia. What do I do next?"

So much of my way had been chosen for me up to this point that I was really ready to make some choices of my own. My mother had had such an overwhelming influence in my life that there came a time while I was still at seminary when I felt rebellion welling up inside. I sat at my desk one night and wrote her a letter. I typed it on my old Smith-Corona with double-shift keys. I lambasted her bitterly and violently.

"You denied me the opportunity to have a normal childhood. You put me to work at the age of ten, working from 3 PM to 7 PM, five days a week, and on Saturdays from 9 to 9. You put me on the mourners' bench so that I would become converted and join the church by the age of ten. When my playmates understood that they should quit school in grade eight to begin working and I wanted to do the same, you packed me off to live with your sisters in another environment. I had to wear knickers when my friends were wearing long pants."

I went on to accuse her of caring more for me than she did for my sister. My sister would say many times, "I am not a Matthews [my mother's family name]. I am a Washington. I am my father's child." The result had been a very distant relationship for me with my sister, who was my only sibling.

Last of all, I wrote my mother, I was uncertain about my own manhood. My mother actually used to take me to monthly meetings of the Clover Leaf Art Club. The members were all her old high school mates. There I would sit, the only boy, with women who knitted, crocheted, and embroidered. I had my own bureau cover to embroider. Would all women have a special agenda that would control my life? If it were possible for parental or other influences to determine one's sexual identity, today I would be gay.

I cursed my mother, called her all kinds of names, and finally it was all out. After completing my catharsis, I sat and read the letter; then I tore it up and threw it in the trash basket.

But that was far from the final resolution of the ambivalent feeling I had toward my mother. In later years, when everyone else in our small family had died and my mother was slowly becoming blind and senile, my wife and I decided to bring her from Charleston to live with us in Philadelphia. Within a couple of years of coming to us, my mother was totally blind and had all but regressed to her childhood. I listened with fascination as she talked with her sisters and brother; I heard her calling her mother and father. She reached a stage where I had to bathe and undress her at night to prepare her for bed. At times I fed her. I found myself caring for her as she had cared for me as a child. Words cannot describe what that experience meant to me. Mother adored me. She could be sitting in her chair, having the time of her life, hallucinating about her childhood, but when I walked in and said, "Hello, mother," she would immediately return to the present and respond, "Is that you, my son?" And we would talk. My mother not only set me on the path that I was to travel, but she always made me feel that I was really somebody special. My earlier resentment was converted into unadulterated love, and I was blessed to become a mother to my mother. It was a sublime experience.

While I was in divinity school and assisting Fr. Davis at his parish on weekends, a girl who was a member of his parish and a student at Temple University called me aside one Sunday after church and said to me, "I am in love with you, and I don't know what to do about it." She was considered to be a beautiful young woman. She had won second place in a Miss Sepia America beauty contest. I responded to her, "There is nothing you can do about it"; but I found myself attracted to her and began "going with" her. Our relationship continued through my graduation from the divinity school, ordination to the diaconate, and appointment at the Crucifixion as curate to Fr. Tabb. However, I found her demands upon me to be more than I could handle.

College students were always partying, especially on weekends, and I could not cope with my responsibilities as curate and at the same time hang out at the weekend parties. I told the young woman on one occasion that I could not be expected to be always at her beck and call, weekend after weekend. We had also talked about marriage, and our relationship had become all-inclusive. She was deeply crushed when I told her that she had to be less demanding, and then she began questioning whether she could become a minister's wife. From that point on, the relationship went downhill until it hit bottom; but even before it ended, I was taking particular note of a girl at the Crucifixion who had just graduated from high school in 1946, the year I went to that parish fresh from seminary.

Christine Jackson had invited me to her graduation party, and as I danced with her she asked, "Father Washington, how do you like my curls?" I responded with a question, "How do you like them?" I found her attractive, appealing, and delightfully naive. Christine's mother looked upon me almost as a son, and I spent much time in the Jackson home. Mrs. Jackson had taken note of the young minister who lived above the parish hall, cooking his own meals, washing his own clothes, out visiting the sick and making parish calls every day. She began inviting me to her home for Sunday dinners regularly, where I looked with more than casual interest at her youngest daughter. Christine, like her mother and brother, all but lived at the church. She was in the choir, played piano for the church school, taught in Vacation Bible School, and was a member of the young people's fellowship.

For all our common interests and the strong attraction that I felt, I wondered if she would be able to leave her mother, from whom she seemed to be inseparable. I wondered even more if she would consider going to Liberia as my wife. So, while having dinner at the Jacksons' one Sunday, I told Christine that I needed to take someone with me to Liberia to be my secretary, and asked if she would consider accepting the job. She was awed by the very thought of it, but she enthusiastically said, "Yes, I'd go." It did not matter to me that she had only been out of high school one year. She seemed unmistakably the right person to be my wife.

I had begun assisting Fr. Tabb in May, 1946. Eleven months later, in June, 1947, I told Mrs. Jackson that I wanted to marry one of the girls in the parish. Her curiosity was aroused. Who is it? This one? That one? She went down the list of every girl in the parish, and finally said, "Not my Christina!" I said, "Yes, Christine." I told Mrs. Jackson that I would visit her home the next day, but I would not be coming to see her.

The next night I rang the doorbell and Christine answered. As she was about to call her mother, I told her that I had come to see her. She was visibly at a loss. When we sat down, I went straight to the point. "Miss Jackson [I called all the girls Miss], I have been at the Crucifixion for almost a year. We have seen a lot of each other during that time. You have gotten to know some things about me and I about you. I would like to marry you. I would love you dearly and I would be a good husband. Don't try to answer me tonight. Think about it for a couple of weeks and I will come to see you again to hear your answer."

The visit was brief, but before leaving I wanted her to have more to think about than my few words. She had to know that Fr. Washington, the curate, was Paul, the man. At the door, where she had preceded me, I playfully drew her to me with the handle of my umbrella. I embraced and kissed her and said, "Goodnight, Miss Jackson." She shyly said, "Goodnight, Father Washington." It was approximately two weeks later that I called on her again. It was still "Miss" and "Father," but she said yes! Between June and August 23, our wedding day, we got to know each other as we traveled here and there, planning the wedding, getting our shots, physical examinations, passports, and purchasing tropical clothing. I knew that Christine loved to paint, draw, sew, play the piano, and sing; so I saw to it that we would send to Liberia a sewing machine, and ample paints and canvases. While we were unable to ship a piano to Liberia, I bought her an accordion, which she mastered in short order.

2. From Liberia to Eastwick

Young as we were, we were full of adventure. Our honeymoon was on a very slow boat to Africa, the Del Viento, a cargo ship that stopped in Brazil and Senegal on its way to Liberia—a thirty-day voyage. I remember Christine getting red clay all over her white bucks from Wanamaker's department store when we wandered far from the dock in Belem, Brazil, where we would have been stranded had we not seen the first mate on a passing bus.

Being in Africa was tremendously important for me. I cannot describe the depth of my feeling when we first got off the ship in Dakar in February, 1948. I stood with my feet firmly planted on the land of my fathers and mothers. As I looked at the Africans around me working on the docks, it was as if at long last I had been reunited with the family from which I had been kidnapped three hundred years earlier. I had still another strange feeling, the feeling that I had been there before. I tried to talk with one of the men on the dock, but we could not communicate. He spoke French, the language of the colonizer.

There was something daring about living in the midst of the jungle in Liberia where Cuttington College was being built, in Suakoko, 120 miles from Monrovia. We were there with only the construction workers, the birds, and the snakes for company. Af-

ter the others on the college staff had made excuses, I volunteered
to live on site, where I was responsible for construction materials,
as well as for getting the first coffee and cocoa planted. I remember Bishop Harris turning to me to say, "Well, Brother Washington, I've been trying to get somebody to go to Suakoko, but nobody wants to go. What about you?"

"Sure, I'll go," I said.

"What about the missus?"

"Bishop, wherever I go, she will go."

Even though I went to Liberia to teach, my first four years were
given almost entirely to other jobs. Beyond my responsibilities for
construction and planting, I was the first business manager of the
college, supervising fifteen to twenty men who worked on the
campus. I made regular trips to Monrovia to get the payroll—
thousands of dollars, all in silver because the men would not accept paper bills. I was also acting president when the president
was on furlough.

Eventually I was free to take on a full teaching load and to
serve as pastor to two congregations: one English-speaking and
the other a congregation of Kru people to whom I preached
through an interpreter, whom I suspected of preaching his own
sermons as well as mine. The faith of the people was often touching. Once a barefoot woman, dressed in white, brought her sick
baby to the altar for prayers. It happened after the sermon, when
the woman and her child accompanied the ushers who were bringing the alms and oblations to the altar. I didn't understand why,
so I asked the interpreter. With a broad smile, he responded, "Her
baby is sick. She wants you to pray for it to get well."

I looked at the mother and then at the congregation. They were
all smiling. They were waiting for the miracle, because the Bible
told them that Jesus heals the sick. I took the child, raised it toward heaven, and said, "Jesus, we have preached that you heal the
sick. These people believe it. Don't let them down. Heal this baby.
Heal this baby!" I commanded that it be done, and I saw Jesus
say, "O, woman, great is your faith; be it unto you as you will."
The baby's eyes opened; it stirred. The people laughed and cried. I

was astonished. I was incredulous. It was absolutely not my faith that mattered, but theirs.

I learned so much in Africa about Christine—the woman who would go wherever I would go. She rejected the normal arrangements for American families on our college campus, which provided for three houseboys, as they were called, to do all the work in the home. The steward cleaned the house, another did the cooking, and one was the washboy. Christine wanted to clean her own house and make her own beds, and she did—to the embarrassment of our cook and washboy. The other houseboys on the campus ridiculed our two because their "Missie" cleaned her own house. She could have proudly written home to family and friends, boasting of having three servants, but she wanted some of the satisfaction of being a housewife. Cooking and laundry, however, were out of the question in that torrid zone.

Both our first and second sons were born in Liberia, and Christine had to leave Cuttington College a month before the time for the delivery of Marc, our firstborn, staying meanwhile in the bishop's guesthouse in Monrovia. There was no hospital or doctor in the hinterland where Cuttington College was located. But by the time Kemah was born, we had a doctor on campus, so he could be born in our home.

Kemah is a Buzzi name. It means Big Brother. Kemahquay, which means Little Brother, had been suggested to us by Belema, Marc's babysitter, but we liked the sound of Kemah better, so the little one was called Big Brother. Far removed as we were from any pediatricians, we relied entirely on Dr. Spock's *Baby and Child Care* in bringing up our boys, just as so many parents in the States did in those years. The book served us well, as I told Benjamin Spock when I met him as a peace activist many years later.

When Marc contracted malaria, we felt the need of expert help. He experienced extremely high fevers during the attacks, and then had to endure many hypodermic injections of liquid atabrine. For sake of his health, both physical and emotional, Christine and I decided to return to the States after six and a half years of a challenging ministry in Liberia. Bishop Harris was very disappointed that we were leaving. He said he had hoped that I would succeed him as Bishop of Liberia.

Bishop Hart welcomed us back to the States and gave me an appointment as vicar of St. Cyprian's Church, a black congregation in the extreme southwestern corner of the city of Philadelphia. This half-developed area, called Eastwick, was perhaps the only part of Philadelphia that was thoroughly integrated, with the well-to-do living next door to the poor, whites next door to blacks. There were both beautiful homes and humble shanties on the Eastwick streets, many of which had yet to be paved. And there were many gardens, of both flowers and vegetables, which Christine and I loved. The church was called St. Cyprian's-in-the-Meadows. We happily lived and ministered in those urban meadows for eight and a half years.

Bishop Hart had placed us well, but there came a time when he unfortunately gave way to the racism that underlay his paternalistic concern for this "colored boy" from Charleston. It happened when his assistant, Suffragan Bishop Gillespie Armstrong, decided that I should serve not only St. Cyprian's but also St. Titus', another mission church in the area, where the congregation was white. I readily agreed to the added duties and expected to receive appointment as vicar of St. Titus' very quickly. I even canceled vacation plans so I would be ready immediately to greet my new parishioners. But the appointment was never made and I was not told why.

Months afterwards, when my path crossed that of Bishop Armstrong, he told me that he had been avoiding me because he felt badly about what had transpired. He had indeed made the recommendation to Bishop Hart, but when Hart informed the congregation of St. Titus' of the decision to appoint me, a delegation of lay people visited him to voice objections: "Bishop Hart, we know Father Washington and we like him, but as our vicar he would have to be our pastor, and we have *daughters*." The bishop had given way to the racial prejudice of the white church members, and that was why the appointment had not been made. That experience left an indelible mark within me. To this day, I live with the feeling that whites whom I consider to be friends can come to a line of race that they cannot cross.

I learned a lot about being a pastor at St. Cyprian's. I learned often enough from my mistakes, as when I turned away a young couple wanting to be married after I found that the young woman was already pregnant. I told them I was sorry but I could not perform the ceremony. They left, obviously hurt and filled with guilt. But within two minutes of their departure, something exploded throughout my being, and I asked myself, "Paul Washington, what have you done?" I rushed to the door to call them back. When they returned, I told them I had rethought my decision and I would perform the ceremony. Thirty-four years later they are still married and their five grown children have given them grandchildren.

It was at Eastwick that I began the prison ministry that would be a part of my life for years to come. I was a chaplain for Episcopal City Missions, first at Moyamensing, the county prison, then at Eastern State Penitentiary, that large and forbidding structure of concrete and steel in the heart of Philadelphia. It was at Eastern State that I met Herman Rucker, who was awaiting execution for two brutal murders.

Herman had come up from Charleston, South Carolina, to Philadelphia, looking for work but finding none. Desperate and destitute, he broke into a mom-and-pop butcher shop to steal. When the owners walked in, he killed them both with a meat cleaver. In prison, he wrestled in a childlike way with his sins, telling me, "Father, God and Jesus know that I did not mean to kill those two people. When they walked in and saw me stealing from them, I couldn't stand it. I had to stop them from looking at me."

I judged Herman to be truly repentant. He had been baptized in the county prison before his trial, and I prepared him for confirmation. Bishop Armstrong came to the prison to confirm him as he awaited execution. The bishop was so moved by Herman's simple faith that he immediately called the Rev. Arthur Barnhart, director of the Christian Social Relations Department of the diocese, asking him to do all he could to save Herman's life. Those efforts failed; but Herman was not afraid to die. In fact, he wanted to be executed as soon as possible so as to get to heaven with "God and Jesus," where he could watch over and pray for us. We had helped him; he wanted to help us. He said to me countless times, "Father, when I die, if you ever need me to talk to God and Jesus, just call, 'Herman, I need you to talk to God and Jesus for me.' " A time would come, much later in my life, when I would have to call upon my personal intercessor.

Whenever I entered Herman's cell on my Tuesday and Thursday visits, his face would light up with a great gap-toothed smile. He asked about all my activities and seemed to live vicariously through whatever I did. If he sensed anything was troubling me, I could always expect a prison epistle later from death row: "Dear Father, When you came to see me Thursday you seemed burdened. Don't worry, Father. I'm praying to God and Jesus, asking them to take care of you."

On January 8, 1961, a terrible prison riot occurred at Eastern. I heard about it on my car radio and went directly to the penitentiary. It was a bitter, subzero night, and the scene that awaited me was horrible. State troopers had moved in to restore order. I saw how they had stripped naked every man who had been out of his cell. The men lay on the concrete floor, some with broken bones, many covered in blood. I went straight to Herman's cell, which the rioters had opened. They had invited him to come out, but he refused. Why should he go running from cell block to cell block at 11 P.M. with nowhere really to go? Eastern State was escape-proof. They had seen to that after Willy Sutton's famous escape through the sewer.

I went on with prison chaplaincy at Eastern until it closed in 1970, and then at the Philadelphia House of Correction. Ninety-nine percent of prison ministry is listening, I discovered. In the listening, I found revealed the darkest and the brightest images of humanity. In these men I saw all of mankind; but most important, I saw myself. I discovered that we are all more alike than unlike each other, except that by the grace of God or by accident, circumstances, or luck, at a crossroad one of us turned to the right and the other to the left.

Herman Rucker died one day of natural causes in the back of a sheriff's van, while being transported from one prison to another. I have kept alive the memory of his childlike faith and I know that in me, probably for the first time in his life, this man had found a father, while I had found a son and brother.

In May, 1958, the Philadelphia City Council voted to condemn the neighborhood in which we lived and ministered. Eastwick was to become the site of a $100 million municipal redevelopment program, designed to win back to the city many of those who were fleeing to the suburbs by providing moderately priced housing within city limits. One of the reasons Eastwick had been chosen for this program was that it was not a politically important neighborhood, nor was the community able to mount much organized resistance.

I felt I had to speak out on behalf of the residents, who were devastated when they heard this news. But it soon became apparent that the plan could not be halted. Once the razing of homes got underway in 1960, the residents' demand became adequate compensation for all who would be displaced. I spoke out publicly, calling for "a house for a house," since "fair market value" could never really be fair to a family forced to move and purchase a home on the open market. I accompanied families to the agency in charge of relocation, helping them to get even $500 or $1,000 more for making the move. With Maurice Fagan of the Philadelphia Fellowship Commission, I advocated nondiscrimination in the sale of the new homes being built.

In one face-to-face meeting with the sales supervisor, we discussed the case of a woman, by chance a member of St. Thomas' Episcopal Church, who was seeking to buy a corner house in the new development. The supervisor explained his predicament to me: "It is the worst thing to sell a corner house to a Negro, because then whites will refuse to buy any house in two whole blocks." He had a very convincing manner, and as he spoke I began to shake my head slowly, in apparent sympathy for the man, until Maury Fagan yelled at me across the table, "Paul, what are you doing!"

During this period of community struggle, two more children were born to Christine and me. To Michael, our third child, we gave the middle name Bravid, in honor of the Bishop of Liberia. Donya, fourth-born but first daughter, was given a name from the African Basseh tribe, meaning "gift."

Bishop Armstrong was now in charge of the diocese, and he had his eye on me for another assignment. The urban strategy of the diocese had led to special attention being paid to the Church of the Advocate in North Philadelphia. The congregation there was racially integrated, as members of a black parish had been added to the dwindling white base when the Rev. J. McNeal Wheatley was rector in the 1950s. The National Council of the Protestant Episcopal Church, U.S.A. had designated the Advocate a pilot parish in urban work and had begun to subsidize community outreach programs there. Soon the diocese assumed the subsidy, which amounted to $26,500 per year.

In designating pilot parishes, the Episcopal Church in fact was asking whether a WASP denomination like itself could minister meaningfully and effectively to Negroes, in particular to those who were handicapped by severe unemployment, underemployment, and poor education. These oppressed people were conscious at all times that it was whites who were responsible for putting them down and surrounding them with an army of occupation, the police, to keep them down. I had no trouble identifying with the people who struggled in this North Philadelphia ghetto. Bishop Hart had only too recently decided to keep me in my place, reminding me by withholding an appointment that, though I was a priest of the Episcopal Church, I was still a Negro. I hardly needed to be reminded of this. Becoming a priest in this white, Anglo-Saxon, Protestant denomination never caused me to feel within myself that I should abandon who I was and take on the identity of the institution that had ordained me. Had I done so, my sacramental functions would indeed have been valid, but politically and socially I would nevertheless be void. Many others had found this out before me.

When the Rev. George Davidson decided to resign as rector of the Advocate, Bishop Armstrong decided that I was the only priest around who could do the job. I suppose that my public involvement in the Eastwick redevelopment struggle contributed to that judgment. In any case, he said that if I decided not to become rector of the Advocate, he was ready to recommend that the diocese withdraw its "pilot parish" support. He caused me to be the one to decide the fate of this ministry.

I told him that I would accept the position, on one condition only. He must promise to give the people of St. Cyprian's another pastor immediately. The bishop promised and he soon made good his word by appointing Fr. Robert DuBose, then curate to Fr. Jesse Anderson, Sr., at St. Thomas' Church in West Philadelphia, to shepherd the flock of St. Cyprian's, which was being scattered by urban renewal.

My new work would begin on June 15, 1962, and as the day approached, Bishop Armstrong personally commissioned me with these liberating words: "Paul, when I die I don't think the Lord will ask me much about what I did as Bishop of Pennsylvania. But I do think he will ask me, 'What did you do for my people in North Philadelphia?' I want you, Paul, to go to North Philadelphia and love my people." Little did Armstrong realize that within two years he would be facing his Lord.

3. Arrival at the Advocate

When I first drove Christine through the neighborhood of the Advocate, around 18th and Diamond Streets, she wept. "Is this where we are going to live?" she asked.

"Yes, this is where we are going to live," I said.

"Paul, there's not even a blade of grass between the concrete slabs," she said through her tears.

But within a few days the tears were dry and her attitude had changed remarkably. Saturday shopping in the neighborhood began the change. Christine found the people to be up-front, honest, warm, and unpretentious. The members of the congregation received us warmly, too, and our children seemed to fit in well at the neighborhood schools.

In those days Philadelphia Police Commissioner Orlando Gibbons had nicknamed North Philadelphia "the Jungle." That name reflected racial prejudice and fear. There was reason for fear because of the explosive combination of social pressures that racism had created here. There was poverty, joblessness, broken homes, overcrowding, and landlord neglect. But there were then, just as there are today, proud blocks with well-tended rowhouses, churches full on Sunday morning and active in good works during the week, and neighbors who looked out for neighbors. Perhaps

North Philadelphia, figuratively speaking, was a jungle. It was indeed a tangled mass of all sorts and conditions of people. It contained every ingredient necessary to make a world.

I began my ministry at the Advocate by taking stock of the relationship between the church and the community. There was a gap to be overcome and we would all have to play a part in overcoming it. I decided that the rectory where we lived, right next door to the church, should have an open-door policy. It was our family home, but no one who needed to see me was going to be turned away from it.

I had heard so many stories of how the poor were treated by welfare agencies and others that were supposed to give services to people in need. So often the needy were treated almost like trash, blamed for being poor, dehumanized, and always kept waiting, waiting. Few realize that if the "haves" are to have, there must be the "have nots." The rich are rich at the expense of the poor. Poverty in our society is systemic.

I decided to give myself—my soul, my time, my resources—to everyone who came to see me. Every person was Christ: "Inasmuch as you have done it unto one of the least of these," Jesus said, "you have done it unto me." So I instructed my family: "When someone rings the doorbell and asks to see me, don't come to me and describe him—clean or dirty, drunk or sober, white or black. Just tell me, 'Someone is at the door to see you.'"

On my first Sunday at the Advocate, my text was not taken from the Bible. I instead quoted an inmate who was in my Bible class at Eastern State Penitentiary. "I searched for my God, but my God I could not see. I searched for my soul, but my soul eluded me. Then I searched for my brother and I found all three." I told the congregation the source of my quote: "This young man, named Isaac, is in prison, banished by a society that includes all of us, and this morning he is saying: 'I am Isaac your brother.'" The Advocate had to become a church that accepted all people as brothers and sisters, particularly the people of the community in the midst of which we sat.

I knew that the church buildings themselves hardly seemed welcoming to those who lived around them. The church proper was such an imposing structure that when our family first entered the huge sanctuary and stood staring up at the one hundred-foot ceiling, Kemah got frightened. "I'm scared, Daddy. This is spooky!" he said. "I want to get out of here."

I was at war with this beautiful church from the beginning. I resented the fact that most people thought of it simply as big buildings that had little real relevance to their surroundings. The church complex had not one but five very big buildings. The church itself looked like a cathedral. The Philadelphia Historical Commission has described it as "the finest specimen of French Gothic architecture in America, a copy, in reduced proportions and with some changes, of the Cathedral of Amiens, France." It had taken seven years to construct (1890–97), at a time when wealthy merchants and professional people lived in North Philadelphia. It is 165 feet in length and reaches 165 feet to its topmost tower, above which stands a magnificent copper statue of the archangel Gabriel sounding his horn. The building can easily hold 1,000 worshippers and in the days of its founder, George W. South (it is the George W. South Memorial Church of the Advocate), it did. I was told by the daughter of the Advocate's second rector how on Sunday evenings there was standing room only in those days.

When I arrived, there were some six hundred members on the rolls. My first Holy Week services were my high-water mark in terms of attendance: 450 on Palm Sunday, five hundred on Easter Day. Of these members, only about one hundred were white, but I was the first black priest ever to serve as rector at the Advocate and I had to feel my way.

It happened that the first pastoral visit I made was to an elderly white parishioner in a hospital. I was uncertain about how she would receive her new pastor, but all went very well. As I was praying with her, she took my hand and tears came to her eyes. I was so impressed that I wrote to Bishop Armstrong to tell him there could not have been a better experience to show me that white people could receive the ministrations of the church from a Negro priest.

If my race was not an issue for the parishioners, my community advocacy would be. The membership of the church was fairly typical for an Episcopal Church at that time: teachers, doctors, city and social workers, and others with "positions." Of course, there were some with just "jobs." It was a fairly class-conscious group of people and they had no great desire to be involved in controversy of any kind. Over the years many would leave because they disagreed with the new course of ministry at the Advocate or simply because they were moving into neighborhoods like Mount Airy and Germantown, where black professionals had become able to purchase some of the fine old homes in neighborhoods some distance from North Philadelphia.

In the congregation there was a group of accomplished bridge players. They participated in tournaments, and every week they played in each other's homes. I recall a bridge tournament at the church on a day when a group had gathered to board a bus for some civil rights demonstration. I did not accompany the demonstrators but said a prayer on the bus before they left. A young man on the bus said to me sarcastically, "You are sending us to the front lines with a prayer, but you will remain here with your real flock—the bridge players." I never forgot that.

At the time when I arrived, the great Selective Patronage Campaign was underway. It was led by a group known as the Four Hundred Negro Ministers, who had been organized by the Rev. Leon Sullivan of Zion Baptist Church. The campaign was a boycott of particular businesses until they agreed to hire and promote more black men and women. The boycott targets were announced from the pulpit by the participating ministers, who had received letters naming the business to be boycotted. One such letter said simply: "Please announce to your congregation that we are not to buy the products of the Tasty Baking Company [one of the major targets] until they agree to hire more Negroes." Those pulpit announcements were very effective, and it did not take long for Tasty Baking or other companies to agree to talk with the leadership group of Negro ministers and with Rev. Sullivan. When I read such an announcement from the pulpit of the Advocate, I was called aside by one of the white vestrymen and told: "We never talk about race in this church."

As a pilot parish in urban ministry, subsidized by the diocese, the Advocate had programs and activities that I had not expected to see. There was a day care center; a community center, open in the evenings for young people; a daily Vacation Bible School for the first two weeks in July, and a summer day camp from mid-July to the end of August. The Advocate had a staff of thirteen for its programs: six in the day care center, five for the community center, and two caretakers. In addition, I had the services of a curate, a full-time secretary, and, of course, the church organist. In all, counting me, we were seventeen.

For some reason, I never felt overawed or inadequate for the very complex and challenging ministry that was now under my direction. But I shall never forget the assistance I received from the curate who was in place when I went there—Jesse Anderson, Jr., now the rector of St. Thomas African Episcopal Church in Philadelphia, the church served then by his father, Jesse Anderson, Sr. Jesse, Jr., had been responsible for starting some of the programs now underway at the Advocate. He introduced me to the staff and labeled about a dozen keys to the Advocate's many doors for my use.

I needed all the help I could get in administering church and community center activities, especially in dealing with the clashes among the various groups that used our facilities. I had hoped for a little time to get acquainted with all the activities before having to deal with conflicts, but that luxury was denied me.

There were two groups using the gymnasium, boys playing basketball and Theater XIV, a very serious and sophisticated group of men and women who regularly presented top-notch plays. The boys resented the theater company using "their" space and preventing them from playing ball. To harass them and drive them out, the boys would identify the cars of the actors and actresses and let the air out of their tires. This was a problem waiting to be solved on my arrival. Fortunately, we had another unused space, an auxiliary chapel. I moved the pews from the chapel into the church proper and gave the chapel over to Theater XIV.

Such problems were interminable. I invited an Alcoholics Anonymous group to hold their meetings at the church a few years after I arrived. They began to meet in the parish hall, but their meetings were invaded by people involved in the Black Unity movement, who preached to them about the need for racial unity and urged them to meet with the Black Unity group upstairs. I had to find another church to provide space for the AA group.

Then there were "the church people" who resented "those other groups" taking over "their space." The Women's Auxiliary had a room that was exclusively for their use, but soon "those outside people" began to congregate there. This conflict was never really resolved, but as time went on a few on the inside began to realize that the outsiders were their raison d'être. I preached to them constantly that the diocese was not giving its substantial grants to the Advocate just for Sunday services or for church people to do "churchy" things. Without the "outsiders" they could not exist as a church. At the same time, the "outsiders," the community people, were often critical of the church people. I had to get them to understand that were it not for the church people, they would not have a church in which to meet. It was a perfect example of what Episcopalians called in those days MRI, mutual responsibility and interdependence in the Body of Christ.

The Diocese felt proud to have a church with a ministry like ours. The diocesan *Church News* boasted that "that 'rumble' or knifing that you did not read about on 18th Street" may have been due to the outreach ministry that touched and influenced the Advocate neighborhood. That same article quoted me explaining our ministry: "Our job is one of constantly revealing to those who feel they are the unwanted outcasts of God's family that God does care and that his acts of redemption were for all."

I did not come to the Advocate with an agenda for social change. I came to be a pastor and, as always, I tried to listen and learn from the people who turned to me for help. My best teacher was a woman named Jackie, who one day came to my office literally crying for help.

She was extremely distraught, and as she sat in my office crying, I saw in her an incarnation of all the ills of North Philadelphia and of the inner city. She was a product of a home for delinquent girls. She had had seven children, all by different fathers, some of them white. The children had all been placed in foster homes by the Department of Human Services. At that point Jackie had been evicted, and she was hungry.

As I listened to her, I asked God, What will I say to this woman that will soothe her, comfort and help her? I soon stopped listening to her and tried to "prepare my response." Finally her story ended and I began telling her the story of God's love, for even the sparrow that falls to the ground. As I spoke I found that she was not comforted but was becoming aggravated and agitated.

Like a bolt of lightning, she leapt from her seat and exploded before my face. "Listen, mister, you can talk about God's love because obviously he loves you. You live in that big, comfortable house next door, you have food for your children, and you are pastor of this big church. Now you just show me how God loves me!!"

There it was. "Go and *show* John again those things which you hear and see" (Matthew 11:4). "The Word became *flesh*" (John 1:14). At that moment I knew that I had to *show* Jackie how God loved her. The Advocate had to be an incarnation of the Word. I knew from that moment that we had to act out God's love, and it began right there. Christine and I gave her a room in the rectory and she stayed with us until she found work. To this day, twenty-nine years later, she calls at least once a year, thanking me for helping to put her on her feet.

Shortly after my encounter with Jackie, I added to the sign on the church's lawn at the corner of 18th and Diamond, "This church lives the Gospel." For God does not appear in words, but in action. "The Word became flesh."

4. Into the Streets

On October 29, 1963, a riot broke out on Susquehanna Avenue, a block from Diamond Street, where the Advocate was located. I went to the scene to see what was happening. I was simply walking up and down dressed in my clerical attire. And people looked at me and wanted to know: Preacher, what are you doin' here? And it was a sort of joke: I wasn't supposed to be there among "the rioters."

It was lucky for one white motorist that I was there. He had found himself surrounded by hundreds of agitated people on the avenue at the height of the disturbance and was unable to move his car. I called to the crowd, "Open up and let the man get by!" They promptly responded, because they really had no interest in the car and its driver. When I got home I heard that man calling in on Frank Ford's radio talk show to tell how some Negro minister had saved his life from an angry mob. I smiled to think that I was regarded as some kind of hero for simply directing traffic. Can it be that the guilty fear when no man threatens?

More important, because I got out on the streets, I was able to piece together what had really happened to spark the riot. A twenty-four-year-old named Willie Philyaw, Jr., had been shot and killed by police after he allegedly stole a watch from a drugstore. The police said that he had lunged at them with a knife. The district attorney accepted the police account and ruled the killing a justifiable homicide. But from what I learned from eyewitnesses, the police were clearly in the wrong.

Willie was lame. He certainly couldn't run. A policeman must have told him to halt, but he kept hobbling away. Another man who was crossing the street at the time walked between Willie and the policeman. At the moment the officer shot, this man threw up his hand, and the bullet went through his hand into Willie's body. If a man could walk between the policeman and his target, how could the policeman have been in imminent danger of being knifed?

The public statements I made about this incident brought me to the attention of Mayor James H. J. Tate, who invited me to become a member of the Commission on Human Relations of the City of Philadelphia. I joined the commission in January, 1964, and served until 1971. Sadie Alexander was the chairperson when I joined, and a very strong leader. It was Sadie Alexander who, along with the mayor, summoned me home from a vacation in August, 1964, when a much larger-scale riot broke out on Columbia Avenue (just four blocks south of Diamond Street).

This riot, too, was sparked by a confrontation between police and residents of North Philadelphia. It began with the arrest of a woman named Odessa Bradford for a traffic violation. A fight with police following her arrest led to large-scale looting and attacks on property on Columbia Avenue. Rumors fed the riot, rumors that the police had killed Odessa and others.

When it was over, the damage was calculated at $3 million, six hundred people had been arrested, and nearly 340 had been injured, including one hundred police officers. There had been one death, not of Odessa Bradford but of one Robert Green. The newspaper account gave only his name and address and his age, twenty-one, reporting that Green "was shot Sunday night after he attacked an officer with a knife, police said."

In the aftermath, a period of great tension, the Advocate became the scene of many community meetings. Our various programs continued, even as the church became a crossroads where police patrolling the neighborhood could drop in for a cup of coffee and, while they were there, watch rehearsals of the Arthur Hall

Dance Troupe. I tried to be a constant presence at the church and in the neighborhood during those troubled days. I joined with other clergy and community leaders in presenting to the city administration a twelve-point plan for easing the tensions in North Philadelphia. We called for job creation, the enforcement of housing codes, the rehabilitation of homes. "Repression through law enforcement is not enough," we said.

Not only was law enforcement not enough, but the police themselves had to be checked. Too often they behaved like an army of occupation and not a protective force. One of the direct action groups that used the Advocate as a base attempted to curb police brutality and illegal arrests by acting as citizen observers. On Friday and Saturday evenings these volunteer members of "Operation Alert" would gather in the parish house to listen to radios that picked up the police band. When they heard of arrests being made, they rushed to the scene in automobiles to observe. It did not take the police long to realize how closely they were being watched. The possession of police band radios by the general public was made illegal in Philadelphia by action of the City Council.

The year of the Columbia Avenue riot, 1964, was also the year when Bishop Armstrong died and a new bishop took his place. The Rt. Rev. Robert L. DeWitt came from Michigan, where for years he had served as a priest to the very wealthy in Bloomfield Hills, a suburb of the Motor City. That wouldn't seem to qualify him for leadership in Philadelphia in such troubled times, but he surprised us all by his willingness to learn. Here's how he describes his early days in our diocese:

"The first day I was on the job as bishop coadjutor of the diocese, several of our clergy were in jail, arrested because they had been involved in demonstrations [for racial desegregation] in that racial powder keg known as Chester, Pennsylvania. In the days, months and years that followed, I was to learn the authenticity of the title of the landmark book by Gunnar Myrdal on racism in America, *An American Dilemma*. Race riots more than a decade earlier in Detroit had been for me a baptism into a consciousness of racism. But Philadelphia was to be my confirmation."[1]

The bishop and I became very close. He came to regard me as one of his instructors in that "consciousness of racism." Bishop DeWitt chose the Church of the Advocate as the site for his service of installation on October 31, 1964. Since the diocese at that time had no cathedral church, the bishop was free to choose where major celebrations were to take place. Choosing the Advocate sent a message that this bishop intended to give priority to issues of racial justice and to the needs of the poor. He selected as preacher for the occasion someone who could put that message into words, Paul Moore, then Suffragan Bishop of Washington, D.C., and well known throughout the Episcopal Church as a champion of civil rights.

The installation service began with a great outdoor procession led by the cadet band and choir from the Valley Forge Military Academy and including eight other Episcopal bishops along with over a hundred vested clergy. What Bishop Moore said in his sermon echoed through the church and was read by church members throughout the Delaware Valley when excerpted in the *Evening Bulletin*:

"Encircling this church are mile after mile of houses in which Negroes are caught in the pressures of ghetto life. Into these streets and houses we must go together, not in a spirit of fear, but in the apostolic spirit of power and love. . . . A bishop is without color. When his Negro people are oppressed, so is he, and their fight for freedom is his."

Deeds followed words when, in 1965, Bishop DeWitt gave his backing to demonstrations calling for the racial integration of Girard College in North Philadelphia. The Girard College struggle has been called Philadelphia's Selma, and the bishop would later say that it provided "the most contentious focus the racial issue had in my years in Philadelphia."

Girard College, in reality an elementary- and secondary-level boarding school, was founded in 1848 on what was then forty-three acres of farmland but by 1965 was in the center of black North Philadelphia, entirely surrounded by a ten-foot-high stone wall. The founder was Stephen Girard, one of America's richest men, who has been described as "a one-eyed sea captain, merchant, and opium trader." He stated in his will that the school was to enroll "poor, white, male orphans." The issue in the 1960s was whether such racial discrimination could be tolerated any longer.

From May 1 (Law Day) to December 17, 1965, there were daily demonstrations outside the massive Girard College wall, a structure that became a perfect symbol of continuing segregation and exclusion in our city. Cecil B. Moore, the flamboyant, cigar-smoking criminal lawyer who was president of the Philadelphia Branch of the NAACP, led the marches, assisted chiefly by young people like "Freedom George," "Freedom Smitty," "Freedom Frank," Mary Richardson, Dwight Campbell, and a long list of others whom I came to know and love over the years. A North Philadelphia street gang called the Moroccos also participated, delighting in running along the wall, shouting that they would go over it. Philadelphia police responded brutally at times, on one occasion knocking out Freedom George's front teeth.

But the clergy were present, too, often organized for picket duty by the Rev. Layton Zimmer, who was on Bishop DeWitt's staff as urban missioner. America's best-known clergyman, the Rev. Martin Luther King, Jr., put in an appearance in August, even though Cecil Moore had told him to stay out of town. What need did Cecil or "Cecil's people" have of outside assistance? Moore relented and joined King on a flat-bed truck when he proclaimed, as only Martin Luther King could, that the walls of segregation would come tumbling down.

I took my turn in the marches and pickets, and was proud indeed of my bishop, who resisted great opposition from white clergy and laity who thought that "wills are sacred and inviolable." In 1968 the Supreme Court of the United States found otherwise. The justices ruled against racial discrimination at the school and made it possible for black orphan boys to attend. When the issue was moved off the streets and into the courts in December, 1965, Bishop DeWitt personally led a service of thanksgiving at the wall.

The bishop felt there was only one moral stand to take. "The issue involved 'our people,'" he said. By that he meant the 18,000 black members of the Diocese of Pennsylvania. But, more than that, he was making a claim of justice, "a claim the church could only ignore at the cost of surrendering its vocation, relinquishing its claim to be the people of God." He paid a price for this stand in the years that followed, in terms of loss of membership in the diocese and reduced giving in support of its programs.

For me, December 17 did not mark the end of the struggle to get Negro fatherless boys into Girard College. The governor of Pennsylvania had appointed William Coleman as a special assistant attorney general for the purpose of preparing a complaint to present in court on behalf of the excluded boys. People to be named as plaintiffs were needed, so when a mother came to tell me she wanted to enroll her two fatherless sons in Girard College, I was advised to bring her to see Mr. Coleman's assistant, a young attorney named Thomas Gilhool, at the offices of the Dilworth, Paxson law firm in downtown Philadelphia. Those offices were on the sixteenth floor of the Fidelity Bank Building.

On the appointed day, I took the mother to Broad and Walnut, where we entered the lobby and stood with others waiting for the elevator. As the doors opened and people stepped in, I nudged her arm and said, "Well, we're almost there." She did not move. Again, I spoke, "This is our elevator." She was frozen, and with eyes cast down to the floor, she said, "I'm afraid of elevators." To which I replied, "Well, it's only sixteen floors, and I can use the exercise." This turned out to be the most arduous segment of the march. Mr. Gilhool received us graciously, and when the last dot was in place, we marched downhill to the first floor, then returned to North Philadelphia. I thought it was a fitting and satisfying end to a long, painful, and at times violent struggle.

Meanwhile, resentments within the diocese toward the bishop continued to be voiced. One expression of opposition came from a secretive lay group that called itself "The Voice from the Catacombs." These disgruntled church members distributed thousands of mimeographed leaflets outside Episcopal churches, handing them to parishioners leaving Sunday services or placing them under automobile windshield wipers. The first set, distributed on June 13, raised concerns about Fr. Zimmer's activities at the Girard Wall as well as concerns about the sanctity of wills. "If the will of Stephen Girard can be broken, the next may be your own," they warned.

Another leaflet asked: "Do you want your money to support the Church of the Advocate?" These leaflets gave no name or phone number, just the name of the group and a post office box. I wrote to the group at their post office number, asking them to identify themselves. "Let us walk together," I asked, "pray together, break bread together." I received no reply.

When complaints came to Church House about my activities, as they often did, Bishop DeWitt would simply say: "He is the rector of a parish, and bishops don't tell rectors what to do." The Advocate was in reality an aided congregation, not a self-supporting parish, so the bishop could very well have told me what to do. He chose instead to honor the leadership that I was providing and to accept as an imperative that we had the right of self-determination.

There were other signs of support from the church. I was elected to serve as a deputy representing our diocese at the General Convention of the Episcopal Church in 1964 and would be almost routinely reelected in succeeding years. This led to my being appointed to a number of committees and commissions at the national level of the church, while in the broader community of Philadelphia over the years I received appointments to the Board of Trustees of Philadelphia Community College and other boards of civic groups and foundations.

Becoming a part of such prestigious bodies in the church and in society, one may be perceived to be an extraordinary person. There is a temptation to be proud of reaching "extraordinary" status, but few realize how deadly and dehumanizing it can be to abandon our given identity and take on the identity of the institutions with which we are affiliated. I have never abandoned the place where God put me nor the personality God chose to give me. Therefore, no matter where I sat, or with whom I sat, everyone was made to know that there was a North Philadelphian in their midst, someone who represented the oppressed.

Mattie Humphrey, who was working then as youth coordinator for the Philadelphia Council for Community Advancement, called me "the legitimizer" for a lot that was going on in the community. Aurelia Waters, educational director for a self-help center at 15th and Diamond, said she could use my name to open doors. That was my goal, that the work that Aurelia and Mattie and so many others were undertaking should go forward. I tried to be in the boardrooms for them and stay in the streets with them, too.

5. Black Unity, 1966

It was in the year 1966 that "Black Power" became a slogan for many in the civil rights movement. Stokely Carmichael, its chief proponent, spoke at the national convention of the Congress of Racial Equality (CORE) that summer and flatly said: "We don't need white liberals. We have to make integration irrelevant." Younger black men and women were challenging the political and moral wisdom of their elders and, in the process, were shattering the ideals of many white sympathizers.

Much of the new awareness had surfaced early in the year in Philadelphia in a rally held at the Church of the Advocate on February 4 where "black unity" was the theme. This event was a turning point for me and for the way in which many people viewed the Advocate. John Churchville was the rally's organizer.

It was at Mattie Humphrey's recommendation that I had hired John to be a "gang worker" at the Advocate, funded by a grant from the Phoebe Waterman Foundation (later called the William Penn Foundation). Richard Bennett, the foundation director, had sought me out to offer me the grant. His foundation was concerned that something be done to reach the young men on the street corners of Philadelphia, too many of whom were involved in brutal gang fights and killings. John Churchville seemed right for the job.

John was a thin, intense, bespectacled young man who had

ended his music education studies at Temple University to go south in 1962 to take part in the voter registration drives. On his return he became active in the Northern Student Movement, which challenged northern college students to work in their own cities to combat racism and which in our city had established the Philadelphia Tutorial Project. John set up the Northern Student Movement Freedom Library in a storefront on Ridge Avenue. The library would evolve into a day school and attract national attention because of its heavy emphasis on instilling black pride in its young pupils.

After John came to the Advocate to do his gang work, he was frequently visited by his friend William Strickland from New York City. Strickland was the national director and the theoretician of the Northern Student Movement. In his writing and speaking he left no doubt about what he thought was wrong with American society. In his eyes, the society was fundamentally racist.

I found myself in frequent conversation with John and Bill. I felt two pairs of young eyes measuring me and everything I did in terms of an analysis of racism in society that was more thoroughgoing than any I had heard before. One conversation with John, after he had been on the job for two months or so, had particular importance for me.

John sat down with me one day and said that he felt that gang activity was not the problem in itself. It was only a symptom of a much deeper problem: the feeling of powerlessness among black people. He suggested that the solution was to work for black unity, to the end of achieving black power and ultimately self-love and respect. Only when we gained power through unity would our problem be solved.

I think I was ready to hear this because of what I had learned in my prison ministry. One Sunday morning at the House of Correction, I had asked young black prisoners what they felt about taking part in gang activities that resulted in killing young black brothers like themselves. Their answer left a deep impression on me: "They always sayin' we ain't worth nothin', so when we kill somebody, it's like we ain't killin' nothin'."

While I believe that no one can blame others for one's own behavior, I am convinced that family, peers, the community, and the society at large can influence tremendously not only the image people have of themselves but their behavior as well. I am convinced that Dorothy Law Nolte's words are true: "If a child lives with criticism, he learns to condemn. If a child lives with hostility, he learns to fight." If he lives with ridicule, he learns to be shy; with jealousy, he learns to feel guilty. Who tells kids that they "ain't worth nothin'"? Are they a prophecy fulfilled? So John made sense to me, but I realized his proposal was a big order. How do you get black people to unite for the total good of all rather than follow the path of "rugged individualism"?

He suggested that we call a Black Unity Rally and that we announce it to the black community on the Joe Rainey talk show on radio station WDAS, which reached the largest black audience in Philadelphia. This made me a bit nervous and uncomfortable. How would it sound for a Christian minister to take to the air waves to talk about "black unity"? Negroes still hated that word "black." It had always been an insulting word, used to cause shame and make us feel worthless, ugly, and dirty; and here I was being called upon to talk to thousands of Negroes about the need for black unity. I had cringed myself the first time I heard Malcolm X say "black" on a radio broadcast I was listening to at home. Later on, when I used the term from the pulpit for the first time, it was received like profanity.

I always had the feeling that John had serious reservations about my sincerity and commitment. He saw my anxiety about what he was asking and he said something to me that I shall never forget. He said, "You are an Episcopalian. It is a church that represents the white establishment and racism in its most sophisticated but vicious fashion. You are going to have to make a choice, to fight for the liberation of our people and maybe get kicked out of this church, or you may reach a point where you have to leave." I felt that I had to prove to both John and myself that I was not a hypocrite. I answered very quietly and simply, "I'm going all the way."

I appeared twice on the Joe Rainey show with John and his

friend Bill Strickland, to explain the need for a Black Unity Rally and to invite people to attend. As we spoke on the air, somewhere an FBI agent was listening and transcribing everything we said. Thanks to the Freedom of Information Act, I now have his transcript. When I read now what I said then, I am amazed. But I had given the issues much thought. I had tried first to think them through theologically.

I was preparing in my mind what I came to call the Theology of Black Power, the conviction that the omnipotent God and Father of us all intends that all his children, black and white, should be vessels of his power. I was trying to bring God's word and not just my own when I spoke. From the pages of the FBI transcript, here is some of what I said:

"I think we have power. There is power in the ghettos, but most of the time this power has been demonstrated destructively. To the tune of say $200 million in the Watts community last summer, and millions in Philadelphia a couple of years ago. If a people in a ghetto can affect the economy of a city at that rate, then this same power can be used constructively in order that the lot of the whole might be better.

"There is a need for a change in our own consciousness of ourselves, a need for a change in our image. . . . There is no reason why we should look upon blackness as being a stigma. But you mention the word black and people's stomachs turn, they become frightened. This was perpetrated upon us, we were taught to despise ourselves. . . . In our schools our children must learn the truth about themselves. . . . You see, we have been taught that we are nothing, we have no worth. We have no faith in ourselves. But this land was built with our labors, built on our broken bodies. So we are not asking for favors, we ask for that to which we are entitled. We can do it if we are united.

"It is my contention that the persons who really enslaved and have a campaign of continued enslavement of black people are not in a position to actually help our ultimate liberation. . . . Even white friends look upon us as being poor things, still boys and girls but never men and women.

"We have looked upon integration as being the highest good.

But I have always discovered that somehow I have been tricked whenever I got too close. Because when I got too close I was always being told I could solve my problems, but not much credence was ever given to my own solution to my problem. . . . I feel we discover ourselves first of all within the family and after having discovered ourselves in the family we move on to the larger and larger communities. . . . We need to call the plays instead of being the reactors. We will call the plays and others will react to us."

Bill and John then addressed the issues in their own ways. John introduced a note of cynicism when he spoke about the 1963 March on Washington. "We went there like children and were treated like children on a picnic," he said. He suggested racist motives behind President Johnson's War on Poverty and raised the issue of the participation of black youth in the war in Vietnam. Both he and Bill branded it a racist war, with the Vietnamese being regarded "as niggers." Talk of the war was relevant to the upcoming rally because Julian Bond, who had been invited to be the featured speaker, had been refused a seat in the Georgia legislature in January because he had endorsed an antiwar statement of the Student Nonviolent Coordinating Committee (SNCC).

The phone callers' response to what we had said on the radio talk show was animated. All these questions were in the air and people seemed eager to discuss them in public. I tried to move the discussion beyond anger and cynicism to offer hope for the future, but a hope based on black unity and pride.

"I would say that America needs the black man because there is something which America is lacking which only we can give. . . . It needs a realization that we are all human beings and that we must learn to deal with each other in this manner. I think God has given us a gift, a gift of being able to recognize another's humanity; so instead of speaking of man's inhumanity to man as has been the case in the past, we can teach this nation how to be giving, man to man."

On February 4, some two to three hundred people came to the parish hall of the Advocate for the rally. Julian Bond was there and, as expected, he spoke out clearly against the war; but the emotional flash point of the rally came before Bond spoke.

As the hall was filling up, I told John how pleased I was to see so many people in attendance—black and white, members of CORE, members of SNCC, and other activists. I thought we had really pulled off a good rally. But he was frowning and telling me he didn't like it. I exclaimed, "Why not?" He responded, "Look at all the white people here. How are we going to begin talking about racism totally surrounded by racists?"

My heart fell, but once again I faced a moment of decision. I responded simply: "I am the first black rector of this church. Before I came, there were white ministers who discouraged blacks from worshipping here. Negroes were told: 'There is a church at 27th and Girard, St. Augustine's; that might be the Episcopal Church you are looking for.' It was a way of saying, 'This church is for white people; you are not wanted here. Go with your own kind.' I made up my mind and established a policy—no one would ever be put out of this church!" John said he accepted my policy, and then proceeded to start the meeting.

He stood before the large crowd, held up a flyer, and read it: "Black Unity Rally—of, for, and by black people." He continued: "It is obvious that white people were not invited. I can't ask you to leave, because that is against the policy of Father Washington, the pastor of this church, but I can say you were not invited and are not welcome. And I am asking that all of the white people who are sitting while black people are standing get up and let black people sit at their own rally."

As I listened to John, I found myself called upon to weigh the thesis of Martin Luther King, Jr., and the antithetical position of Malcolm X. Martin would see that night as a night when "all God's children, black men and white men, Jews and gentiles, Protestants and Catholics" were holding hands. Malcolm would see it, at one point in his life, as the white liberals once again saying that they are our friends, but far from ready to accept us as equals, the only condition under which genuine friendship and brotherhood can exist.

That night, John synthesized these antitheticals. We did not ask the whites to leave, but he made it emphatically clear that on that night in Philadelphia we were embarking upon a journey of self-discovery and self-determination. White participation was not desired.

I sat motionless and in dead silence, but in that moment I had made one of the most profound statements in my whole ministry. There is a time for separation (not segregation). Wholeness cannot exist unless there is integrity of its parts. From 1630 to 1966, we as a people were denied the right to live with integrity. That night I was saying we must learn the truth, for it is the truth that will make us free. But the ultimate truth is that America itself cannot be free and whole until all of its parts are free and whole.

The FBI informant who was present reported it this way: "Prior to the beginning of the meeting there were some 20 to 30 white people in the audience and these individuals were requested by Churchville to stand up and give their seats to Negroes who had arrived late and were standing in the back. This was done without any altercation resulting; however, there was much murmuring and evidence of surprise and indignation exhibited by both whites and Negroes."

In the next day's paper, the stuff hit the fan. Strangely enough, I felt no pain. I did not feel that I had to be defensive and I was not afraid. The moment of truth had come and I had recognized it and stood with it. I knew that there were whites there who had marched at the Girard College wall and in other ways had taken a stand for justice. I knew that their feelings had been hurt. But the strongest public reaction came not from them but from some leaders in the black community.

The *Philadelphia Tribune*, the city's leading black newspaper, and radio station WDAS both editorialized against what they called "reverse discrimination." *Night Life*, a tabloid for black café society, complained about a "lynch whitey!" mood at the rally. The Rev. Jesse Anderson, Sr., rector of St. Thomas' Episcopal Church, the oldest incorporated black church in the nation, expressed his "shock and horror" in an open letter to Bishop DeWitt.

Father Anderson condemned what he called "segregation and

hatred in the House of the Lord," and said he was writing to newspapers "in order to express, as a Negro and an Episcopalian, to the white people involved my apology and heartfelt chagrin at this attempt to vilify a set of people because of the color of their skin."

These were words well said, words faithfully representing the convictions of Fr. Anderson and his generation. It is amazing, however, how perspectives can change from one generation to another. It is said that "circumstances are the shaping hands of God." God had placed me squarely in the midst of a set of circumstances that shaped me for this moment in time. It did not take long for Fr. Anderson to realize that "time makes ancient good uncouth; they must upward still and onward who would keep abreast of truth." Very soon he would not only defend my stand, but our stand would become one and the same. It was important to me that the two of us should be on the same side.

Mattie Humphrey responded to all this in a reasoned letter to the *Philadelphia Tribune.* What had happened was no more discrimination, she argued, than it would be for the Sons of Italy to reserve spaces at one of their meetings for fellow Italian-Americans. "Those who came were fortunate enough to be permitted to remain, and there is no indication that they asked for more." But Mattie's reasonable approach did not persuade many people. A real nerve had been touched.

At my next vestry meeting it was hell. Not only had I hosted a meeting calling for black unity in a Christian church where God is no respecter of color, but I had insulted white people, people of the Episcopal Church (most of whom were white), and members of the Advocate (some of whom were white). It was shameful and unchristian. Someone moved that the subsidies from the foundation be sent back, John fired, and all such activities cease and desist.

Once again, I sat, listened, pondered these things in my heart, and then I spoke: "I have been called to and I am participating in Christ's ministry of redemption, and God knows that Negroes are in need of redemption. I know what I am doing. I shall continue doing as I am doing, and when you reach the point where you can no longer accept this ministry, ask me to leave. I will leave and not even protest or fight you."

No one took me up on it. But these were strong words and I meant them. So often our decisions are based on, What can I say that will not threaten my security, my very survival? I had a wife and four children. What if the vestry had asked for my resignation? Where would I have found a job to take care of my family?

I felt almost certain that I could get a political appointment, no matter who the mayor was. Had not Mayor Tate appointed me to serve on the Human Relations Commission even after I had condemned the police for the killing of Willie Philyaw in 1963? And if it came to that, I could work on the waterfront as a stevedore. Having been a chaplain for so long in county and state prisons, I knew many men working on the docks who "owed me one." I am physically strong, and the kind of pride I have is not the kind that would cause me to feel ashamed to be working on the waterfront. In fact, I would feel proud. That is where Jesus found some of his apostles—on the waterfront.

6. Survival of the Parish

One direct result of the Black Unity Rally was that the second half of the foundation grant for John Churchville's work ($2,500) was not forthcoming. The foundation director told me simply but coldly: "There is no more money. You have not used it for the purpose for which it was given. It was given to work with gangs. You used it to call black unity rallies." At this point, his money didn't matter. Little did he realize what had been the real mission of that foundation grant. It had been to launch BPUM, the Black People's Unity Movement, a movement that would cause black people to sing, "Deep in my heart, I do believe, we shall overcome some day."

I was much more worried about the annual diocesan grant, and so was the bishop. This grant appeared as a separate line item in the diocesan budget, which had to be approved each fall at the diocesan convention, with clergy and lay delegates from each parish in the five-county diocese casting their votes. We had our opponents there; one of the strongest and bitterest voices in the diocesan convention against funding the Advocate was that of a black priest. But the bishop devised a strategy to safeguard the funding.

The 1966 convention would ask Diocesan Council, the ruling

body between conventions, to reevaluate "the experimental diocesan program at the Church of the Advocate" and report its findings to the convention of 1967. This move would cut off any hasty action by 1966 convention delegates upset by recent events at the Advocate, allowing instead for thoughtful reflection and, the bishop hoped, the development of a solid rationale for the church's work at 18th and Diamond.

We gave the members of the diocese even more to think about during the summer of 1966. Teenage counselors in our summer day camp, who had been recruited from churches around the country, got involved in demonstrations at the main Post Office Building at 30th and Market sponsored by CORE to protest discrimination in hiring. In June, I was the spokesman in Harrisburg at a rally to launch the Crusade for Children, aimed at raising the state welfare grant for a family of four from a pathetic $1,800 per annum to an established poverty level of $3,600. But what drew the most attention were the two appearances of Stokely Carmichael at the Advocate in July and August.

John Churchville, who had arranged for Stokely's visit, had not been surprised to find that of the pastors he approached, I was the only one in town who would consider hosting the apostle of Black Power. On July 18, Stokely spoke to a large crowd in the parish hall, while our youth counselors, mostly white, observed discreetly from the balcony. When reporters interviewed me about his message, I said that Black Power gives shivers to some people, but it gives hope to others.

In his return engagement in late August, Stokely gave a lot of people the shivers when he addressed a crowd of some 2,000, this time outdoors, from the steps of the church. "Philadelphia is a racist city run by police gestapo," he said. "The next time racist Rizzo tries to march 1,500 cops into our community he's not going to get away with it."

He was referring to police raids on three SNCC meeting places earlier that month. Two and a half sticks of dynamite had been seized in the apartment of Freedom George Brower, and he and three others had been arrested. The dynamite, however it had found its way into George's apartment, was not part of some anarchist plot. But these arrests allowed Police Commissioner Rizzo to advance himself further as the savior of the community from riot and rebellion. (Mary Richardson tells me that it was Bishop DeWitt who put up bail money for Freedom George, who was a close associate of Fr. Layton Zimmer.)

Black pride was Carmichael's theme in his outdoor address. "We're going to say to our children, 'You're black and you're beautiful,'" he proclaimed. Both Carmichael and James Forman, also of SNCC, were dressed in flowing white robes given them by Sekou Toure, premier of Guinea, earlier that year. Walter Palmer of the Black People's Unity Movement opened the meeting by saying that "American black people are the chosen people of the world." Bill Mathis of Philadelphia CORE, calling for black unity, said, "There ought not to be one man in this crowd who is afraid of what the white man can do to him."

I was closely in tune with what Bill and Walt and Stokeley were saying. In a talk to a student group at Temple University in the same year, I argued that integration was not nearly as important to us as the new image we were creating for ourselves: "Black Power has alerted the world that the black man is changing. The white man may not like what we're saying, but at least he has to deal with us because he knows we are not going to shuffle our feet and submit feebly to injustice anymore."

My FBI files for 1966 reveal the nervousness of the authorities and their complete misunderstanding of what we were saying and doing. On August 17, 1966, FBI agents were advised to be alert to my influence and that of John Churchville: "You should be particularly alert for any indications that black nationalist leaders or individuals are influencing Negro street gangs to engage in riots or racial disorders." This FBI advisory made reference to a "meeting and rally of street gangs sponsored by Groovers Social Club at the Church of the Advocate," and was filed under the heading "Northern Student Movement."

NSM, SNCC, CORE, BPUM—all these groups were using the Advocate for meetings that year. It was BPUM that became the agent of shaping and defining ourselves as a people; it was more a movement than an organization. We of the BPUM met monthly, and month by month we grew to realize that we had a right to participate and share in every aspect of life in America. We had a right to be chief executives, legislators, officers of the police force, principals and superintendents in the school system. We had a right to employment and good housing, and the responsibility to enter into the political arena to cause decisions to be made that did not overlook us but instead respected us. BPUM showed us that we should love ourselves because "black is also beautiful." It spoke about family values, and it reminded us of the words of Frederick Douglass: "Power concedes nothing without a demand." We had to realize that our cause had to be a struggle and that we all had to join in. As Douglass also said: "We may not get all in this life that we pay for, but we must certainly pay for all that we get."

Walter Palmer and Mattie Humphrey; Ed Robinson and Ed Sims; David Richardson and Saladin Mohammed (Phil White); John Churchville and Bill Strickland; Bill Meek and Bill Mathis; Jimmie Lester and Rose Wiley; Alice Walker, Almanina Barbour, and Richard Traylor—I name only a few who were part of that movement. And very much in harmony with those who embodied BPUM were supporters and leaders who were with us in spirit though not in body: the Revs. Marshall Lorenzo Shepard, Jr., Jerome Cooper, and Jim Woodruff of the bishop's staff; educator Bernie Watson; attorneys Oscar Gaskins, Charlie Bowser, and the "irreverent" Cecil B. Moore, revered by all. These and scores of others were among the sung and unsung heroes who moved us and Philadelphia from "before the sixties" to a new day. In the words of an old man speaking to Martin Luther King: "We ain't what we used to be and we ain't what we ought to be, but, thank God, we ain't what we was."

Not all of them called "the Name," but they made my ministry whole, for there are those who say "Lord, Lord," and there are those who do his will, some of whom, in this case, paid dearly for their convictions. They were beaten by police, charged, tried, and jailed for various offenses. On some occasions, white sympathizers and supporters in Chestnut Hill and on the Main Line provided bail for those arrested. In fact, so close was our communication and relationship with the Chestnut Hillers that we adopted the name "The North Philadelphia/Chestnut Hill Pipeline." We were by no means alone in our struggle. We realized that separation did not have to mean that we were disjoined. So often the cause of evil prospered, yet we knew that "truth alone is strong, and behind the dim unknown" there stood a man of God, "within the shadow, keeping watch upon his own"—Robert L. DeWitt, the Bishop of Pennsylvania.

The Advocate was the place where those who advocated good and right causes met. But there was one group I turned away, and I feel guilty to this day for doing so. Some antiwar University of Pennsylvania students wanted to use the church for a rally on February 19, 1966. I first said yes but reconsidered after receiving a phone call from a member of the diocesan committee that supervised the annual grant to the Advocate. He had heard of the planned event and advised against it. His words were, "Paul, if I were you, I would not permit them to use the church."

Up to this point in my life, I had always tried to examine my fears and realize the truth of what President Roosevelt had said, "There is nothing to fear but fear itself." But I had not anticipated this issue. The man who had phoned was on the committee to recommend to the diocesan convention for or against continued funding for the support of the work of the Advocate. He sat in our vestry meetings as I battled with my vestry about black self-determination and black power, and he had never once said a word. But when I decided to extend our ministry to include opposition to America's war in Vietnam, I discovered something I had never thought about before.

Without having realized it, I was following the same path that Martin Luther King was on, as his growing opposition to the war led him finally to speak out so eloquently on April 4, 1967, in Riverside Church in New York City. King knew that we are all caught up—along with the people of Vietnam—in a single garment of destiny. The rights of Negroes in America could not be separated from those of the Indochinese, and King knew that he would have to answer not only to his own people in America, but to history and, above all, to God.

Because of his outspoken stand, King fell out of the graces of President Johnson, Roy Wilkins of the NAACP, Whitney Young of the Urban League, and many of his white supporters. He saw $332,000 being spent for every "enemy" killed, while so little was spent on every person in poverty. He saw Negroes being killed in disproportionate numbers to those of whites. And he saw through the self-serving philosophy of those who manufactured war, which was "the war is the white man's business."

That is what the white committee member was saying to me: "The war is our business, not yours." I would come to realize all this later, and conclude that I had to join forces with those who acted against America's destruction of Vietnam, even if it meant causing the Advocate to lose support; and I would open wide the doors of the church to students and others who were antiwar protesters.

The incident of the phone call requires me to say something about the complex governance of the parish at that time. First, there was the all-male vestry. That was typical for those days; the charter of the church specified the election of men only. I decided it would be too cumbersome to change the charter, so I created an auxiliary vestry made up of women, appointed by me. In addition, there was a board of trustees, rather like a cathedral chapter, which was responsible for administering our small endowment fund and looking after the physical structure. These trustees were white men from churches on the Main Line and Chestnut Hill.

To top it all off, a Bishop's Committee of five (including the member who made the phone call about the student rally) had been appointed to supervise the expenditure of the diocesan grant. Bishop Armstrong had instituted this committee when I was sent to the Advocate and he did it entirely for reasons of race. The bishop knew and I knew, and we both accepted the fact, that the people of the diocese would openly question the ability of a Negro priest to administer a grant of that size. He suggested the appointment of a Bishop's Committee, its members to come from some of the wealthiest and most prestigious parishes in the diocese. They would attend all vestry meetings at the Advocate but were advised to speak only sparingly, and when I reported to Diocesan Convention they would stand with me, certifying that the handling of "their" money by this Negro priest met with their approval.

I should have found this arrangement totally revolting, and I should have rejected it with deepest indignation, but the year was 1962. Race relations were the way they were almost as if ordained by God. What is stranger than fiction is that these committee members were present during some of the most dramatic confrontations which I had with my vestry as I moved into the theology of liberation. They did not participate in the conflict. It was as though it was irrelevant to them, or perhaps they agreed with the stand I was taking. I hope it was the latter. The only time I was ever challenged—or, better, threatened—by a committee member was that one phone call about the antiwar rally. Bishop DeWitt dissolved the committee not long after he became diocesan bishop, since he found no need for it.

The worship life of the parish had its own complications. My accomplished organist and choir director, Edward Collins-Hughes, and I had very different ideas about the appropriate style of our liturgy. I wanted a liturgy that would reflect the black experience, but the choir director and the choir wanted to maintain a tradition of music and worship befitting a great Anglican cathedral. The choir won out; but I got my way at least with respect to where the altar should be located.

The architectural design of the Advocate spoke to the transcendence of God. The chancel is three steps above the nave, and the altar five steps above the chancel. Both theologically and psychologically I was uncomfortable being locked into this transcendent position in relation to the congregation. I felt the liturgy should symbolize the immanence of God in the midst of his people. That was central to my theology. That is why I was in the midst of the people during the North Philadelphia riots and their aftermath.

When I proposed to my curate, the Rev. Lloyd Winter, that we should have a free standing altar in the nave, he was very supportive of the idea. My talented curate himself built a beautiful altar of solid oak, and I had some of the men of the church build the platform where it still stands today, on the same level as the people.

As one would expect, there were those who felt that I had done violence to one of the most beautifully designed specimens of French Gothic architecture in the country. Why would I come down from "on high" and celebrate the Mass in the midst of the people? One of my older members told me that when *he* died he wanted me to use the high altar. I did.

My preaching became an issue for some as well. When I told the congregation that racial unity was of the essence, and that there was more similarity than difference between black people who lived in poverty around 18th and Diamond and black people who lived in comfort in Germantown and Oak Lane, that was hard for some to accept. Even the Afro haircuts of Marc and Kemah, my sons, and of some of the other teenagers who attended church could be a cause of offense to someone. The congregation decreased in size, and for the longest time I was deeply troubled.

Like all other American institutions, the church is expected to show annual growth both in members and in monetary income. But soon I began to realize that, while on Sunday mornings at 11:00 the numbers were going down, often on a Sunday afternoon at 4:00 I would be standing before two hundred people or more. They were often angry, indignant, hurting people, who wanted to do something about the injustices to and the oppression of blacks in America. Eventually I came to realize that this was precisely what the church should be about. God was made known through Moses to the Hebrew people in Egypt who were oppressed. Jesus quoted Isaiah, when he began his ministry: "The Spirit of the Lord is upon me. He has anointed me to preach good tidings to the poor, to bind up the brokenhearted, to proclaim liberty to the captives, the opening of prison to those who are bound" (Luke 4:18). During the week our daily ministries would touch the lives of many. After a while, when people asked me, "How big is your congregation?" I would answer, "Well, only about a hundred congregate at the Advocate at 11:00 on Sundays, but during the week (and this was true especially after we opened the soup kitchen) we have a congregation of about 1,500."

Our Sunday services were never sheltered from the life of the streets. Dorothy, who was mentally disturbed, frequently interrupted services with long harangues. I would wait until she finished or sometimes come down from the altar and put my arm around her to calm her down. But one Sunday, Dorothy grabbed a handful of envelopes from the offering plate and ran out of the church. I ran out and caught her. She then stuffed the envelopes into her brassiere. I said to her firmly, "Dorothy, you'd better take them out, or I am going in after them." She gave them to me. On that morning we had some white visitors worshipping with us. They were obviously startled by such bizarre actions in church. I explained briefly that being a Christian does not mean that we should sit passively in the face of wrongdoing, and I proceeded with the service.

Something similar happened on January 1, 1967. I felt very pleased to see a young man about seventeen years of age attending our eight o'clock communion service. Suddenly he snatched two purses from two women who were kneeling in prayer. I saw the young man bolt through the door and I ran right out after him. People on the street were stunned to see a priest fully attired in ecclesiastical vestments pursuing a youth through the slushy, mud-packed snow. After chasing him for a few blocks I was ready to quit, but I had narrowed the gap between us and I called out, "You better drop it, kid, because I'm gonna catch you." He dropped the purses and went on running.

I picked up the purses and made my way back to "the flock," who were just standing and waiting, momentarily speechless. They voiced their exclamations, hugged and kissed their rector, and then I said, "Let us pray for the whole state of Christ's church," and we prayed and broke bread together on our knees.

The committee appointed by Diocesan Council to study the work of the Advocate liked what they saw. The report prepared by these three laymen from suburban parishes (John Ballard of Whitemarsh, John Newbold of Radnor, and Stephen Gardner of Gladwyne) was so strongly supportive that it ensured the continued funding of our programs by the diocese.

So Stokely's appearances and John Churchville's activities ended up being validated by a blue-ribbon committee of ranking Episcopal laymen from the white suburbs who were not afraid to say that my participation in the Black Power movement was "a legitimate expression of [my] ministry." They hedged their support only a little by recommending that meetings of a controversial nature might be held in churches of other denominations as well, and that we should take care to ensure unsensational reporting of such events in the press. That would be almost impossible to do, because the Philadelphia press seemed to enjoy writing about Episcopalians doing unconventional things.

The committee's report included practical recommendations, most of which were not acted upon, I am sorry to say. They thought I should have both a curate and a parish visitor on staff so that I could be more free to work on community issues and to interpret those issues to the larger church and society. They noted that my discussions of Black Power in suburban congregations (their home turf) were contributing greatly to understanding in the diocese.

I was certainly pleased by the report and its positive reception at Diocesan Convention. My survival tactic then and in the years that followed has been never to allow the question of diocesan support to be framed in terms of whether the diocese could afford to keep the Advocate open. Instead, I wanted to force them to ask: "Can we afford not to keep it open?"

But as the work expanded and costs kept rising, church funding alone, which reached a high-water mark of $60,000 per annum, would not pay all the bills. Another tactic was necessary. Turning to the Bible, I found a passage which I called "making shields of brass": "So Shishak, King of Egypt, came up against Rehoboam and took away the treasures of his house . . . and he carried away also the shields of gold which Solomon had made. Instead of which Rehoboam made shields of brass" (II Chronicles 12:9–10).

What do you do when you find your staff is dwindling but your program is not? Make shields of brass to substitute for the shields of gold. Secular sources of program money began to open up and we took advantage of them. The Crime Prevention Association asked permission to place up to ten persons in our parish house as staff for some very creative programs. Then Model Cities came up with a cultural arts program. From that source the parish house was refurbished, rent was paid by the square foot, and staff of good quality could be hired to run the programs. The Urban Coalition, under the direction of Charles Bowser, came across with as much as $13,000 a summer for us to run summer programs.

I would not accept all secular sources of program funding, however. They had to be consistent with the Advocate's goals and with my own sense of God's purpose for this church. I said no, for instance, to the managers of the Joe Frazier Corporation when they asked for the use of the parish gymnasium as the heavyweight fighter's training facility.

The spokesman for the Frazier Corporation was a white Episcopalian who thought surely he could convince me to sign on. The training facility would be used not only by Joe Frazier but would also be available to young men from the community, steering them away from idleness and developing in them discipline and pride. The corporation would pay us handsomely, enough so that the diocese would be freed of any further need to subsidize the church.

I admitted that the money could certainly be used, but I told the spokesman there would be no boxing at the Advocate, because I believe the sport is dangerous, destructive, and immoral. He was upset and angered by my rejection and went to the bishop to complain about how the church had turned down this marvellous opportunity. The bishop gave him his standard response: "This is Father Washington's prerogative as rector of the parish. I will not and cannot violate the authority given to him under the canons."

It was more difficult for me to say no to Stockton Strawbridge, a leading merchant and worthy recipient of the Philadelphia Award, when, as chairman of the United Way fund drive, he asked permission to use my name and photo on some of the campaign literature. This could have raised awareness of the Advocate in the community and might have resulted in more support for us. The United Way was supporting two agencies on whose boards I sat, but I was known more for my identification with the less sophisticated, small and humble community groups. My photo would have implied that United Way supported those groups, and I could not honestly say that it did. Stockton Strawbridge is widely recognized and respected for his untiring efforts to enhance the attractiveness of Market Street East, where Strawbridge and Clothier's department store is located. He has done all of that, but I could not say that he was doing the same for North Philadelphia.

I had another hard decision to make when the Police Athletic League asked to set up one of its PAL centers at the church. I knew they had a good youth program that had helped many young people in city neighborhoods, but I felt we could not have it at the Advocate. It was a case such as St. Paul spoke of when he said he would not eat meat offered to idols (I Corinthians 8). For him, eating it would mean nothing; it could do no harm. But there were people who would not understand and would feel that he was an idol worshiper; therefore, he would abstain. While I knew that the PAL programs were in many instances good, there would be those who would believe we were in alliance with "the enemy." I could not afford such a misunderstanding.

It had been much easier to say no to the police when, during one of the periods of great tension in the neighborhood, they asked me for permission to station armed officers in the church's steeple. There was no way that was going to happen.

The Advocate had become an important symbol for the whole church and for the community around it. We had to be clear about what it was we symbolized. The diocesan committee expressed it well by saying that the Advocate had become an "outward visible sign" of the commitment of the diocese "to involvement in the struggle against race hatred and poverty in the slums of Philadelphia." They went on to say: "A commitment to the struggle against color as a barrier to the love of man for his neighbor is right and proper—a necessary concern of the church." We would survive and gain what support we could for the sake of that struggle.

7. A Divided City

The rising black consciousness was everywhere. It was certainly being felt in the public schools, where it would come to a head in one of the most polarizing events in recent Philadelphia history—a demonstration by black city high school students in front of the offices of the Philadelphia Board of Education at 21st and the Parkway on November 17, 1967. When Police Commissioner Rizzo ordered a brutal billy club charge against those young people, it set back race relations in the City of Brotherly Love for years.

I had sensed some of what was coming because both Kemah and Marc were high school students. Kemah was the one most caught up in the ferment of the times. As a student at the Saul Agricultural High School, he had been refusing to salute the flag at school assemblies. When I was informed of this and brought the matter up with him, Kemah said to me, "Dad, do you really believe that this country intends for *us* to be included in this 'liberty and justice for all'? You talk about integrity and honesty all the time. What do you expect me to do?" I didn't discuss it any further with him.

My two sons were keenly aware of the effects of racism. They could see it all around them where they lived, and each had experienced his own share of discriminatory treatment. Kemah was once picked up by policemen who had taken offense because he was standing observing them as they were arresting other young people. The police put him in their car, drove him to another neighborhood and dumped him there, fully aware of the tense gang situation that made it extremely dangerous for any young person to be found in a territory not his own.

In the summer of 1966, son Marc was working as a counselor for the Advocate day camp. He was sixteen at the time. He decided to take his group of nine- to twelve-year-old children to police headquarters (the Roundhouse at 8th and Race) to witness a hearing on charges arising from the police raid on SNCC when dynamite had been found. While waiting to go into the part of the building where the judge sat, Marc said offhandedly to the young campers, "Now you are going to see American justice in action." A plainclothes policeman hearing this immediately came over and took Marc into custody, saying, "You're under arrest for corrupting the morals of a minor."

Marc was handcuffed, fingerprinted, and photographed in the basement of the Roundhouse. When I found out, I hurried down and, with the help of Clarence Farmer, director of the Human Relations Commission, was able to have the arrest quashed and Marc's photograph handed over.

Kemah very much wanted to be a part of the November 17 demonstration. It had been widely publicized in the community. The students were demanding the teaching of black history in the public schools and other reforms they thought long overdue. But Kemah did not make it to the demonstration. When he and two other classmates left the Saul school that morning to make their way downtown, they were followed by a school counselor in an automobile. He stopped them, loaded them in his car and returned them to school. All the school doors at Saul were then locked to prevent further escapes.

In spite of precautions like that, the number of students at 21st and the Parkway grew to about 3,500. I was there early on, along with a number of other adult community leaders, to show my support and to be of assistance. I made the great mistake of leaving the site at midmorning. I thought that everything was proceeding so peaceably that my presence would not be needed.

School superintendent Mark Shedd, while apprehensive about so many students leaving school to demonstrate, recognized the importance of the issues being raised and had decided to meet with student leaders to discuss their demands. He asked Mattie Humphrey, then a consultant to the Community Relations Service of the U.S. Justice Department acting as a liaison to high school students, to identify ten students on the spot to come in and talk with him. While this discussion was going on inside, the demonstration outside grew ever larger.

School board officials had asked the police to be present only with plainclothes officers who were part of the Civil Disobedience Squad, led by Lt. George Fencl. The police kept that bargain only until noon, when Commissioner Rizzo showed up with hundreds of uniformed police who took up riot formation. What happened then I did not see and can only report second-hand. The police reports say that two officers attempted to arrest some unruly students and then found themselves facing a large number of young people who moved threateningly in their direction.

Whatever the provocation or lack of it, all agree that Commissioner Rizzo ordered a billy club charge. "Get their asses!" he shouted, according to a reporter standing near him. Students, school administrators, and anyone else in the crowd then came under the swinging nightsticks. Pandemonium ensued. One reporter saw six police converge on a fallen youth and begin pounding him with their nightsticks. The Rev. Marshall Bevins, a white Episcopal priest, tried to intervene when he saw an officer dragging a young black woman down the sidewalk by her hair. He was arrested and hauled away himself.

Mattie Humphrey recalls the shock that she and others in the negotiating session felt when they looked out the window and saw the police attacking the demonstrators. She was so distraught herself that she ran out into the street gripping a fireplace log from the conference room in her hands. She saw Lee Chapman and "Doc" Holliday, two rising young black educators in the Philadelphia system, in tears. That they would do this to the children!

Groups of students, now very agitated, fanned out through center city, some engaging in acts of vandalism as they went. At City Hall, one such group was reportedly met by police with submachine guns and dogs. Fifty-seven arrests were reported, and at least twenty were injured, including bystanders and some police.

According to Frank Rizzo, the police had done "a beautiful thing." Many white Philadelphians must have agreed, as the police claimed that their switchboard was kept busy receiving congratulatory calls. The general fear of potential riots was leading some people to look for a strong man who would keep the city from going up in flames the way Detroit had that very summer. Frank Rizzo put on that mantle on November 17; some think it was his actions that day that made it possible for him to become mayor of Philadelphia only a few years later.

Others were horrified by the police action. Richardson Dilworth, former mayor of Philadelphia, then president of the school board, said, "That charge by the police triggered the violence. We did not ask for this large mass of police!" Judge Raymond Pace Alexander, leading black jurist in Philadelphia, spoke in very strong terms after he lowered the extremely high bail that had been set for my friends Walt Palmer and Bill Mathis, two of the adult leaders on the scene who had been charged with inciting to riot. The judge said: "The mere display of brute force with 300–400 armed police encircling youngsters—easily excited school children—will in itself cause the explosion that occurred Friday afternoon."

Ron Miller, a TV reporter for one of the local stations (later to become a national network reporter), came to our house to unload emotionally after observing the calamity at 21st and the Parkway. He needed to pour out what he had experienced; it was something his normal apparatus could not handle. He described to me what he had seen and heard, and in another language communicated what he felt. Then he left, and at six o'clock, the "professional" Ron Miller reported the news of the day.

The Rev. Henry Nichols, black Methodist minister and vice president of the school board, also criticized the police action severely. "F—— Reverend Nichols!" was Rizzo's reply as reported by the press. The police commissioner's later words of justification were a classic example of what many in the white community felt in the late 1960s: "We are going to stop all this lawlessness. We are going to maintain law and order. Nobody is going to make a patsy out of the Police Department."

The students who had met with Mark Shedd gathered the following evening at the Church of the Advocate to consider what to do next and to draw up a statement of purpose. Their demands were these: (1) More black representation on the school board. (There were only two black members at the time.) (2) Exemption from saluting the flag in classrooms, since "liberty and justice" do not exist for all. (3) The teaching of black history in all schools, by black teachers, as a major subject. (4) The removal of all police and nonteaching assistants from school buildings. (5) The assignment of black principals to run predominantly black schools.

What the students were asking for, apart from the particulars of their demands, were schools that would affirm them as full human beings. The police attack was doubly tragic both because it was a brutal denial of that underlying appeal for respect and because it frustrated the efforts of educational leaders like Dilworth, Nichols, and Shedd, who were looking for ways to respond honestly to the students' needs. Many parents were so shocked and dismayed by what took place on November 17 that they did not want their children returning to classes in public schools.

Ed Robinson of the Black People's Unity Movement and other black leaders organized "learning centers" to provide alternative places of instruction, with a curriculum based on black history. One such center met at the Advocate and the Washington children were a part of it. A parents' group that formed around this effort at community-controlled education included Christine as an active member. This was her first step on the way to becoming a leader in the community.

A personal incident that same year may be a good illustration of the gap that existed between many white school administrators and black students and parents. I had been summoned to the high school counselor's office to talk about a problem concerning

Kemah's behavior in class, and I cannot recall that interview without experiencing the feelings that it evoked.

As I sat talking with the counselor and expressed some disagreement with him, he said to me: "You know, Reverend Washington, there's one thing that you people must remember. You can't afford to become emotional." The man was sitting there just as cool and calm as could be, and he was trying to disintegrate me. I thought I was pretty much together that day. My mind was clicking, my heart felt just right. There was a certain amount of aggressiveness throughout my being, but well under control. I was together; but this man was trying to put me in the same box he was in, his white, professional box.

"So you must remember, Reverend Washington, you people must function only with your mind"—that's what he was really saying to me—"but don't, for God's sake be whole; because we don't know how to deal with wholeness."

It was not only members of the black community who responded to the police attack on the students on November 17 and all that it symbolized. Two new organizations that I would work with very closely were formed over the next few months. One, called People for Human Rights, was only for white people who wanted to work against racism in their own community and to be a support group for Black Power activities. The other, called Philadelphians for Equal Justice (PEJ), was a racially mixed group of citizens who decided to band together to protect black Philadelphians in particular against "illegal intimidation and arrest and almost daily episodes of police brutality."

PEJ recruited a battery of volunteer lawyers to represent people in situations of police brutality or false arrest. A phone call to PEJ's number at the church (a number widely distributed in the community) would bring a lawyer to a preliminary hearing at a district police station to represent someone who thought he or she had been falsely charged. It was all too typical for the police to cover up their own misbehavior by charging a citizen with disorderly conduct or assault and battery against a police officer.

A phone call to PEJ in the middle of the night could result in several people (black and white, from different parts of the city) showing up at a police station or at the Roundhouse to demand information about the whereabouts or the physical condition of some arrested person. On call that particular evening might be a black lawyer like William Akers or a white lawyer like Jack Levine. Certainly one of the most responsive lay volunteers was Joe Miller, who became a close friend and associate in many later projects. This short, white-haired, dignified-looking mortgage broker and I put in a lot of appearances at police stations together to inquire about the fate of persons known to us only because of a call to LO 3–1388.

November 17 so clearly showed the division in our city. On the one side were those white people who feared a revolt, and instead of working to eliminate the causes, were calling for police repression. On the other side were black people, with some white allies, who were searching for new institutional forms to express their own identity and worth. On April 4, 1968, the day that Martin Luther King was killed, our divided city was tested once again.

Washington, D.C., and other major cities went up in flames and riot when word came of the assassination of Dr. King; but Philadelphia did not. I think that had very much to do with the peacekeeping efforts of so many in the black community who went out into the streets as I did, encouraging others to return to their homes and watching for any disruptive acts by the police or by overwrought citizens. I think it had very little to do with the "law and order" response of City Hall and Commissioner Rizzo.

Mayor Tate proclaimed a limited state of emergency, forbidding the gathering of groups of twelve or more on the city streets. The ACLU challenged this as unconstitutional, and People for Human Rights formed groups of more than twelve to demonstrate in front of the homes of members of Congress in white neighborhoods, courting arrest and exposing the racist nature of the mayor's proclamation.

On the night of April 4, we opened the doors of the church and called people in for reflection and prayer. The service was led by Fr. Winter, while I remained on the streets. The next day, Dr. Paul

Anderson, president of Temple University, asked me to address Temple's student body. I told them that it was up to us now to embody the spirit of Dr. King and make his dream a reality. Immediately following my talk at Temple, I hurried to Independence Mall to speak along with others to a great crowd assembled there at 6th and Market Streets. Through such public gatherings and a well-organized march through the streets of center city, Philadelphians peaceably expressed their grief and tried to renew their spirits.

On the Sunday following, Palm Sunday, we made our own statement about the limits on public gatherings by purposely expanding the route for our traditional Palm Sunday procession through the streets around the church. Civil liberties attorney Henry Sawyer called me to say that if the police interfered with our march, he would defend the church. Deeply moved by the death of Dr. King, many more people joined us in that procession and the worship service afterward than had been seen on a Sunday morning at the Advocate for a long time.

8. The Black Power Conference, 1968

Increasingly I found people turning to me to explain what was going on. What was this new black consciousness? How could we understand the explosions rocking our cities? Why was there such a spirit of revolt in our young people, black and white?

In media interviews and speeches I tried to speak as directly and clearly as I could to the questions that were coming from white America. In a feature article in the *Evening Bulletin* in 1968, I fielded questions that were typical for that time.

"Riots? You ask why? I don't think the riots today have a calculated aim any longer. People riot, not for the right to get a better job or a better house—but because they've already found there is no job, there is no house. They've been promised and they believed, and then they found there is nothing.

"Most white people now fear a real revolt. So, instead of working to eliminate the causes, they advocate more police. But the tighter you press the lid down, the greater the explosion."

When asked if I thought there was a chance for improving black-white relations, I replied in the affirmative.

"Yes, I think there is a chance. It's like the relationship between a man and a woman. You can either have a relationship based on integrity or one based on force. Either you respect her or you rape her. Now, black people are not willing to be raped any longer."

The racist nature of the war against Vietnam was something I also tried to make clear. In a speech at an antiwar rally of 750 people at Arch Street Methodist Church in February, 1968, I spoke of the paternalistic attitude of white America, toward black people here, toward Asian people in Indochina. "Instead of eliminating the cause of revolts, the U.S. government simply sends more and more soldiers abroad, just as they beef up police forces to maintain men like Rizzo here at home."

All of these quotations are from press reports in the metropolitan dailies, but I was called upon to speak frequently in the suburbs, too, and the suburban press took note—in particular the *Main Line Chronicle*, which was edited by the arch-conservative known as "Uncle Ben."

One talk at St. Mary's Episcopal Church in Ardmore was covered fairly objectively in the news section of the paper. Integration was one of the themes of my talk, and I was quoted accurately as saying, "Integration is not the answer to the racial problem. The black man is developing a heritage of his own through black nationalism."

On the editorial page, however, Uncle Ben quoted from the notes taken by the *Chronicle* reporter: "Rev. Washington rambled on and on. He seemed bitter, and gave me the impression he doesn't like white people. He was better received than I thought he would be. They applauded rather generously. No one asked any good questions." Uncle Ben found the applause, as well as some reported laughter, to be patronizing. "In 1968," he wrote, "a Negro speaker is automatically correct because he is black. And all his jokes are funny."

Speaking hard truths to white people in the church and the larger community did not guarantee a good reception, but I kept receiving invitations to speak, and I kept at it because I believe that improved relations between the races can only be based on hearing each other's truth. There were times when a word of rebuke had to be spoken within the black community, too. This was usually because of the growing strain between the generations. Too many older people were alarmed by the radical politics of their own children. And sometimes young radicals failed to honor the struggle of their parents.

On June 23, 1968, a rally was held at the Girard College wall to celebrate the decision of the U.S. Supreme Court earlier that month to open the gates of Girard College, after 137 years, to black orphan boys. All those who had contributed to the efforts to desegregate the school were to be honored.

Cochairmen for the event, which drew some six hundred people, were attorney Cecil B. Moore, the Rev. Marshall Lorenzo Shepard, Jr., and the Rev. Jesse Anderson, Sr. When Judge Raymond Pace Alexander, who had begun the legal effort to integrate Girard College back in 1954, took the mike, he was heckled by some young people in the crowd. Both Cecil Moore and I rebuked these young people who thought they were so much more militant than previous generations had been. "He was out there fighting for freedom before you were born!" I told them.

Because it had become known around the nation that the Advocate was the center of the Black Power movement in Philadelphia, I was asked to be the host of the Black Power Conference, an event that would bring almost 8,000 participants from around the country to Philadelphia on August 29–September 1, 1968. It was the third in a series of conferences attempting to actualize in political and economic terms the growing black consciousness in America and to organize the black community for self-determination.

The previous conferences had created tensions with white power structures fearful of disruptions in the cities in which they were held. The conferences had also revealed tensions among black people who had varying understandings of the meaning of black power. I realized that someone was needed as host who could support the just demands of the militants and yet be a peacekeeper. But beyond this, I deeply believed in the purpose of the conference. I had reached a point where I felt there was a moral imperative to fight for freedom and the wholeness of our being, shattered by the violence of racism, and to achieve this, the power that the omnipotent God had breathed into our black beings had to be released. So I said yes to the Rev. Dr. Nathan Wright when he asked me to serve as national vice-chairman in charge of hospitality. Dr. Wright was a brother priest in the Episcopal Church who was becoming well known as a theologian of Black Power. I offered him the Advocate as the center for registration and as one of several community meeting places for workshops and rallies.

I said yes to Nathan without first consulting either my bishop, my vestry, or anyone else. There was just nobody else who was where I was at this moment. Bishop DeWitt proved to be very supportive. The vestry went along, but without much enthusiasm and with a degree of apprehension. But I had learned that leaders cannot always be democratic. Moses did not consult with the Israelites in Egypt before he led them to freedom, and there were times when Harriet Tubman demanded that her followers follow at the point of a gun. My vestry had no experience that would have prepared them to make such a decision.

I thought of the text from John's Gospel: "Other sheep I have, which are not of this fold; them also I must bring, and they shall hear my voice; and there shall be one fold and one shepherd" (John 10:16). The people who would gather at the Black Power Conference were sheep that I as a shepherd knew. They knew my voice and I knew theirs. But let no one think for a moment that there were not times when I felt strongly moved to "plead the fifth" lest I found myself being incriminated. Black Power meant different things to different people. Some gave it a very sinister interpretation.

J. Edgar Hoover, FBI director, chose to understand it simply in terms of urban riots. In his annual report to the U.S. attorney general in 1968, he said that Black Power had "come to mean to many Negroes the 'power' to riot, burn, loot, and kill."[1] President Nixon, interestingly enough, had chosen to interpret Black Power in what, to him, was a very positive sense. In a speech on March 28, he defined it as "the power that people should have over their own destinies, the power that comes from participation in the political and social processes of society." In another address he identified Black Power with black capitalism. "What most of the militants are asking is not separation but to be included in . . . to have a share of the wealth and a piece of the action."

Black social theorist Harold Cruse, a critic of the Black Power movement from the left, went at least partway with Nixon. He saw the movement as a mixture of conservative reform politics and "black revolutionary anarchism." "It is nothing," he wrote, "but the economic and political philosophy of Booker T. Washington given a 1960s militant shot in the arm and brought up to date."

The Second International Black Power Conference, which had been held in Newark, New Jersey, in September, 1967, had been financed by fifty major corporations. They, like Nixon, must have understood what was going on in terms of black capitalism. Yet it was "revolutionary anarchism" that caught all the headlines and determined how most people perceived the proceedings in Newark.

Newark at the time of the conference was a city still extremely tense after rioting that very summer, which had resulted in twenty-six deaths. The conference itself ended in a small riot when some delegates reportedly smashed a dozen TV cameras and drove newsmen out of a scheduled press briefing in a back room of Episcopal Cathedral House. News coverage of the Newark conference had been biased and inflammatory, which explained the delegates' anger; but their actions only served to confirm fears of a black revolution. The fact that members of the Harlem Mau Mau Society had appointed themselves conference guards and were to be seen wearing helmets and carrying machetes lent credence to the alarms of Hoover nationally and Frank Rizzo in the City of Philadelphia.

In August, 1968, Rizzo brought a bill to Philadelphia City Council to ban the carrying of long knives on the streets of the city. The fine would be a minimum of $300 plus ninety days in jail. The bill became law promptly by a vote of 13–1. Thacher Longstreth, the lone dissenting council member, said it was obviously timed with the forthcoming Black Power Conference in mind.

Once he was finished with his political posturing, Commissioner Rizzo was more restrained. When members of the Guardian Civic League, black police officers dedicated to fighting discrimination in the department and improving police-community relations, volunteered to police the conference events, Rizzo did not interfere with the arrangement. The Guardians said they would do it on their off-duty hours and as a project of the league. Uniformed, on-duty police kept a generally low profile throughout.

Internal security was to be handled in Philadelphia by the Black Panthers, who had emerged on the scene in Sacramento, California, the year previous when they entered the state capitol bearing arms, in order to make a statement about the right to self-defense of black people. The Panthers at the conference were unarmed but had a military appearance, wearing black trousers and shirts with Panther insignia as shoulder patches. They were from the West Coast, the Panther organization not yet having been formed in Philadelphia. Some served as the bodyguards of Ron Karenga, leader of the organization US, from Watts, the suburb of Los Angeles where the urban uprisings of the 1960s had begun. Karenga was a dominant personality at the conference, as were playwright LeRoi Jones (Imamu Amiri Baraka) and the Rev. Jesse Jackson, then running "Operation Bread Basket" in Chicago. Mrs. Rosa Parks was among the well-known participants. Stokely Carmichael did not attend.

The conference theme was "Black Self-Determination and Black Unity Through Direct Action." Dr. Nathan Wright set forth the goal as devising methods to "forge a black nation." Black people would be mobilized, he said, to resist the "genocidal tendencies of American society." What all this meant was to be developed in the workshops held in churches and schools in black neighborhoods of Philadelphia. This sampling of workshop topics shows the breadth of concern:

A Black Nation: A State or a State of Mind?
Black Economic Control of Black Communities

Black Labor Unions
A Third Black Party or Third Black Independent Force?
Black Education in Black Schools and Black Curriculum in
    White Schools
Formation of a Black Militia
A Black Foreign Policy

Was this separatism or a demand to be included in the government and the marketplace? A writer named Debbie Louis said that in the late 1960s "the black community stood as a conglomeration of often contradictory interests and directions, dubiously tied together by a common mood which combined centuries of anger with new hope, increasing desperation with new confidence."[2]

There was indeed ambiguity and contradiction. W. E. B. DuBois had described it earlier as "two souls, two thoughts, two unreconciled strivings; two warring ideals in one dark body whose dogged strength alone keeps it from being torn asunder." And again in the 1960s, in this "one dark body" were taking place the conflicts and contradictions between Malcolm X and Martin.

The media and the civil rights leaders presented Malcolm as a black segregationist, despite his contrary claims. "Many of you misunderstand us," Malcolm often said to black audiences, "and think that we are advocating continued segregation. No! We are as much against segregation as you are. We reject segregation even more militantly than you do. We want SEPARATION but not segregation." According to Malcolm, "Segregation is when your life and liberty is controlled (regulated) by someone else. . . . Segregation is that which is forced upon inferiors by superiors; but SEPARATION IS THAT WHICH IS DONE VOLUNTARILY."[3]

In the conference workshops, where we came together voluntarily with one another, our new confidence was expressed in new ideas for common action. Of special relevance for the future ministry of the Advocate was the housing workshop, a stimulus toward what would become the Advocate Community Development Corporation, under Christine Washington's direction. As a workshop participant, Christine was learning her first important lessons about how to obtain government funding for housing development in North Philadelphia. From another workshop came the impetus for Frankie Davenport and her husband David to begin publishing the *Voice of Umoja* in an attempt to meet the need for a periodical that would inform and inspire the black community toward the goals set by the conference. Sister Frankie would soon assume a new identity as Sister Falaka Fattah, founding the House of Umoja, a Boys' Town for black youth, as part of her campaign to bring gang violence to an end in Philadelphia.

Other workshops allowed for analysis and critique of patterns of racism throughout society. Andrew Freeman, executive director of the Philadelphia Urban League, told participants in a workshop on "The Control of White Violence" about the behavior of Philadelphia police on November 17, 1967. He lamented the fact that the Philadelphia Police Department had actually been receiving awards, commendations, and overwhelming support from the white community for beating black schoolchildren.

My greatest concern at the conference was that all should proceed peaceably, that this attempt at forging greater black unity, with its internal contradictions and its real promise, should not be disrupted nor experience anything like what had happened at the close of the Newark gathering the previous year. On the third day of the conference there came a time of testing when three white city policemen shouted racial obscenities and slurs at a group of conference delegates who were standing outside a Methodist church at 17th and York Streets.

News of this incident spread quickly and feelings were soon running high. I called Clarence Farmer, director of the Philadelphia Human Relations Commission, to urge an immediate response by city authorities. To the relief of us all and the astonishment of many, the police department announced the suspension of the offending officers within five hours of the incident, a response so quick it had no precedent. Along with the Rev. Claude Edmonds, pastor of the church where the incident occurred, Clarence Farmer and I were able to announce this suspension to a workshop session at the Advocate and cool everyone's temper.

Press relations were handled by Chuck Stone, a black journalist in Philadelphia who had been an aide to U.S. Congressman Adam Clayton Powell. White newsmen had to get their information from Chuck, since they were not invited to cover directly what was going on in the conference sessions and workshops. One white reporter vented his feelings at being shut out in a column that ran in the *Philadelphia Inquirer*:

He had stood on the corner for only ten minutes but already he had ceased to exist. It was loneliness heightened, but there was more. It was first his face that was lost, then his form. He became invisible and then was gone.

They were lined at the Church of the Advocate where 18th meets Diamond. It was here they would meet in a Black Power Conference to agree they were right because they were black. All around him was black. The police were black and the men were black and the children were black. They had come to celebrate that blackness and refused to dilute it with even one white.

He was white. He saw but was not seen; spoke, but was not heard. He felt intense presence around him but affected no one with his. For them, he was not there.

He could not stand it any more and walked to the corner where a black man in beads and dark glasses was standing. "Hello," he said, and the word choked in his throat, for it was stupid and hollow and a plea, not a greeting. The black man folded his arms on his chest and looked through him and past him without blinking. He walked away, defeated.

On the next corner, a black man in sandals stood impassively. The white man approached, then stopped, waited what seemed like hours, then said: "Are you forbidden to talk to me because I'm white?"

"Yes," the black man said, without looking at him.

The white man waited a minute, then said haltingly, "Does it make sense? Is it right that you judge me without knowing my name?"

"That's the way it is, baby," the black man said.

The columnist doubtless expressed the resentment of many whites who did not venture to the corner of 18th and Diamond but simply read about the event at home or on the suburban trains on the way to their racially segregated neighborhoods. Being white had never before meant being invisible or automatically excluded. Aware of this resentment, the Diocese of Pennsylvania tried to reason with those members of the white community that it could reach.

A public relations bulletin was prepared by the Rev. Francis Hines, a priest and publicist whom the bishop had hired to interpret events like this one that involved the participation of some part of the church, in this case the Advocate.

"This will be the most widely representative meeting of black people at a national level in the entire history of the U.S.," Hines wrote. Taking pride in the role of the Advocate and the Episcopal Church, he continued: "The Presiding Bishop [John Hines] has committed our Church to the cause of self-determination of peoples. Some years from now when the history books are all rewritten and this time of turmoil is analyzed a bit more objectively, they will have to note this fact and, also, because of our prayerful and tangible support to black people at this time, that our role in this process of history was not insignificant."

The bulletin, which was sent to diocesan clergy at the time of the conference, dealt mainly with the issue of the exclusion of whites from the event, arguing that this was not racist exclusion, even though some "black racist types" might be in attendance at the conference. It was simply one minority group doing what many minority groups in our country's history have had to do, that is, "organize ethnically to break the bonds of prejudice."

I was pleased that the diocese was being so supportive and was doing its best to interpret those aspects of the conference that most agitated white church members and others. My job as the host was to make sure that peace prevailed. I was tense and worried on the inside but projected the image once described by a reporter for the *Evening Bulletin*, who pictured me as "a sinewy man with a deep voice who exudes a Bogart kind of toughness." The mood of the conference seemed to call for Bogart toughness.

Usually when large crowds of black people get together, the atmosphere is festive, with warm greetings and laughter; but nowhere was there to be found among the 8,000 conventioneers even the slightest smile. I tried to be present everywhere, workshops, plenaries, and just walking around clerically attired, to say, I am your host. I fixed the muscles of my face to a look of seriousness, determination, and commitment. I was approachable, but only for the mission of the moment. In fact, unconsciously, I must have felt that this gathering was in my hands.

The burden was heavy. Thousands of black power militants from all over the country, ready to "take over" the country! I knew the Philadelphia leaders, and I felt that I could trust them to act within reason, but I did not know the Chicagoans, those from Oakland, New York, Newark, Boston. I was glad that they were all here, but I wanted it to be over and done with.

It should have been over on Sunday afternoon, but Amiri Baraka had arranged to present one of his plays on Sunday evening at a local school. I could not be relieved of the burden of my role at this conference until the play ended, the school doors were closed, and everyone was en route home, wherever that might be.

I stood outside the school where Baraka was presenting his play, still binding the remaining few conventioneers in my heart lest something break loose and there be hell to pay. There were also three or four black plainclothes policemen who were waiting for the final event to end.

At last, the people opened the doors and began pouring out, and then Baraka himself. The lights were turned out and the doors locked. When all had walked out, going in all directions, and there was no one left in sight, I collapsed, falling to one knee on the concrete pavement. I began crying uncontrollably.

The policemen ran to me and one held me like a child and said, "Don't cry, Father Washington, it's all over now. Everything is all right." They understood. I suspect they were as relieved as I. I got myself together and went home. Christine asked, "Well, how did it go?" I said simply, "O.K."

One of the effects of the conference on those of us who took part was to cause us to look more closely at our own practices with regard to black self-determination. At the Advocate that meant making a decision about the clergy team. My curate, Lloyd Winter, had stayed away from the church during the conference. He had come to me prior to the event to suggest that it might be best if he did so. I was glad that he had brought it up because I was thinking the same thing. It became clear to both of us that I needed a curate who was black; so Lloyd, who had served so faithfully, spoke to the bishop, and he gave him a new assignment at another inner-city location, as priest-in-charge of Christ and St. Ambrose Church, at 6th and Venango.

Of course there were two sides to the question of whether white clergy and volunteers should be prominent in the work of the Advocate in 1968. I had argued the opposite side myself when eight black young people had met with me the previous year to ask that all the counselors in our summer day camp be black. They were convinced that this should be our policy.

In previous years, white students had "invaded" the inner city, working in ghettos across the country. Their schools would put up lists of places that offered opportunities for summer service. Our day camp, with an enrollment of around two hundred children, had counselors who came from as far away as Paris or Turkey and from all over the United States. All these outside volunteers were white.

I told the young people that I understood their concern but could only agree with them in part. I knew that our children should have young role models with whom they could identify, but I also felt that it was important for some white teenagers to come into the inner city to learn from personal experience what life is like in the black ghettos of our country.

The young black people were uncompromising. They did not want white girls and boys picking up our children, holding them in their laps, with our children running fingers through their hair as if they were God's chosen people. These white kids don't learn anything, my young group said. They just leave when the summer is over, feeling they have stooped to bless us with their presence.

In the end they would not appreciate us, but pity us, and we don't need their pity.

I continued to argue for only just a few white camp counselors, but I realized that the "movement" was giving birth to a black identity and an insight into racism that someone of my age had not yet attained. Moreover, I had the distinct and unmistakable feeling that if we had white counselors at the Advocate during the coming summer, there would be trouble. In the summer of 1968 all of our counselors were black. It was healthy to see our children respecting and learning from their own. This was really a large part of what the Black Power movement was all about.

But black power as we understood it never meant "antiwhite." It was in fact a call and a struggle for the oneness and the wholeness of all of God's children, as in the case of Lil, a Jewish girl who had stayed on the third floor of our home along with other girls who worked in the summer day camp. Many afternoons after camp closing, instead of gathering with the other counselors she would remain with our family. Many times she said, "I like your family." Before the summer ended, she said, "I'd like to stay with you when day camp is over." She would be the fifth person who, for a season, would become a part of our family.

We asked Lil's mother, who was a teacher at the University of Pennsylvania, to come to talk to us about her daughter's request. When she came, she readily agreed; she and Lil did not get along. Lil was overjoyed. She had never experienced "family" the way she dreamed it should be. She found that with us. Immediately, Chris became Mom, I Dad, and our children her sisters and brothers. She came to church every Sunday. Although she did not receive communion, she would come to the altar rail for me to lay my hand on her head in blessing. Today Lil is married, and through her we have a son-in-law and two grandchildren. Her own family is modeled after our family, which became hers too. To me this is another dimension of black power, the power that makes us all one and whole.

I mentioned before the paranoid understanding of black power by J. Edgar Hoover. As can be imagined, the FBI had been watching the proceedings of the Black Power Conference with special interest. There were people there, like Max Stamford of the Revolutionary Action Movement (RAM) and Milton Henry of the Republic of New Africa (RNA), who had been placed on the FBI's "Agitator Index." An FBI memorandum dated April, 1968, had included me in a rather rambling report on "Black Nationalist Movement; Racial Matters." The memo discussed everything from the alleged plot by RAM to assassinate members of the Philadelphia police force by means of cyanide poisoning, to the "noticeable increase in the African hairstyle on the city streets, in restaurant waitresses, and among Negro youth." I was identified in this memo, right after mention of the alleged RAM plot, as having "consistently made the facilities of the church available to Black extremists."

For someone so closely associated with extremists and agitators, I certainly lacked some important credentials. For instance, I had never been arrested, not even in a demonstration. But before the year of the Black Power Conference was out, that lack was remedied, although I had to argue myself into the arrest.

At 8:30 on the morning of November 14, Philadelphia Welfare Rights Organization (WRO), led by Roxanne Jones, began a sit-in in the third-floor offices of the State Department of Welfare at the State Office Building in Philadelphia. Five hundred or more took part at the outset, mostly women and children, black and white, who were welfare recipients. Their demand was a $50 Christmas bonus for each recipient. It was an appeal that aimed to dramatize the plight of families living at such a subsistence level that gifts for children at Christmas and needed winter clothing were out of the question. As there were 425,000 welfare recipients in the state, meeting the $50 demand would have cost a total of $21.2 million. The action meshed with similar Welfare Rights demonstrations that season in Ann Arbor, Michigan (where a $70-per-child emergency allowance for school clothing was achieved), in Newark, in Toledo, Ohio, and elsewhere. In New York City there was a demonstration at the Macy's Thanksgiving Day parade.

When Roxanne Jones phoned me to say her group had taken

over the Welfare Department offices and wanted me to join them there, I left home immediately for Broad and Spring Garden. When I arrived at the office building, I found all the doors guarded by state troopers, who allowed no one to enter. Lt. George Fencl, in charge of the Civil Disobedience Squad, saw me and told the troopers to let me through. He thought that I could help to resolve the conflict.

I went up to the third floor, where I was surprised to see all of the chairs and all of the desks occupied by Welfare Rights members. They were making outside calls on the state phones and receiving incoming calls. There were many children there. It was a wonderful sight to behold all those poor people in charge of things for a change.

About midnight, twenty-five state policemen moved into the building. Those who wanted to avoid what seemed imminent arrest left. The remaining group of about 250 went on singing songs and sharing food that had been brought in for the siege. At 2 AM the troopers made their move to clear the building of all demonstrators. Roxanne Jones was carried away, kicking and yelling. The Rev. David McI. Gracie, urban missioner for the Episcopal Diocese, went limp and was taken out on a stretcher. David was as relaxed as ever, smoking a cigar. The Rev. Robert Strommen of the United Church of Christ was arrested too. The two of them were already in the police wagons by the time I got down to the first floor exit.

When the police accompanied me to the front door, they tried to send me on my way. I said no. If I have broken a law, I must be arrested. Once again they tried to push me out the door. I caught the sleeve of an officer and insisted: "If I have broken a law, arrest me!" Lt. Fencl stood by. He looked at me and I at him. I did feel as if I had betrayed his trust.

In the paddy wagon on the way to the Roundhouse at 8th and Race, the spirit of the action remained upbeat, with WRO members singing gospel hymns as we were driven away: "Precious Lord, take my hand; lead me on, let me stand." At the Roundhouse, Clarence Farmer of the Commission on Human Relations

appeared. He made his way to where I, one of his Human Relations Commissioners, was standing, waiting to be processed along
with the other arrestees. He told me that he had arranged for the
matter to be quashed. I could simply leave with him. But I refused
this easy way out and joined my clergy colleagues to be photographed and fingerprinted.

"It breaks my heart to do this to you, Father Washington," said
the black officer who was taking the prints. But my heart was
glad. I was proud to have my mug shot taken at last, be fingerprinted, and put into a cell. It was an experience I felt was overdue.

9. Reparations

The next phase of the Black Power movement was inaugurated early in 1969, when James Forman, a civil rights veteran of the Student Nonviolent Coordinating Committee, walked down the aisle of New York City's Riverside Church during a Sunday service to demand a payment of "reparations" to black Americans. The case for reparations had been made in the document called "The Black Manifesto," issued by the National Black Economic Development Conference in Detroit in April 1969. The manifesto used the language of socialist revolution ("an armed confrontation and long years of sustained guerrilla warfare inside this country"), but it presented what amounted to a modest proposal for reform based on the undeniable fact that exploited black Americans needed capital: "for the establishment of cooperative businesses . . . a Southern Land Bank . . . publishing and printing industries . . . a research skills center."

The manifesto stated: "Racist white America has exploited our resources, our minds, our bodies, our labor. For centuries we have been forced to live as colonized people inside the United States, victimized by the most vicious racist system in the world. We have helped to build the most industrial country in the world.

"We are therefore demanding of the white Christian churches and Jewish synagogues which are part and parcel of the system of capitalism, that they begin to pay reparations to black people in this country. We are demanding $500 million from the Christian white churches and the Jewish synagogues. This total comes to 15 dollars per nigger."

Both the manifesto's frightening rhetoric and Forman's dramatic New York City challenge to white church-going America had tremendous shock value. The media were more than ready to publicize the campaign for as long as members of the Black Economic Development Conference (BEDC) could keep walking down church aisles, forcing white churchpeople to struggle with their consciences. Was this extortion, plain and simple, or was it a prophetic call to move beyond charity to a just sharing of resources with those who had been shut out of the system for so long? I heard it as prophecy.

Surely something was owed to a people who had been enslaved, set free, yet never given the "forty acres and a mule" they had been promised as their stake in the economy. Instead they had been further exploited under all the many forms of racial discrimination that continued to this day. Now was the time to pay what was owed to those whose labor had first been stolen from them and then systematically undervalued for generations. The debt should be paid with no strings attached, for the purpose of black control of economic and social institutions in the black community. If the church could not understand the moral basis of this claim for reparations, it seemed clear to me it would once more be rejecting the prophets in its midst.

It was a particular prophet who first got me involved in this campaign. In the Philadelphia area the BEDC organizer was Muhammad Kenyatta, a young Baptist preacher only twenty-five years of age, of medium build and a winsome manner, with weak eyes behind tinted glasses. He had worked with James Forman in civil rights activities in the South and then had become involved in community struggles in Chester, Pennsylvania. "Mo" Kenyatta had great charm and a gift of persuasion the likes of which I had never experienced before.

Our first meeting was at my initiative. I asked him to bring me a copy of the Black Manifesto. The words on the page engaged me much less than the presence of the messenger. For years I had been listening for a prophetic voice, perchance that of a pastor as well as a prophet, someone who would call us to repentance. Was James Forman "one who should come"? I wondered. Was Mo Kenyatta? Both seemed to have the courage to overturn the tables of the money changers. I didn't know the answer for sure, but I allied myself with them and the issues they raised—not so much for the issues themselves, but to say: "I affirm these men." I wanted to drape my mantle over their shoulders.

I must admit that Kenyatta and the little cluster of reparations activists who worked with him were not a prepossessing group when looked upon as potential investment brokers for the large sums of money being demanded from the churches. BEDC operated out of a humble storefront office, which was the scene of numerous press conferences called by Kenyatta, who had tremendous public relations skills. He used his ability to communicate through the media not only to press the demands of BEDC but to call attention to other issues of injustice in the community, notably cases of police brutality. The small band of activists included some very strong women, whose strength was difficult for Kenyatta to adjust to, and a group of men, none of whom could make the impression that he did; but Woody Woodland, the Revs. Dwight Campbell and Wycliffe Jangdharrie were loyal and staunch supporters of Mo and BEDC.

Bishop DeWitt became very interested in the reparations concept himself. At his behest, I arranged a meeting at the Advocate rectory for him, Kenyatta, myself, and a few others, so that the bishop could become better informed about BEDC goals and tactics. During the meeting, the front doorbell rang and when I answered it I found myself facing a man who identified himself as an FBI agent. He asked if Bishop DeWitt was in a meeting here, then left, asking for nothing else.

The bishop's prophetic imagination was immediately captured by Kenyatta's presentation of the ideas of the Black Manifesto, and he decided that he would champion this cause in his own diocese and in the national church, as a member of its Executive Council.

On May 1, James Forman had gone to the Episcopal Church Center in New York City to present the manifesto's demands. On May 13 he wrote to Presiding Bishop John Hines demanding $60 million, plus 60 percent of the church's profit on assets each year, along with an accounting of the total assets of the Episcopal Church in all its dioceses. John Booty, in *The Episcopal Church in Crisis*, writes about the siege atmosphere that developed among church leaders as "plans were made, in cooperation with civic officials, for dealing with the possibility of unfriendly occupations of churches and church offices."[1] By contrast, Bishop DeWitt suggested a positive response to the demands: Why not mortgage the Episcopal Church Center itself to raise a significant amount of money for the purpose? And as for the demonstrations, disruptions, and occupations of sacred places, why not value them as modern-day examples of the prophetic acts we so cherish in the Biblical tradition? The bishop's enthusiasm is evident in his description of this movement years later:

"And then came the Black Manifesto, and its demand for reparations for generations of injustice done to Black people by Whites. It was a bold, imaginative effort. And bold and imaginative was the local spokesperson for the Black Manifesto, Muhammad Kenyatta. I will never forget when he intruded into a communion service at Holy Trinity, Rittenhouse Square. After interrupting the service and speaking to the demands of the Manifesto, he strode to the altar and picked up the alms basin. He flung the money on the floor of the sanctuary, dramatizing the sacrilege of a religious offering to God which belied and denied the weighty matters of the Law of God, such as racial justice. That was religious poetry acted out, worthy of a Jeremiah."[2] Perhaps I need not add that the Rev. Cuthbert Pratt, rector of Holy Trinity, did not appreciate the poetry.

In July, 1969, Kenyatta formally wrote to Bishop DeWitt demanding reparations from the Diocese of Pennsylvania. The bishop invited him to the July meeting of the Diocesan Council to present his demands in person. I was a member of the council and was there to hear his presentation, which deeply pleased and impressed me because of the reasoned manner in which it was made.

Kenyatta left immediately after he had spoken, and no sooner had the door closed behind him than the council erupted like a volcano. He was attacked as a person, and the call to us as representatives of the church was denounced as though he had called upon us to crucify Christ himself. This was violent and vicious stuff. Finally I spoke and expressed my hurt, my anger, and my sorrow. I pointed out that Kenyatta had come to us with respect and in love. He was calling us to repentance and rectification of undeniable sins and wrongs, and we were treating him as though he were an enemy. Following my speech, I told them that I could not be associated with this body any longer, and I shook the dust off my feet and stormed out. I formally resigned from Diocesan Council. In a letter to Bishop DeWitt, I wrote that while patience and understanding were virtues, there was a point beyond which patience could become apathy and understanding a disguise for cowardice.

Still, the bishop would not let go. He called the Council to meet on August 6 to reconsider its decision. This meeting, held at the Denbigh Conference Center of the diocese, lasted past midnight and resulted in the appointment of a committee, chaired by the Rev. Richard Hawkins, rector of St. Thomas Church, Whitemarsh (a very well-to-do white suburban congregation), to study the matter further and report to the Diocesan Convention in October.

The convention then created a "Reconciliation Committee" to report to a special diocesan convention in May, 1970. Through this long and sometimes very difficult process, many members of the diocese, both black and white, lay and clergy, were pressing for a positive response to the reparations demands. What united those of us who lobbied and demonstrated at Denbigh and at Valley Forge Military Academy, where the May convention was held, was a sense of how terrible it would be if the demands were flatly rejected. It would signal a kind of final insensitivity to racial injustice and an inability of Christian people to repent.

The moral issue of repentance became the dominant issue in the discussions as the debate went on. The convention of May, 1970, decided to commit $500,000 (the profit from the impending sale of the diocesan headquarters building) to a grant program to be administered by black Episcopalians in the diocese. The decision to do so could be made after the Rev. Jesse Anderson, Sr., put the question in acceptable theological terms.

"Since the word 'reparations' is a stumbling block to so many," he said, "I propose we not use that word, but rather substitute another word, hallowed by centuries of usage in the Anglican *Book of Common Prayer*. That word is 'restitution.'" He referred us to the "Exhortation for the Celebration of Holy Communion" in the prayer book, which contains these words:

"And if ye shall perceive your offences to be such as are not only against God, but also against your neighbors; then ye shall reconcile yourselves to them; being ready to make restitution and satisfaction, according to the uttermost of your powers, for all injuries and wrongs by you to any other . . . for otherwise the receiving of the Holy Communion doth nothing else but increase your condemnation."

The fund established by the Diocese of Pennsylvania in response to the reparations demand was thus called the Restitution Fund and the body of black church members administering it the Restitution Fund Commission. It was a very encouraging moment when Fr. Anderson's motion was passed. The actual working of the Restitution Fund was, however, most discouraging, and ironically, of all the grants eventually made, not one cent went to BEDC. Before telling that story, however, which stretches over a few years, it is important to look at the very similar process that was going on in 1969 in the national church.

Presiding Bishop John Hines had called a special convention of the Episcopal Church for August 31–September 5, 1969, in South Bend, Indiana, on the Notre Dame campus. The convention was to deal with more than just the issues raised by BEDC. At the 1967 General Convention in Seattle it had been decided that more frequent meetings were needed "in this age of ceaseless change." The age was the late 1960s. A war was going on overseas, there were racial rebellions in the cities, and issues of justice were being raised within the church by racial minorities and by women.

As an elected deputy to the General Convention from the Diocese of Pennsylvania I had been in Seattle in 1967, where I was deeply impressed by the leadership of John Hines, who had gone out into the streets and neighborhoods of the cities that had exploded, so that he could listen to the people there describe their own hopes and fears. The General Convention Special Program, which was authorized in 1967 to give grants to community organizations to assist them in achieving some degree of political and economic power, had my full support. It had the flavor of a new age in which each person would know that he or she was a child of God and entitled to the good things of God.

Yet, when the Executive Council of the Episcopal Church issued its "Response to the Manifesto" on May 21, 1969, indicating that it would simply continue the work of the special program of 1967, I believed that was not enough. I went to South Bend as a deputy, committed to assist Kenyatta in his demand for recognition of BEDC by the church and for payment of reparations to that body.

Matters quickly came to a head at the Sunday night opening plenary session when Kenyatta seized the microphone from the chairman of the Committee on Clergy Deployment as he was making a committee report. A tussle ensued, involving the presiding bishop, who tried to take the microphone back.

I was late for this plenary session, having been in a meeting of the black caucus of the convention. We were discussing the refusal of the chairs of the two houses of convention to place a report dealing with the reparations issue on the agenda early enough to allow it a full hearing. A small group of us, including Barbara Harris, a lay delegate from the Diocese of Pennsylvania, and the Rev. Jesse Anderson, Jr., entered the top level of the stadium together.

Looking down to the stage below, we saw Kenyatta at that point taking the microphone away from the presiding bishop. We immediately descended to the floor level alongside the stage. Perhaps never again in the history of the church will we see a presiding bishop tusseling with a dashiki-clad black man in a plenary session of a General Convention!

Fr. Jesse Anderson, Sr., climbed the stairs to the platform and asked Bishop Hines for permission for me to speak, explaining that I was a deputy to the convention. I was totally unprepared to speak in the midst of such confusion—nay, chaos—and I turned to young Jesse Anderson and asked him in desperation, "What must I say?" He quickly replied: "Call all black people to leave this convention."

Meanwhile, Bishop Hines was putting the question to the joint houses of the convention there assembled: "Shall we allow Father Washington to speak?" After a quick show of hands, he immediately ruled that the answer was yes, and I had the floor. Never before in all my life had I been called upon to muster up the authority of voice, the power of spirit, and the stature (in that moment I grew from 5 feet 9 inches, 155 pounds, to 7 feet, 290 pounds) to move people to an action that no one had time to cerebralize. If they had, they would have thought about how blacks had waited a lifetime in the church to be deputies to General Convention, yet a Fr. Washington was commanding them to leave the place for which they had longed!

I can remember only saying: "White people cannot set the agenda for this church. Black people must set the agenda for this church and for this nation. And since you refuse to deal with our agenda, I have no choice but to call upon all blacks to leave this convention." With that said, I stormed from the platform and started climbing tier by tier to the exit at the top level of the stadium. That was the loneliest and the longest walk of my life.

Barbara Harris was at my left, the two Jesse Andersons and a few others followed, but I was pleadingly asking myself, Will the blacks follow? Lord, will they follow? If they did not, the name of Paul Washington would have gone down in disgrace. He had dared to presume to lead, then found no followers. But young Jesse Anderson and his father were looking to the right and to the left and commanding: "You all come, come! Get up, come!" It was a dramatic, moving moment, enough so that some felt impelled to move out with us.

Not only did enough blacks follow, but some whites also. We had precipitated a crisis, enough of a crisis to cause Bishop Hines and the Rev. John Coburn, chairman of the House of Deputies, to meet immediately after that joint session and decide to place our issue on the agenda the very next morning.

In an open hearing on Monday, the convention discussed the recommendations of a committee chaired by John Coburn that said BEDC should channel any requests for money from the Episcopal Church through the General Convention Special Program, which had been established for that very purpose. That seemed reasonable enough to some, but it did not meet the approval of the Union of Black Clergy and Laity in the Episcopal Church or other supporters of BEDC. After all, BEDC was making not requests but demands for reparations, and in an amount that would be beyond the capacity of the special program.

The Union of Black Clergy spokesperson, the Rev. Joseph Pelham, asked that $200,000 be given immediately to BEDC and that a process of dialogue be established toward making further church resources available, without reducing the church's responsibility to fund the special program. The $200,000 would go for administrative and development expenses of BEDC nationally—seed money, in effect.

Discussion from the floor revealed strong support on the part of some, including a white lay delegate who said he acknowledged the debt and was making a personal pledge of $1,000. Opposition came from those like Bishop Stuart Wetmore of New York, who said, "Jim Forman is seeking our guilt money. . . . We should not play the game of trying to buy him off." Others expressed confusion about BEDC. Was it a reliable organization? Was it violent, as the prologue to the Black Manifesto seemed to indicate? (Kenyatta had said that people could write their own prologue using Biblical texts to replace James Forman's words.) What would the people back home make of the delegates' actions in Notre Dame? How could they understand what was going on?

The final action of the special convention on this matter was to vote for giving the $200,000, not as reparations but as seed money. The money would not even go directly to BEDC but would be channeled through the National Committee of Black

Churchmen, a group with recognized, respected members from various Christian denominations. In spite of all this maneuvering, the story that appeared in the *Chicago Tribune* on Thursday morning had the subheading "Church Unit Votes Reparations." It appeared that Thoreau was right when he said that "a moral minority can precipitate a revolution." That the Episcopal Church had voted to respond, even to the tune of $200,000, to a moral imperative it was forced to confront by the minuscule Union of Black Clergy and Laity indeed seemed revolutionary to some.

The session of the convention held on Tuesday evening was the most remarkable of all. It was a time of debate on BEDC and related issues when black convention delegates announced our intention to remain silent. Joseph Pelham said, "We have made our positions quite clear. This is your debate. We will sit and listen and watch very carefully." The result was a session during which white delegates experienced a relationship with black church members never known before. At the close, I had been selected to rise and speak a final word on behalf of the black delegates.

I told the white people in that hall that in all love and gentleness we had offered them an opportunity to "rise up as men of God," but that they had been afraid to love, afraid of freedom, afraid to be beautiful. I told them that I pitied them. In their dealings with me, it was as if they had tried to squeeze me a little bit too hard and I had slipped through their hands. They still had a chance for greatness, I said. If they took it, I knew it would mean they would go home to be crucified, but in doing that they could follow in the steps of Jesus.

After the Notre Dame convention, there was backlash in the church in any case. Even the appearance of the church yielding to the reparations demand caused some to leave the church and others to cut their giving to its national programs. John Booty explains the motives of the critics: "some of those reacting against Notre Dame revealed strong racial prejudice. Others were reacting to what they saw as rampant liberalism."[3] But neither liberals nor conservatives were pleased with the outcome. The demand for reparations had been neither accepted nor clearly rejected. The desire in the hearts of many to take seriously the commands of the Bible as framed in the prayer book's call for restitution was frustrated on the one hand by fear and racist attitudes and on the other by the limitations of the instrument that had been offered to enable restitution for acknowledged injuries and wrongs.

While some of us in the church attempted to understand the challenge of Forman and Kenyatta in theological terms, law enforcement agencies understood it in their own way, as this FBI bulletin of September 11, 1969, makes clear: "9/11/69 Urgent to Dir., Phila., Pitts., Det. NBEDConf Det. Apr. 25–27. Extortion; Conspiracy. Dept. has requested Bureau to determine contents of speech by Muhammad Kenyatta at South Bend, Aug. 30–Sept. 5. Grand jury proceedings contemplated."

The Rt. Rev. Bravid Harris, Bishop of Liberia (seated, front row, center), and faculty of Cuttington College, Liberia, 1952. (Personal collection of Paul Washington)

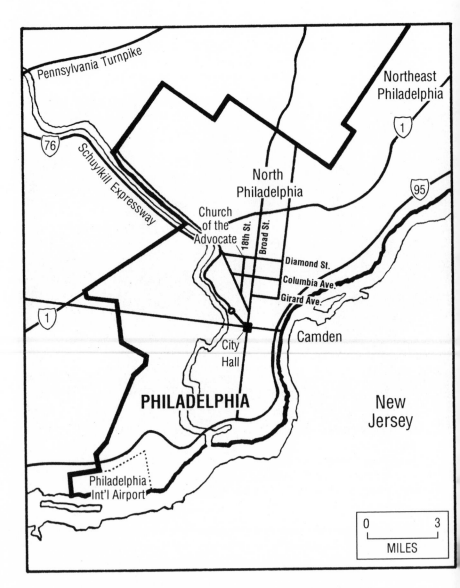

Map of Philadelphia, showing the location of the Church of the Advocate at 18th and Diamond Streets.

Judge Joseph Sloane swearing in Fr. Washington and Sydney Orlofsky as new members of the Philadelphia Commission on Human Relations early in 1964. (*Philadelphia Evening Bulletin*, Urban Archives, Temple University Libraries)

Philadelphia police in action during the disturbances on Columbia
Avenue, August 28, 1964. (*Philadelphia Evening Bulletin*, Urban
Archives, Temple University Libraries)

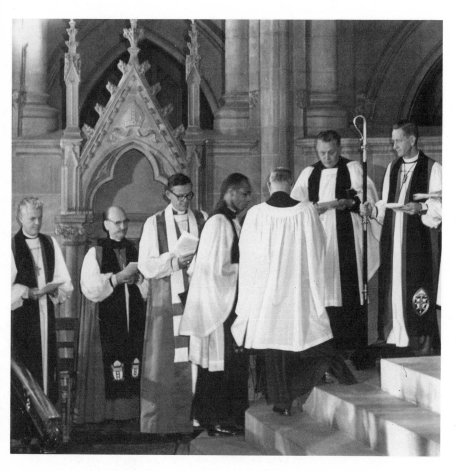

Service of installation for the Rt. Rev. Robert L. DeWitt as Bishop of
Pennsylvania, held at the Church of the Advocate on October 31, 1964.
Left to right: Bishop Brooke Mosley, unidentified bishop, Bishop Paul
Moore, Fr. Washington, unidentified priest, Fr. Hugh White, Bishop
DeWitt. (Personal collection of Paul Washington)

Procession around the Girard College wall in Philadelphia, led by members of St. Thomas Episcopal Church, in September, 1965. (*Philadelphia Evening Bulletin*, Urban Archives, Temple University Libraries)

Stokely Carmichael addresses a crowd of 2,000 from the Gratz Street steps of the Church of the Advocate in August, 1966, his second appearance at the church. *Upper-left-hand corner,* Freedom George Brower; *upper-right-hand corner, in African dress,* Walter Palmer. (Jack T. Franklin, courtesy of the Afro-American Historical and Cultural Museum, Philadelphia)

Part of the crowd listening to Stokely Carmichael at the corner of Gratz and Diamond Streets, August, 1966. (Jack T. Franklin, courtesy of the Afro-American Historical and Cultural Museum, Philadelphia)

Muhammad Kenyatta interrupts a session of the Philadelphia Yearly
Meeting of the Society of Friends to deliver the "Black Manifesto,"
demanding reparations from the churches and synagogues of America,
June 19, 1969. *Also standing*, Francis Brown, General Secretary of the
Philadelphia Yearly Meeting. (*Philadelphia Evening Bulletin*, Urban
Archives, Temple University Libraries)

Bishop Robert L. DeWitt leads a meeting of the Diocesan Council of the Episcopal Diocese of Pennsylvania at the Denbigh Conference Center on August 7, 1969, discussing the reparations demand from the Black Economic Development Conference. *At rear, far right*, Fr. David McI. Gracie; *in shirtsleeves, with pipe*, Dean Edward Harris. (*Philadelphia Evening Bulletin*, Urban Archives, Temple University Libraries)

Fr. Washington speaking at Arch Street United Methodist Church at a meeting held to discuss US-USSR relations after the shooting down of the U-2 spy plane in September, 1969. (*Philadelphia Evening Bulletin*, Urban Archives, Temple University Libraries)

Members of the Black Panther Party, stripped and handcuffed following Philadelphia police raids on Panther headquarters in August, 1970. (*Philadelphia Evening Bulletin*, Urban Archives, Temple University Libraries)

Participants in the Black Panther Party's Revolutionary People's
Constitutional Convention, McGonigle Hall, Temple University,
September 6, 1970. (*Philadelphia Evening Bulletin*, Urban Archives,
Temple University Libraries)

Member of the Black Panther Party distributing free lunches to North Philadelphia residents in August, 1971. (*Philadelphia Evening Bulletin*, Urban Archives, Temple University Libraries)

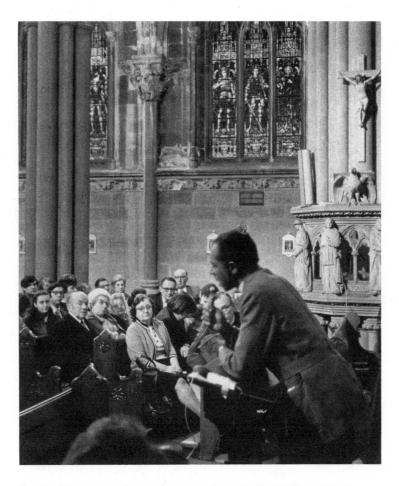

Fr. Washington speaks at the memorial service for William "Pop" Seidler, North Philadelphia merchant killed in his store on Columbia Avenue in March, 1971. (Personal collection of Miriam Seidler)

Fr. Washington with Miriam Seidler at the memorial service for her husband, William, March, 1971. (Personal collection of Miriam Seidler)

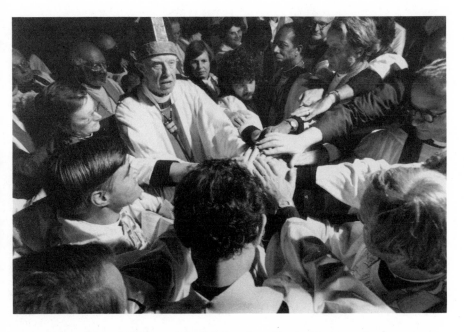

Bishop Edward Welles ordains his daughter, Katrina Swanson, in the historic service of ordination of women to the priesthood at the Church of the Advocate, July 29, 1974. (Personal collection of Paul Washington)

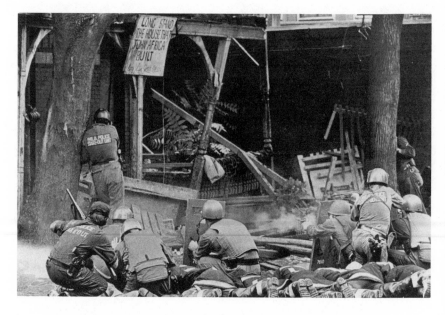

Police sharpshooters in the raid on the MOVE residence in Powelton Village, Philadelphia, August 8, 1978. (*Philadelphia Evening Bulletin*, Urban Archives, Temple University Libraries)

MOVE members giving clenched-fist salute in a demonstration protesting arrests and trials, August 12, 1980. (*Philadelphia Evening Bulletin*, Urban Archives, Temple University Libraries)

Fr. Washington in April, 1979, with the murals in the Church of the Advocate painted by Philadelphia artists Walter Edmonds and Richard Watson. (*Philadelphia Evening Bulletin*, Urban Archives, Temple University Libraries)

Philadelphia Mayor W. Wilson Goode speaks at "Tribute to the Man" banquet held at the Bellevue Hotel in honor of Fr. Washington on February 21, 1985. *Lower left*, Christine Washington. (Personal collection of Paul Washington)

Bishop Barbara Harris celebrates Holy Communion at the Church of the Advocate on the Sunday following her election on September 24, 1988, as Suffragan Bishop of Massachusetts, the first woman bishop of the Anglican Communion. (Episcopal Diocese of Pennsylvania)

Fr. Washington, flanked by the four women priests sponsored for ordination during his tenure at the Church of the Advocate, officiates at the service of ordination for Ann Robb Smith on June 15, 1991. *Left to right:* the Rev. Smith, Bishop Barbara Harris, Fr. Washington, the Rev. Mary Adebonojo, the Rev. Suzanne Hiatt. (Personal collection of Ann Robb Smith)

Christine Washington, Fr. Washington, and Mayor W. Wilson Goode at the dedication of the mural at Ridge and Cumberland Streets in the Strawberry Mansion neighborhood of Philadelphia, December, 1991. (*Philadelphia Daily News*)

A Washington family gathering in Cape May, New Jersey, August, 1990. *Left to right*: Kemah, Lil, Donya, Michael, Christine, Paul, and family friend Delores Dow; *behind them*: Kemah's wife, Sandy, Louis Dow, Agnes, and Marc; *in foreground*: Akeem and Kemah, children of Kemah and Sandy. (Personal collection of Paul Washington)

The Church of the Advocate in the 1960s, as seen from the corner of 18th and Diamond Streets. (Personal collection of Paul Washington)

The Angel Gabriel, atop the Church of the Advocate, watches over the City of Philadelphia in a photo montage created by Charles Penniman. (Charles Penniman)

Mural at Ridge and Cumberland Streets in the Strawberry Mansion neighborhood of Philadelphia, not far from the Washingtons' home. (Personal collection of Paul Washington)

10. The Black Panther Convention

"Just as I cannot escape the fact that I am in America but I know I am not of America, I feel also that I am in the Episcopal Church, but not of it. I feel like an organ which has been transplanted into an organism, but where the 'rejection syndrome' is still at work to destroy a foreign invader."

I wrote those words in a letter to one of the leading white liberals in the Episcopal Church shortly after the convention in South Bend. The Rev. John Burt was director of the Clergy Deployment Office for the national church, and I felt moved to tell him I thought it presumptuous of the Episcopal Church to think that it could make any decisions about deploying black clergymen.

I had resigned from Diocesan Council and was expressing sentiments like this to anyone who would listen, yet the rejection I experienced was not total. I was finding a great deal of support and affirmation for the ministry of the Advocate from some quarters in the church. My own seminary, the Philadelphia Divinity School, which in my student days had made me feel at times like a foreign invader, awarded me an honorary doctor of divinity degree in May, 1970. In the citation they called me "disturbing prophet, healing priest." I felt they understood the roles I knew I was called to play in my ministry.

In that very year of 1970 there would be plenty of disturbing events providing more than enough opportunities to prophesy. It was the year of the special diocesan convention that dealt with reparations (or "restitution" in the acceptable prayer book language). It was another year of war, and the antiwar movement had grown to such an extent that on Tax Day, April 15, I found myself speaking to a crowd of 3,000 demonstrators at J.F.K. Plaza in downtown Philadelphia. It was above all the year of the Black Panther Party's Revolutionary People's Constitutional Convention. Held in Philadelphia over the Labor Day weekend and headquartered at the Church of the Advocate, this gathering of black and white political radicals gained national attention, not least because of the repressive measures taken against the Panthers by the Philadelphia police. In the week prior to the convention, Police Commissioner Frank Rizzo had staged dawn police raids on all the Black Panther Party offices in the city, putting their leaders behind bars. But many of us stood up for the constitutional rights of the Panthers, including their right to hold their own "constitutional convention," and we prevailed.

The Black Panther Party had its local Philadelphia headquarters in a storefront office on Columbia Avenue, from which a group of young black men and women went forth to sell the party's newspaper and in other ways agitate for the Panthers' Ten Point Program, calling for "land, bread, housing, education, clothing, justice and peace." The Panthers were distinguished from other activist groups by their willingness to defend themselves and their community against police brutality, even murder. In East Oakland, California, they had organized armed patrols to this end. In Philadelphia, too, the rhetoric of a self-defense against the "pig" could be heard; the party chapter trained members in the use of weapons, and on at least one occasion went armed to defend four black women who had been fired upon by racists after they moved into a formerly white neighborhood. But in all my experience with them, the Philadelphia Black Panthers were essentially a nonviolent movement. Reggie Schell, local Panther defense captain, organized marches and demonstrations, often in coalition with other groups (white and black), whenever Philadelphia police shot down someone in the streets or engaged in brutal acts. Along with the demonstrations, the other distinguishing activity of the Panthers was their free breakfast program for children, which had begun in September, 1969, in a building near their Columbia Avenue office.

Reggie Schell and I came to know each other because of our shared participation in meetings and activities dealing with the issue of police brutality. I had agreed to the use of the church on December 14, 1969, for a memorial service for Fred Hampton and Mark Clark, murdered by police in a surprise attack on Black Panther Party headquarters in Chicago early on the morning of December 4. When 1,000 people attended the service, we could see the level of sympathy and support the Panthers were gaining from people who believed in their message and from others who were simply revolted by the nature of the police repression they faced. The deaths of Hampton and Clark were widely believed to have been political assassinations carried out by Chicago police in conjunction with the FBI. A federal grand jury ruled in May, 1970, that "the police fired eighty-three shots into the apartment while only one shot was fired toward the police."

At the Hampton and Clark memorial service and similar events at the Advocate on behalf of other people killed by the police, I would usually conduct a simple memorial service, after which Reggie and others would speak. Reggie was a very articulate and convincing speaker, but with very informal manners. At one service I remember Reggie swinging his leg over the side of the elevated pulpit at the Advocate as he spoke. The audiences were always mixed, black and white, because while membership in the party was reserved for black people, alliances were continually sought with any who would work with the party on the basis of its political program.

"We feel that in order to be effective in the black community, the party must remain black, but we will align ourselves with any group working for basic changes in this country." That is how Reggie explained the philosophy of the party the day following the killings of Hampton and Clark, in a talk given for a downtown luncheon group at the Central YMCA on Arch Street—undoubtedly arranged by Pete Weimer, a YMCA staffer active in groups against police brutality. The press reported "a generally friendly audience of businessmen and professionals." That Reggie could receive a friendly reception in such a downtown gathering was due to his own evident sincerity. He was a man totally dedicated to improving the lot of the poorest in the city. In a printed interview, Reggie described himself as "a street nigger" who had become a Panther because the party "symbolized this new human being, ready to fight."[1]

Reggie could also get a favorable hearing because many who were neither black nor poor recognized the reality of police oppression in the ghetto. The shocking killing of a high school student named Harold Brown in 1969 had led to a major campaign by the Panthers, which included the circulation of wanted posters for the four policemen who had been accused of taking his life. The need for the other changes the Panthers were calling for was also obvious to many, even if they could not join in the rhetorical denunciations of the "fascist government" and the shouts of "Off the pig!"

When the party decided on Philadelphia as the site of its Revolutionary People's Constitutional Convention—to begin to draft "a constitution that serves the people, not the ruling class"—it needed the help of all in the city who had any sympathy for its goals. It was to be a major gathering over the Labor Day weekend, with invitations going not only to Panther branches but also to other black groups, antiwar organizations, and the plethora of political groups on the left across the country. A highlight of the convention would be an address by Huey P. Newton, one of the West Coast founders of the party, who had just been released from three years in prison, most of it spent in solitary confinement. Thousands were expected, and in fact more than 6,000 would take part.

Meeting space was the first order of business, and Reggie

wasted no time in asking me if the Advocate could be both a location for large assemblies and the center for registration. It seemed logical to me that the Advocate might serve in this capacity. It would be similar to the role the church had played in the Black Power Convention of 1968, and I knew that many of those who had attended that gathering (especially the young people) would also be involved in the 1970 convention. But while I could justify Black Power on theological grounds, how could I justify the use of the church by a group that committed itself to attain rights and justice for black people "by any means necessary," not ruling out violence? The Panthers dared to say openly, We will defend ourselves by arms if driven to that point.

I could certainly identify with the rejection, the pain, the anguish, and the anger that the Panthers expressed. Recalling my experiences as a child in Charleston, I still felt ashamed, embarrassed, as well as enraged, remembering how we had to "make peace with the oppressor" if we were even to survive. Elderly Negro men and women had been "boys" or "girls," who had to stand up to give their seats to the white folks on buses and trolleys. And I will never forget how afraid I was when my mother exploded and told that white insurance agent to "get your feet off my table, get out of my house, and never come back again." My father, a "colored man," could have been lynched for talking to a white man in that way. He would have been charged with "not knowing his place."

Even when there was a lynching, domestics had to go to work, smile, and be pleasant, just as though our very humanity no longer existed. No matter how deep the insult, how painful the slap, how barbaric the deed, we were expected to smile as though insensitive to acts of inhumanity. I was confronted with the same spirit of racism at Beaver College, outside Philadelphia, when I addressed a class about the strategy of Martin Luther King. To protest violently, I explained, would make enemies, not brothers. Whatever we did had to be governed by an ethic of love. To which a young lady said, during the discussion period following my talk, "We don't want you as brothers, and we don't need your love."

Whites really had come to believe they had recreated us in an image that complemented theirs. That is why, when we "got out of place," they always blamed the influence of "outside agitators." After all, whites had destroyed our humanity, they thought. For this reason, many blacks came to see Malcolm and the Black Panthers as true liberators. They dared to express that which for so long we had to suppress. They boldly spoke that which we dared not even let whites know we were thinking. With rifle in hand, the Panthers proclaimed that "by any means necessary" we will obtain our liberation and our rights.

I felt in tune with Martin, but also with Malcolm and the Panthers. For me it became not a matter of one or the other; within my "one dark body" the two represented what for me was wholeness, even if I could not intellectually resolve all the contradictions they raised.

I knew that in spite of any threatening rhetoric we had not reached a point where we were ready for a violent revolution. Yet the question nagged me. When one is faced with a life-threatening situation, is it not both normal and natural to defend one's self, and is it possible to defend one's self against violence without resorting to violence? Sometimes those who violate others condemn them for reacting violently in defense. Martin Luther King was condemned even for nonviolent direct actions in Birmingham and other cities across this nation. In his "Letter from a Birmingham Jail," April 16, 1963, he wrote: "It is unfortunate that demonstrations are taking place in Birmingham, but it is more unfortunate that the city's white power structure left the Negro community no alternative."[2] Like Gandhi and King, I believe that the cycle of violence can end only when moral power overcomes evil. But my questioning continues.

There are times when moral theologians resort to the field of natural theology in their search for answers, and I am led to ask: Why did God implant within my white corpuscles phagocytes, able to destroy that which would destroy me? I ask further if we are willing to condemn Dietrich Bonhoeffer for volunteering to be a part of the conspiracy to kill Hitler, a crime for which he was condemned and executed. The life that I have lived places me with

Gandhi and King, but would I be with them if I found myself where Bonhoeffer or Nat Turner was? I feel ready to allow my life to be taken rather than take the life of another, but I might well be ready to take the life of someone wantonly engaged in destroying the lives of others.

Whenever I heard Reggie speaking for the Black Panthers, I heard him describe plans to seek a solution to our grievances through a perfectly acceptable, nonviolent, political process. I thought at first this attitude seemed out of character with the Panthers. But what he said was based on a radical understanding that the U.S. Constitution seemed impotent when it came to including the Negro among those who were entitled to the full rights of citizenship. (What most people did not know was that this convention was to have been followed by an even larger convention in the nation's capital in 1971, when protesters would petition Congress to guarantee us our "inalienable rights." The follow-up never happened. I conjecture that the reason was that Washington did not have the respected and well-known black leaders and white supporters to make it happen. Nor did Washington have an institution with the respectability and credibility of the Advocate.)

I decided to open the doors of the Advocate to the Black Panther Party's Revolutionary Constitutional Convention. But the church alone would not suffice. A much larger public space was needed as well, and it was decided that Temple University, in the heart of North Philadelphia and only a few blocks distant from the Advocate, should be asked to make available its large new gymnasium, McGonigle Hall.

I joined a group of citizens, which included my friend Joe Miller and Philadelphia Bar Association president Robert Landis, to meet with Temple officials to win their cooperation. From my FBI records I learn that on August 7, the FBI passed the word to "the White House, Vice President, Attorney General, the military and Secret Service" that Temple had made the gymnasium available. The FBI readied its secret agents and informants to attend the events at the university and the church.

On the Saturday before the convention was to begin, a murder was committed. A Philadelphia policeman named Frank VonColln was shot dead in a Fairmount Park guardhouse. His assailant, who also wounded another park officer in the attack, was believed to be a "black revolutionary," not a member of the Black Panther Party but "acquainted with the Party and its activities," police said. The tragic death of Officer VonColln and unrelated attacks on yet two more policemen on the streets stirred the emotions of the city and provided Police Commissioner Frank Rizzo with the cover he needed to directly attack the Black Panther Party in Philadelphia.

At dawn on August 31, 1970, heavily armed police raided the three Panther offices in the city: 2935 Columbia Avenue, 3625 Wallace Street, and 428 W. Queen Lane. Around the world flashed news photos of young black men arrested in the raids and ordered to strip, one photo showing them in their underwear, another showing them stripped naked at gunpoint. The Panthers had become the objects of Frank Rizzo's rage at the "imbeciles and yellow dogs" who shot at his men on the streets and in the guardhouse. For others they became the symbol of black manhood humiliated and stripped of dignity, but fighting back against racist oppression. This is Reggie's own account of the police raid:

"About five o'clock that morning I was asleep, and somebody woke me up (we used to pull guard duty in the Panthers anyway) and said, 'They're here.' I looked out the window, and they're lined up across the street with submachine guns, shotguns; they're in the alley. I saw the head man clearly, he had a pistol and a gas mask strapped to his leg; he was bending down, and then all hell broke loose. Finally, we had children in there and the gas got to them too much so we had to come out.

"Each cop took an individual Panther and placed their pistol up the back of our neck and told us to walk down the street backward. They told us if we stumble or fall they're gonna kill us. Then they lined us up against the wall and a cop with a .45 sub would fire over our heads so the bricks started falling down. Most of us had been in bed, and they just ripped the goddamn clothes off everybody, women and men. They had the gun, they'd just snatch your pants down and they took pictures of us like that. Then they put us in a wagon and took us down to the police station. We were handcuffed and running down this little driveway; when we got to the other end of it, a cop would come by with a stick and he'd punch us, beat us. Some of us were bleeding; I know I was bleeding, but really I thought it would be a whole lot worse."[3]

That raid put local Panther leaders behind bars, with bail set at $100,000 each. Those of us who had been preparing for the upcoming convention faced major uncertainties. Who would be responsible for the thousands who would be coming in a few days to attend the convention? How would these Panther supporters act in response to the raids? And, above all, how would the police behave? The police had not been content to arrest the Panthers in the manner described, they had proceeded to trash their offices and were going door to door in black neighborhoods in search of suspects in the VonColln killing.

An emergency meeting was called by community leaders at the Episcopal Church House on Rittenhouse Square. Muhammad Kenyatta, Sister Falaka Fattah, the Rev. David Gracie, and others held a press conference there to announce that a federal injunction would be sought to halt the continued police "fishing raids on homes in the black community." In attendance was civil rights attorney William Kunstler, who spoke for all present when he said he thought the shootings of the police "were used as an excuse to raid the Black Panthers and interfere with the convention."

Attorneys promptly moved for bail reduction while the Philadelphia Yearly Meeting of Friends, other church groups, and individuals put up property bail for the release of Reggie and the others who had been jailed. Temple University publicly reaffirmed its commitment to make McGonigle Hall available for the opening session of the convention. Most important, federal judge John Fullam issued an injunction against the Philadelphia police that had the effect of dramatically reducing their activities and even their visible presence on North Philadelphia streets over the Labor Day weekend.

On September 4, registration for the convention began at the Church of the Advocate. Everyone who lined up to register was frisked by members of the Black Panthers—a strange experience for some, who had never before been searched for weapons on their way into a church building. The search did have the effect of establishing who was responsible for law and order at this event— the Panthers, not the police. The weekend was not only peaceful, it was extraordinarily so. The streets of North Philadelphia seemed for once to belong to the people of North Philadelphia. It was Huey Newton's and not Frank Rizzo's time to be center stage.

Unfortunately, when Huey spoke, after three years of enforced silence, Reggie felt that "what he said just lost people." Newton didn't present a clear-cut program. If he had, Reggie said later, "I think the corporate capitalists would have had a hell of a war on their hands. At that plenary session there were Indians, Asians, Puerto Ricans, White people, Black people, everybody . . . and any kind of clearcut, basic, fundamental plan to go back into communities—if it was nothing else but to make sure that the government couldn't co-opt what was existing at that point—could have helped us funnel more and more people into our struggle."[4]

If the prophet failed, at least he had been provided a platform and a chance to speak at the Church of the Advocate. That the killing of a police officer, the raids on the Panther offices, and the emotions set off by these events did not tear the city apart showed once again the sense of responsibility of community leaders at all levels, from grass roots neighborhood organizations to the Philadelphia Bar Association, Temple University, and the Religious Society of Friends. The Episcopal Diocese played its part well, and as far as the Advocate was concerned, I thought to myself, "If we could pull off a convention of Black Panthers, we could do anything!"

11. The Power of Women

Our ministry at the Advocate, as the faculty of the Philadelphia Divinity School put it, was both disturbingly prophetic and a source of healing, and there were those who were drawn to the congregation by both aspects of our ministry. One woman who came to us would have a dramatic future in the church that would symbolize for many all that we stood for at 18th and Diamond. In 1970, Barbara Harris was elected to serve her first full term on the vestry of the Advocate. Appointed to fill a vacancy the year previous, she thus became only the second woman member of our vestry. (Rosalie Lloyd, the first, also served along with Barbara.)

Barbara, who had joined the Advocate in the summer of 1968, quickly became active in the life of the church, fully supporting all of those programs that some of our leading members still found too hard to take. She remembers one socially prominent vestryman telling her: "Don't come around here talking any of that 'black stuff'; remember we get our money from the diocese." To which she replied that she was a long-time contributor to the Episcopal Church herself, so some of that diocesan money was hers, and she planned to say whatever she felt she had to say.

Barbara was a businesswoman who had worked with Joseph Baker Associates, a public relations firm, before being hired by

Sun Oil Company as a public relations officer in September, 1968. Black bourgeoise, one would think, judging by her position in life, her smart appearance, her wry sense of humor. She lived in Germantown, where she had attended St. Barnabas Church, a black congregation that merged in April, 1968, with St. Luke's, a largely white, Anglo-Catholic congregation with a splendid church building near Germantown's Market Square. Barbara had been uncomfortable from the first at St. Luke's because of its very formal and inflexible liturgy; so she went looking for a parish church where she would feel more at home.

Any church that would hold her loyalty would have to be about the business of social change, because Barbara was an activist. She served on the Christian Social Relations Committee of the Diocese of Pennsylvania for years, and had represented the diocese as a special delegate to the convention in South Bend, where she helped to lead the walkout of black delegates. As a member and sometime president of the Philadelphia chapter of the Episcopal Society for Cultural and Racial Unity, Barbara had joined the Selma-to-Montgomery march, she had walked at the Girard College wall, and had taken part in antiwar vigils.

While no stranger to political controversy, Barbara was also engaged in the church's pastoral ministry. In January, 1968, in cooperation with Episcopal Community Services, she had begun visiting women in prison on a regular basis, and was able to continue this volunteer prison work when she came to the Advocate. From 1970 to 1974, Rosalie Lloyd and I went with Barbara every Sunday afternoon to the Philadelphia County House of Correction. Rosalie and Barbara visited the women's wing, while I visited the men.

Barbara's concerns and those of the Church of the Advocate were remarkably similar. But there was still something surprising in her being here; for when she found her way to 18th and Diamond for the good of her own soul, she was reversing the trail of all those black professional people who had left the radical church in North Philadelphia for safer and more secure surroundings in Northwest Philadelphia and elsewhere. Barbara vividly recalls her first Sunday service at the Advocate.

"I got up on Sunday morning with no idea where I was going to go to worship, and I dressed very casually. I don't know if there was any significance in this or not, but I dressed in a way that I had never dressed to go to church. I put on a dashiki, flat sandals, and wore no stockings. I had never entered a church dressed like that before. I got in my car and I still didn't know where I was going. And without thinking I drove to the Church of the Advocate. I knew where it was, of course, but I had never worshiped there before. And I didn't know they were on a summer schedule. I arrived in time for an eleven o'clock service, but they had begun at ten. All the doors were open, and I went in the Diamond Street door and found myself walking right toward the altar. I was very embarrassed and made a quick turn down the side aisle. I guess I looked perplexed. Then a woman named Jean Harris extended her arms to me and embraced me, and that was my introduction to the Church of the Advocate. I felt wrapped in love from the moment I walked in there. That very week I requested my letter of transfer. I knew I was home."[1]

Barbara found a home with us and we found a solid supporter in her. She became a pillar of strength to me, serving as my rector's warden for several years. She was joining the small group of dedicated people remaining at the Advocate in 1968. By the time she was elected to the vestry, all but four of the hard-line opposition had left. The vestry member who had rebuked her about "that black stuff" soon left himself. All those who remained either supported the church's programs or kept their displeasure to themselves.

Among the supporters and in the center of the action were some other remarkable women. Barbara recalls getting to know Daisy Lacey, who ran our parish food and clothing cupboard and was living then in what had been the curate's home. Very active with the Welfare Rights Organization, Daisy had formed a chapter of WRO at the Advocate in 1967. She helped that organization, made up largely of mothers on welfare, to wage a successful campaign to get companies to open credit accounts for welfare recipients. With her own new account at Sears, Daisy had purchased a refrigerator—avocado green. She proudly showed it to Barbara, exclaiming, "Lord, now help me pay for this thing!"

It was welfare rights organizing that first brought me into contact with Suzanne Hiatt back in 1966. She had been hired by the
Philadelphia Health and Welfare Council and the Diocese of Pennsylvania jointly to work with Terry Dellmuth in implementing a
strategy aimed at raising the level of welfare grants in Pennsylvania. The grant level was so pitifully low that tactics like a blood
sale in November, 1967, by mothers on welfare who needed
money to buy shoes for their children, seemed quite appropriate.
Sue Hiatt helped organize the publicity for this action, called
"Blood for Shoes"; it was made even more powerful in its effect
when most of the mothers were rejected as donors due to iron
deficiency, caused by their inadequate diets.

Sue was an Episcopalian who had earned a divinity degree at
the Episcopal Theological School in Cambridge, Massachusetts, at
the same time she was earning her master's in social work at Boston University. She really wanted to work for the church and soon
joined the staff of Bishop DeWitt as his suburban missioner,
working with a group on the Main Line called Friends of Welfare
Rights, and maintaining her contacts at the Advocate with me and
the WRO chapter that met there. One morning a week I met with
Sue, the suburban missioner, Dave Gracie, who was the urban
missioner, a few other key players on the bishop's social action
team, and Bishop DeWitt himself. From these breakfast meetings
in 1968 came the impetus for a powerful pastoral letter by Bishop
DeWitt on the issue of welfare rights, to be read from all the
pulpits of the churches in the diocese.

The not-so-hidden agenda of this remarkable young social
worker was to bring about the ordination of women as priests in
the Episcopal Church. Sue felt called to the priesthood herself and
when she knew that she had my support she joined the Advocate
so that we could be her sponsoring parish. She would put into
practice all the organizing skills she had learned and sharpened in
the welfare rights movement to build a national movement for the
ordination of women. It was always important for her (and for
me) to remember that the first movement inspired the second by
displaying the courage of women learning to stand up for their
rights—whether sitting-in at welfare offices to demand just treat-

ment for one of their sisters, publicly selling their blood to dramatize their children's need, or picketing a $200-a-plate dinner for Governor Ronald Reagan of California sponsored by the governor of Pennsylvania (that one got Sue fired from her organizer's job), and in many other ways showing what organized women could achieve.

The woman in my life who emerged most clearly as a new leader in 1970 was none other than my own wife. I had chosen Christine to be my wife because I believed that she could support my special calling, but now she was finding a special calling of her own—building houses for the poor. I watched in amazement as she moved step by step into her leadership role. Although I was supportive all along the way, I admit to feeling some degree of masculine uneasiness at first. I had some growing to do to realize that Christine, in addition to being wife, mother, choir member, and advocate of better education for black children, was called to be a housing developer.

This process all began with the parents' group that met at the Advocate after the November 17, 1967, demonstration at the Board of Education. The fourteen people who met regularly were concerned primarily about their children's education, but they tried to help each other's families when other needs arose. One of the members, a devoted mother with seven fine children, faced eviction because she had stopped paying her rent to protest the landlord's refusal to make repairs on her property—about a half-block distant from the church. Christine and a few others decided they would spend their weekends helping her find another house to live in. It took them two months to succeed.

One real estate agent told Christine that he would rent a house to the woman but would expect Chris to keep watch over the house to see that she did not tear it up. How demeaning, how degrading, we thought. Christine was still fuming when we went to bed that evening. Suddenly she sat up and said: "We are going to have to build houses for our people!" I replied, "Sure, baby," and patted her on her shoulder while asking myself, How in God's name is Christine going to build houses?

The first thing she did was suggest to the parents' group that they incorporate themselves as a housing development corporation. Since they were as naive as she was, they readily agreed. Christine had learned about the Model Cities program in a workshop on housing at the Black Power Conference in 1968. Model Cities sent two consultants to work with Christine's group. They also got help from Philadelphia Council on Community Advancement, directed by W. Wilson Goode, the man who would later become mayor of Philadelphia. These consultants played their part well, being careful to give technical advice but not to substitute their judgment for that of Christine and the other community residents.

I gave the budding development group the first $500 I ever received for a speaking fee so they could pay a lawyer to handle the incorporating. They named themselves the Advocate Community Development Corporation (ACDC), and when they found that the city was planning to build fifteen new houses for low-income families on Page Street, not far from the church, they went into action.

The city housing agency was preparing to sign a contract with a commercial outfit to do this work, but Christine marched down to the city agency and asked, "How dare you sign a contract with an outside group to build houses in *our* community when we have a housing development corporation of our own?" Somehow she convinced them to name ACDC as the developer, although the corporation had never even rehabilitated a house, much less built one.

The project was complicated. The homes were to be built for families receiving welfare, who were to be trained in home maintenance skills and would participate to some degree in the construction of the units. It was ACDC's first effort and it had to go well, so when the contractor failed to perform to the satisfaction of ACDC, Christine decided to take on supervisory duties on location. (This meant that we had to buy another car.)

Every morning after getting the children to school, she went to the 1600 block of Page Street. Home again to make lunch for the children, she would return to Page Street in the afternoon. That close attention to detail paid off as the project moved to successful completion. ACDC had established itself and had begun the work the group continues to this day, with Christine as president and the multitalented Spencer Sewell as executive director. Although Christine goes to work daily she has refused throughout all the years to accept a salary.

I am listed on ACDC brochures as chaplain, and at times I imagine my name and influence, as well as my prayers, have been of some help. On one occasion I confronted the secretary of a state housing agency after he backed down on a promise to Christine and ACDC. Two carloads of North Philadelphians had driven to Harrisburg, the state capital, to sign a contract with the state, only to be told the deal was off. I was angry and I cautioned the official: "Mr. Secretary, you have been playing with my wife, and nobody plays with my wife but me! You encouraged her; you promised her; and today you say you cannot do it. I don't like what you have been doing with my wife." My words to the secretary were so disorienting to him that he placed his pipe in his mouth bowl first. I had thrust the issue, almost rudely, from the ordinary bureaucratic modus operandi and had set it in human, personal terms. He immediately reconsidered his position. "Let's all go to lunch," he said, "and after lunch I'll call in my staff and we'll sign that contract."

But the last thing I want to do is exaggerate my role in ACDC's growth. In fact, I have to confess how hard it was for me at first to adjust to the fact that it was Christine who was making the deals. When she came home to tell me about signing the first government contract in the amount of $250,000, I rejoiced with her, but it was like a blow to my gut. There she was signing a contract for that much money when my parish at that time had never had an annual budget of more than $100,000. I was actually envious.

It was not until later that I realized that another revolution was taking place, one that would force men to realize that this is not "a man's world," but a world where interdependence is inherent in the divine plan and we must all be mutually responsible, one to the other. "My" ministry would not be what it has been without my accepting the fact that we are interdependent. I realize that as I look back upon not only my mother and how she influenced my life, but also my wife, and upon Jackie, who challenged me: "Show me how God loves me!"—revealing to me the principle that would underlie the Advocate's ministry.

Along with them, I think of Sue Hiatt, who motivated, strategized, and became the driving force leading to the ordination of the first eleven women as priests in the Episcopal Church; Barbara Harris, who became the first woman bishop; Mary Adebonojo and Ann Smith, who would recognize their call to the ordained ministry while members of the Advocate, so that I had the privilege of presenting four women for ordination. Beyond the Episcopal Church, I was invited to speak at Philadelphia's Imani Temple in December, 1991, at the service of institution for the Rev. Rose Marie Vernell, the first woman to be ordained in the African American Catholic Congregation, founded by Archbishop G. Augustus Stallings.

I have been privileged to support some outstanding women in politics, too, beginning with Roxanne Jones, the unsurpassed grass roots activist, who called me into the situation leading to my first arrest. A day would come, in 1984, when she would ask me to be chairman of her campaign committee as she ran for a seat in the Pennsylvania Senate. When she asked, I had serious reservations about her being able to win; but I reasoned that if I went to jail with her, then why not be willing to go down to defeat with her if she lost? Well, she won, becoming the first black woman, and only the second woman, in the Pennsylvania Senate. Another unique woman, Ida Chen, invited me to join her campaign for judgeship in the municipal court of the City of Philadelphia in 1989. She became the first Asian American woman to sit as a judge on that court.

Beyond question, some of the most challenging, fulfilling, and significant journeys as I pursued my calling have been with and because of women. Until women, and indeed all of God's children, are allowed to participate totally in church and society, our life together will continue to bear the stamp of mankind and not humankind.

12. "A Castle to Keep Me Safe"

The psalmist cries to God in Psalm 31:3, "Be my strong rock, a castle to keep me safe, for you are my crag and my stronghold." I believe that God's church should be a castle and a stronghold for those in need. By the 1970s, the Advocate had for years been serving as a sheltering place for individuals, groups, and social movements; but, like a castle, it also served as a place from which to move out to challenge the existing racist and sexist order of things. Even at the times when people took shelter at the church to mourn the loss of lives, that dimension of challenge was present. The memorial service for Bill Seidler in March, 1971, was a very moving case in point.

William "Pop" Seidler had run an apparel store at 1937 Columbia Avenue for as long as people could remember. When he was shot and killed in his shop in the course of a robbery, shock waves went through the community of North Philadelphia and beyond. At his memorial service the church was filled with North Philadelphians and Chestnut Hillers, Episcopalians and Jews, people of various political persuasions. They all came to pay tribute to a man who (in the words of a newspaper columnist) "lived his life to eradicate the conditions that produce the person who killed him."

Bill was both neighbor and friend to me. He and his wife, Miriam, lived above the store they had rebuilt after it burned down in the 1964 Columbia Street riot. They had decided not to join the general exodus of shopkeepers but to stay in North Philadelphia and keep on working in the community for justice. Their store was located just a few doors away from the Black Panther Party office, where the Seidlers were no strangers but strong supporters of the Panthers in their various projects. They especially shared the concern to end police brutality, and were active in the formation of COPPAR (Citizens Organized for Philadelphia Police Accountability and Responsibility) earlier in the year in which Bill died.

Bill's wife, Miriam, had seen him murdered in their shop, but even so she refused to leave Columbia Avenue, believing there was more she could do to bring about the political change she and Bill believed was necessary. She told a reporter: "Without black liberation there will be liberation for nobody. I shall stay in North Philadelphia."

In my eulogy for the sixty-two-year-old Jewish merchant who and shown so much love for our community, I said that Bill would not want expressions of concern just for him, but for everyone who is shot down in North Philadelphia. Bill did not consider himself better than anyone else.

In April, a month after Bill Seidler was killed, occurred the death of Jerard Foster Young, a twenty-five-year-old Washington, D.C., police officer, shot down on the streets of that city in the course of a struggle with a man he was attempting to place under arrest. Jerard had grown up in the Church of the Advocate and had been one of my altar boys, so I was asked to preach his funeral sermon at the Washington Cathedral, at a service that would be attended by more than a thousand police from Pennsylvania and Washington, D.C.

I accepted the family's invitation and then thought about what I could say about a fine young man who had accepted such a difficult calling.

I had a great deal of difficulty preparing that sermon. With many thoughts in my mind but little on paper, I mounted the pulpit and looked out at those in attendance.

I began talking about Jerard Young as a Vietnam veteran and a police officer who I knew was personally repelled by killing. I recall ever so vividly the Sunday he came to church after returning from Vietnam. As he was leaving the service on that day, he paused, we embraced one another, and while holding my hand he said to me, "Father, we're killing women and children over there." With his head bowed, he left.

In my sermon I spoke about the deaths of other police on the streets of our major cities and asked if we have become so depersonalized that we can simply put a label on a man and do away with him. Have we really stopped thinking of policemen as people? I talked about the almost impossible situation in which society had placed our police officers by demanding rigid enforcement of law and order in the ghetto while tolerating illegality in high places. And then I asked the police officers present to broaden their sympathies and to think not only of injustice done to policemen, but also to black residents of our cities deprived of their rights and to the women and children being killed at that moment in Vietnam.

Concerned as I was about speaking some healing and challenging words to the colleagues of Officer Young, I was more concerned about his mother, who had kept a round-the-clock vigil at the bedside of her unconscious, twenty-five-year-old son until he died. After the rifle salutes and the playing of taps at Lincoln Memorial Cemetery ended the long ceremony and her long ordeal, I saw her collapse and be carried away to a waiting limousine.

On September 10, 1971, at the Advocate, a thousand people listened while another mother spoke about the death of her young son. Georgina Jackson, the mother of George Jackson, a member of the Black Panther Party killed in an alleged escape attempt from San Quentin prison, told of her loss and of what we had all lost in the death of this young leader. George Jackson's memorial service was sponsored by ten groups, including the Black Panther Party and the Black Economic Development Conference. In the crowded

church and in a march to the Black Panther Party office on Columbia Avenue that followed the service, there was the usual
quota of FBI and plainclothes police agents, although who they
were no one could be sure. On September 27 a similar service and
protest gathering took place at the church, this time remembering
those who had been killed in an inmates' uprising at Attica prison
when Governor Rockefeller ordered that the prison be raided by
New York State Police.

The funerals and memorial services of those years revealed how
we as a society were locked in a cycle of killing and retribution
that was leading to a denial of our common humanity. It was my
job and that of the church to affirm what was being denied, by
being open to the families and friends of all the victims.

I can recall only one time when I said no to a request to use the
church for such a memorial service. That was in May, 1974, when
six members of the Symbionese Liberation Army were killed at
their Los Angeles headquarters in a flaming shootout with police.
Reggie Schell wanted to memorialize their deaths as fellow radicals and participants in revolutionary struggle, but since I knew
that the SLA had been responsible for the assassination of Oakland, California, school superintendent Marcus Foster in 1973, I
refused. Marcus Foster had been an outstanding high school principal in Philadelphia before going to Oakland. He was a black
educator who had won the respect of many, both at Gratz High
School and throughout the city; both Christine and I deeply felt
his loss. I asked Reggie, "If members of the SLA could kill Marcus
Foster and be seen as revolutionary heroes, what's to prevent them
from killing me and being considered heroes for it?"

Our moral authority was all that we had to rely on. Apart from
that we were quite vulnerable. While the church looked like a castle, we had no moat or drawbridge to keep any enemy at bay. Yet,
just as the church in ancient times had been regarded as a sanctuary for those charged with crimes, so the Advocate became a
sanctuary in May, 1971, for a twenty-six-year-old pastor of the
Church of God in Christ. The Rev. Dwight Campbell had been
found guilty of assault and battery on a police officer in an inci-

dent in 1965 during the Girard College demonstrations. Somehow he had never been asked to serve his time. It was six years later that the district attorney discovered the error, after the incident had been mentioned in the Philadelphia mayoral primary as an example of mayoral candidate Frank Rizzo's brutal conduct as a police officer. A photo of Rizzo in uniform raising his billy club to strike Eugene "Tree" Dawkins, who had been sentenced along with Campbell and a third young man named Leonard Hill, had been widely circulated in the community.

Anyone who knew the gentle, soft-spoken, five-foot-tall Dwight Campbell would have to doubt that he was guilty of assaulting police officers. When he learned that a warrant was out for his arrest, Dwight came to the Advocate along with Muhammad Kenyatta, with whom he was closely associated in BEDC. He was seeking sanctuary, and we offered it to him in a very public way.

I introduced Dwight to the Sunday congregation and explained the situation to them in the terms of the African proverb that when elephants fight, it is the smaller animals in the jungle who get trampled. The elephants in this case were the mayoral candidates and the one being hurt was Campbell. Kenyatta was with us that Sunday to preach a sermon on the occasion of BEDC's second anniversary. He called the cases against Campbell and the other two "police skullduggery" and said we were not going to run from that, but were challenging it publicly.

The media paid attention to the case, becoming very interested in the idea of sanctuary, especially since it seemed to work. The district attorney sent no one to the church to make an arrest. In effect, we bought some time, a matter of a few days, during which legal appeals were taken and the issue resolved without Campbell being jailed. Kenyatta told the press: "[Rev. Campbell's] courage has vindicated the notion of the black church as the only available sanctuary for black folk in this time and place."

A few years later, in 1974, my own sense of the church as sanctuary was tested when it was proposed that the Advocate be the meeting place for warring street gangs. Barry Hogan, who made the proposal, could see no reason for my hesitations; but that's the way Barry was—very determined and deadly serious about his mission. I don't think I have ever met anyone like him.

A barber on Susquehanna Avenue now, Barry had once taken someone's life and had done time for it in a state penitentiary. Barry afterward felt a strong sense of responsibility toward the young brothers who were killing each other in gang wars in North Philadelphia, and one day he walked into my office to say that he was going to do something about it.

He was an impressive man. Physically, he looked like a middle-weight Larry Holmes, and his demeanor was always serious. I don't think Barry ever smiled. I remember thinking to myself that the man was crazy to believe he could deal with this problem. When I asked him how he proposed to go about it, he began by giving me his credentials: "Number one, I used to be a runner [a gang leader]. Number two, I spent seven years in the penitentiary."

"And so you think that you can stop all the gang killings?" I asked.

"Yes, I can," he responded with complete confidence.

When I asked why he was telling this to me, he said that he needed a place to meet with the gang members and he wanted to meet at the Advocate. At that point I began to feel anxious. "Wait a minute. These are enemy gangs that have been killing each other off. You want to bring them together here at my church?"

"Yes, this is the only place where we can meet."

"And when do you want to start this?"

"In a couple of days, just as soon as I can get to the corners to talk with all of the runners."

Feeling my hesitation, Barry explained to me the necessity and the logic of his mission. The gang members were young brothers who had absolutely no faith in their elders, neither mothers nor fathers, and certainly not "preachers." They had contempt for cops, whom they called "pigs." And if I or anyone else tried to reach them, pointing out that theirs was a game of Russian roulette, it would only become more exciting and challenging for them. Their violent behavior gave them a feeling of power not only over their territory but over life and death. But for Barry to speak to them was different. He knew where they were because he had been there. He could speak of life because he had taken one; and from personal experience he could say, I am living and life is worth living.

His proposal was dynamite. How could I afford the risk of saying yes? But how could I afford to say no? In the ten years leading up to 1974, Philadelphia gang wars had claimed more than three hundred young lives. This was a problem of immense proportions; but never before in my experience had an older, well-known gang leader had the courage to step forward to do what even the gang control unit of the police had not been able to do.

Feeling led by the Spirit and anchored in faith, I gave Barry permission to bring the 25D's (25th and Diamond Street gang), the 23D's, the Seibert Street gang, the Norris Street gang, and still another, to the Advocate. Perchance there could be another Pentecost: they might be able to be in one place with one accord, "Parthians, Medes, Elamites and dwellers of Mesopotamia" (Acts 2:9). They might be able to hear through Barry, a man who had served time for murder, the wonderful works of God.

It did not take Barry long to get back to me. He said that he had met with five runners and they had agreed to meet with each other at the Advocate. They promised that this would be neutral territory and they would not start a war around the church.

On the appointed afternoon they came from all directions and *on time*. I stood at the parish hall door to greet them and also to let them know they were meeting on my turf. It felt strange as I attempted to greet these young boys, ages fourteen or fifteen to nineteen or twenty, only to discover that they would not even look at me. They passed me by as though I was not even there. The few who did look at me looked with disdain. I sat in the rear of the large meeting room and listened as Barry took over.

He spoke with authority, beginning by presenting his credentials: "I used to be a runner. I killed a young brother. I spent seven years in the penitentiary. I want to make you into a Nation of Power."

There was no dialogue, no questions, no charges by one gang against another. All seventy-five to one hundred of them sat in absolute quiet, and when Barry finished what he had to say and told them to go back to their own corners and not to war around the Advocate, they did as they were ordered.

I attended three such meetings, which never lasted more than forty-five minutes. I never addressed the group. There were no discussions, questions, or answers. Barry's one statement was: "We must stop killing one another. We must stop warring against one another. We must become one nation and in that oneness there is power." After the third meeting Barry told me I had to stay away. "The brothers said they don't want you in their meeting, and if you are in here the next time, they are all going to leave and go back to their corners."

I protested: "They don't want me in the meetings? Don't they know this is *my* house?" Barry didn't argue. He simply laid down the condition, for me to accept or reject. Barry was a man of strength. While in the penitentiary he must have thought a lot about life, the way Malcolm X and others did. And Barry was saying to me something that sounded like what God had once said to the people of Israel: "Behold, I have set before you this day life and good and death and evil." I had to make the choice and take the risk. I chose the hope of life in a situation where the potential for death was written on the face of every child who came through our doors.

I must confess that Barry both challenged and intimidated me. Since I could not always be there to open the doors for his meetings, I had told him that meetings had to be held at my convenience. He informed me that they could not be at my convenience but whenever the brothers wanted to meet, and he suggested that I give the key to the parish house to him. Would you believe that I did? But the Nation of Power was being born. Those little brothers who had been living a day at a time only to die on an appointed day could now choose life.

But where does Christian risk taking become simply foolishness? Where do you draw the line between being a damn fool and what St. Paul called "a fool for Christ"? Just before Christmas, Barry came to me with yet another challenge/demand. "The brothers want to have a Christmas dance," he told me. Once again I looked at Barry with incredulity and I asked: "Aren't you taking this too far? If one brother from one corner says one word, or makes one false move towards a lady belonging to a brother from another corner, you've got an explosion. This is a risk we can't take. Let's not push our luck!"

Once again Barry pulled his credentials on me. "Listen, Father Washington, these brothers respect me. When I tell them something, they obey; and if I tell them not to make a pass at another brother's lady, they will do as I say." By this time I had crossed the line. I was now a complete fool, for Christ, I hoped—or maybe just a damn fool.

The night of the dance came. I was on the church premises but I did not go up to the dance floor. I heard the music blaring, the drums booming, the voices and the laughter of young teenagers having a good time. Of course, Barry totally ignored my ultimatum to close down at 1 A.M. They went on and on.

I sat in my office praying, writing Christmas cards, and waiting for whatever might come. I remember writing a card to Bishop DeWitt. I told him at what time I was writing and how I was praying that Barry had built a Nation where murderous enemies could now share their ladies with each other, bump shoulders, experience that bump as a touch of life rather than of death.

The dance finally ended after 2 A.M. As I sat in my office I heard the loud laughter of youngsters trying to get a word through the noise of a joy-filled little world to the ears of a friend. A few days later when I sang "Joy to the world, the Lord is come," I was thinking of the sounds of Barry's Nation of Power.

Barry met regularly and faithfully with these young fellows for about a year. He did not attempt to build them into an organization, nor did he have the assistance of any other adult. They came together because of him, and their unity was in him. Barry and I never conversed, except for brief moments when he needed my permission to do certain things. Looking back on that event in my ministry, I feel that Barry wanted to atone for his sin. He had killed and he then wanted to save lives, and he did. In that one year he may well have prevented the killing of at least ten children and young men.

In a way Barry was to those youngsters a savior. Christ wears many faces and appears in all shapes and sizes and styles. He might even look like the gardener (as he did in John 20:15). After about a year, Barry said to me, "We don't need any more meetings." He returned the key to me and was gone. He had atoned. He was finished. Every now and then a young man will stop me on the avenue and say, "I used to meet at the Advocate with Barry." The Advocate is the only church they know. They are sheep of the fold.

13. A Pivotal Year, 1971

I must return to the year that Bill Seidler and Officer Young died, the year when Dwight Campbell took sanctuary in the church, because in the incredible pace of events of 1971 many clear turning points were reached. Frank Rizzo was elected mayor of Philadelphia. The reparations struggle in the Diocese of Pennsylvania reached its bitter climax. The campaign to ordain women in the Episcopal Church was well and truly launched.

On the national scene, the divisions in the Christian churches were sharpened because of the Angela Davis case. As usual, the Advocate became the focal point for the controversy in the Diocese of Pennsylvania. A rally held at the Advocate to raise money for the Angela Davis Defense Fund on January 7, 1971, gave offense to many people.

Angela Davis was a young, black, revolutionary woman, regarded as doubly dangerous because she was a member of the Communist Party. She had been fired from her teaching position at the University of California–Los Angeles for her political activities in 1970. Later she became a fugitive from the FBI after being charged with furnishing guns for a kidnapping from a Marin County, California, courthouse. When she was captured and put in jail, many regarded her as a political prisoner who had been framed to silence her views about racial and economic injustice in the United States. When the Rev. Jesse Jackson visited her in prison, he told the press: "She is an avowed Communist, and I am an avowed Christian. Both of these commitments represent threats to the existing social, economic, and political establishment."

I shared Jesse's sentiments, and so I offered myself and the Advocate in the nationwide campaign for Angela Davis's legal defense. I took the appeal for money to members of the Chestnut Hill Pipeline, white residents of Philadelphia's wealthiest neighborhood who had committed themselves to aid the poor in North Philadelphia and with whom I had worked closely on a number of projects. In a letter that appeared in the *Chestnut Hill Local* newspaper, I wrote: "Angela Davis is in isolation, with only one hour of recreation a week. Her health, if not her life, is in jeopardy." Such advocacy aroused the ire of political conservatives in the diocese.

Because of the January 7 support rally, W. Clark Hanna, a layman who led a group calling itself Episcopal Renaissance, sent a letter to every parish in the diocese urging that they withhold funds from the diocese to protest such open support of Angela Davis. Since the Advocate was being subsidized then by the diocese in the amount of $30,000 a year, he argued that any money given to the diocese would amount to indirect support to "an admitted communist," Angela Davis.

At a meeting of the Diocesan Council, Hanna pushed his anticommunist line further, claiming that people like me were aiding the cause of the Antichrist. The ministry of the Advocate was defended by Eleanor Sears, a parishioner, and by most others at the council meeting. The sense of the meeting was that the church must be concerned for all people—as someone said, "even, heaven forbid, a communist."

In the City of Philadelphia in 1971, the race for mayor was a political lightning rod for many of the tensions in the whole country, certainly those between black communities and the police. Police Commissioner Frank Rizzo contested the Democratic nomination with Councilman David Cohen, a liberal critic of Rizzo's record as police chief, and with Hardy Williams, an attorney, who was the first serious black contender for mayor in the city's history. A Black Political Convention was held in February, 1971, at the Benjamin Franklin High School. That convention, which I chaired, served to build the base for Williams's candidacy. Attorney Cecil Moore and playwright LeRoi Jones called for a major voter registration drive. "The ballot not the bullet" was the theme of Jones's address. The Rev. Leon Sullivan, founder of Opportunities Industrialization Center (OIC) and pastor of Zion Baptist Church, projected victory for a black mayor "by the time the Bicentennial rolls around in 1976." His prophecy would fall eight years short, for the first black mayor of Philadelphia, W. Wilson Goode, would not be elected until 1984. Nevertheless, the ball started rolling with the Hardy Williams campaign.

Frank Rizzo won the primary because of strong support from white voters, many of whom regarded him as a savior from riots in the streets. Rizzo's opponents split their votes between the two liberal reform candidates, one white and one black. In November, in the final election, I joined those in the black community who declared themselves in the camp of Thacher Longstreth, Rizzo's Republican opponent. We felt we had no other choice.

Longstreth was a Republican from Chestnut Hill who had directed the Philadelphia Chamber of Commerce and had served on City Council. Personable and outgoing, he was no stranger to the black churches and neighborhoods of the city, where he seemed to enjoy the fact that many called him "Longstretch," a pronunciation that suited his size. I told people that at least we could communicate with Longstreth, while Rizzo wouldn't even enter our communities. "Bozo" was one of the nicknames the police commissioner was given at that time in North Philadelphia.

Although many Democrats voted for the Republican candidate in order to oppose someone who symbolized for us violence and racism, racism was very much in season and Frank Rizzo won. He would serve two terms as mayor, then try but fail to have the city charter amended so that he could run a third time. After his 1971 election victory, the press asked me what I thought would happen.

I tried to be hopeful and said that I couldn't believe any mayor would want to perpetuate polarization. "He will have to begin to establish some rapport and some dialogue. When he does, there will be hope for some mutual understanding."

The years that followed did see some degree of mutual understanding; for instance, the Advocate Community Development Corporation received continuing support from the Rizzo administration for its housing work. Following a devastating fire in our parish house in 1975, he called me personally at dinnertime. "Rev, I heard about the fire at your church. If we can be of any help, just call Goldie [Goldie Watson, deputy mayor] and we'll send people out to give you all the help we can." I did call, and we were provided with a large city truck and three men, who helped alongside the neighborhood people, Temple University students, and members of our church in our cleanup operation.

In my relationship with Frank Rizzo, I have to distinguish Rizzo the police commissioner, Rizzo the mayor, and Rizzo the man. I strongly opposed his statements and his tactics in many situations when he was police commissioner. I also found that many of his political statements were racially divisive. We were at opposite poles and we were both aware of this. Yet when we encountered each other personally, our relationship was cordial, and I might say even warm and mutually respectful. In 1986 he heard that I was undergoing serious surgery in Cape May, New Jersey, following an auto accident. He wrote a brief note to me, expressing his hope for a total recovery and adding, "You mean a lot to our city."

I genuinely liked Frank Rizzo, the man. I did not like Frank Rizzo, police commissioner and mayor. Polarization was never overcome during his administration. Eight years after he was elected mayor, I was a strong supporter of the "Stop Rizzo Coalition" in the vote on revising the charter, while Rizzo was calling for his supporters to "vote white."

Continuing polarization in the Diocese of Pennsylvania made the papers repeatedly in 1971, in particular with regard to the Restitution Fund, which had been set up in response to the reparations demands of the Black Economic Development Conference. A sum of $250,000 had been granted by the diocese and $15,000 came from other church sources. Bishop DeWitt's hope was that the fund would grow well beyond this amount. And, since it would be administered by black members of the church only, he hoped that it would become a model for the church's response to demands for black power.

Tragically, but predictably, the Restitution Fund Commission split along ideological lines. In the internal power struggle, power ended up in the hands of those black church members who feared the BEDC and were looking for the safest and most conservative ways to invest the funds committed to their charge. The struggle became very public in June at a ceremony at St. Philip's Church, 1925 Lombard Street, at which the officers of the Restitution Fund Commission were to be installed.

At the ceremony, fourteen of us, black clergy and laity, announced our resignation from the commission in protest against the leadership of chairman Harold Pilgrim, a vestryman from Calvary Church in West Philadelphia, who, it seemed to us, was simply providing a black face to the forces of reaction in the diocese. Barbara Harris was our spokesperson. She decried the failure of the leadership of the commission to understand what black self-determination really meant. They were "preoccupied with their accountability to the white church," she said, and she assumed that they intended to go on funding only safe projects, as in their grant of $7,000 for air conditioners for OIC training centers. (Opportunities Industrialization Center was a favorite project of many at that time, including the federal government, which had funded it with millions of dollars.)

Muhammad Kenyatta joined in our protest and effectively disrupted the service of installation for one-half hour, preaching against "right-wing Uncle Toms." When I took the pulpit to attack the forty-two member commission for betraying the trust of the black community by sitting for eight months on the money given by the diocese while making only token grants, I broke down in sobs. "If I cry tonight," I said, "understand that my cries are those of our children dying in the streets while we haggle in committee over procedure."

A reporter's story noted that I was speaking from notes written on the back of five "Stop Rizzo" handbills. Yes, I was under the pressure of fighting two losing battles at once. And my bishop was under pressure, too. During the stormy commissioning ceremony he sat in the bishop's chair near the altar, frequently with his head in his hands. A half-hour after the service, he stopped at my home to see how I was feeling and told me to "hold on."

In a later address to the diocese, Bishop DeWitt forthrightly admitted the failure of his hopes for the reparations process. "We now face the paradox," he said, "of giving to a fund for black self-determination the allocating committee of which is seriously divided on the meaning of self-determination. How shall we respond? Conscientiously and openly. Give or don't give 'as unto the Lord', without any gloating or self-righteousness. Let us stay open to the reconciliation God will work among us."

The Restitution Fund Commission eventually began to expend the money, but only after much effort "to certify the validity and veracity of applicants." Harold Pilgrim even hired an agency to investigate the organizations that applied for funds. Needless to say, no funds went to BEDC, which had prompted the whole process. Kenyatta kept up his verbal barrage against Pilgrim and the commission, for he sincerely felt that these black churchpeople were in no way modeling self-determination but were being used as instruments of white churchpeople. "Don't give to BEDC," he said to them. "Crucify BEDC, but don't shut out the black community, don't divide us!"

Amidst the many setbacks and tragedies of 1971, there was one step forward in the direction of equality in the church that would not be reversed, although the participants in the action could not know that at the time. On June 18 I presented Suzanne Hiatt to be ordained to the diaconate. She was the first woman to be ordained a deacon in the Diocese of Pennsylvania and only the second in the Episcopal Church, U.S.A.

The service of ordination took place at the Church of Christ and St. Ambrose at 6th and Venango, where Lloyd Winter, my former curate, was priest in charge. Sue's lay presenter was Jeannette Piccard, a dynamic woman, seventy-six years of age, who had felt called to ordination in the church for most of her life and who would soon be ordained deacon herself in Minneapolis. The preacher was the Rev. Dr. William Wolf, professor of theology at the Episcopal Theological School in Cambridge, Massachusetts, where Sue had studied. In his sermon he issued a clear call for the ordination of women to the priesthood and the episcopate. Not everyone at Christ and St. Ambrose realized the historic importance of that call, and certainly not everyone agreed with what was happening. Sue told me that in the vesting room before the service she experienced hostility from some of the men who were to be ordained deacon alongside her.

That Sue could be ordained deacon at all was due to the actions of the Episcopal Church at its General Convention in Houston, Texas, in 1970. There the position of women in the church had been advanced in two important ways. For the first time, women were seated as lay delegates to the convention, and the decision was made to authorize the ordination of women as deacons. Priesthood and the episcopate were still denied to women, but I along with many other convention delegates sincerely hoped that the remaining barriers would come down at the next General Convention, in Louisville, Kentucky, in 1973. Working closely with Sue Hiatt, I determined to do all I could to bring that about.

In 1972, on the anniversary of Sue's ordination, we held a service at the Advocate that was more protest than celebration. All the other deacons, the men who had been ordained alongside Sue, had since been made priests. The normal practice was to regard the diaconate as a one-year training period leading to priestly ordination. Sue alone remained a deacon, simply because she was a woman. So we planned the anniversary service as a Eucharist that would not be completed. Sue would read the opening part of the service (the ante-communion), which deacons were allowed to do, then stop before the prayer of consecration, making a point of the barrier she faced. No male priest present would complete the service, in this way showing solidarity with her and demonstrating our sense that without the ordination of women to the priesthood, the church's ministry was incomplete.

The service was not well attended. Although I had written a letter to all area clergy inviting their participation, only about seventy people came. Bishop DeWitt's words to those of us in attendance were picked up by the press, however, so others could at least read about what the bishop called "the shame of the church." He pointed out, "The world has long since recognized the validity of the gifts of women in the professions. The Episcopal Church is peculiarly unable to recognize those gifts."

Nevertheless, only three years after Sue Hiatt's ordination to the diaconate, and in spite of the failure of the Louisville General Convention to authorize the ordination of women, there would be women priests in the Episcopal Church. Sue and Jeannette Piccard would be among their number; the Advocate would be where it happened.

14. "Neither Male nor Female"

The struggle for the ordination of women to the priesthood in the worldwide Anglican Communion spans many years, from the ordination of Florence Li Tim Oi in wartime China in 1944 to the decision to ordain that was finally reached in 1992 by the Church of England, the mother church of the Anglican Communion. Our part in that struggle in the Episcopal Church, U.S.A., gained a special impetus from the civil rights movement. In that movement we had learned to hear the call to freedom and human equality in scripture and to act on it, even if that meant violating laws that perpetuated inequality. Practicing civil disobedience prepared us for the day when ecclesiastical disobedience would be required. But as in the case of civil disobedience, one must first try to correct injustice by using legally available means. In the Episcopal Church that meant trying to get the votes at General Convention.

In the General Convention of 1970, a resolution to admit women to all holy orders failed by only a narrow margin in the clergy order. The lay delegates had approved it, but when a "vote by orders" is called a measure must gain approval by clergy delegates and lay delegates counted separately. The approval of ordination for women as deacons was a kind of consolation prize (a "booby prize," Sue Hiatt called it). When the General Convention of 1973 defeated women's ordination by a bigger margin, some people felt that another route had to be chosen. After all, it had taken General Convention from 1946 to 1970 just to decide to seat women as lay delegates; the wait for a positive vote on ordination could be as long as that.

Bishop DeWitt was among those who wanted action at once. He tried to encourage diocesan ordinations of women without waiting for the uncertain outcome of the 1976 General Convention vote. He argued that the canons of the Episcopal Church did not forbid the ordination of women (the "he" in the canons could be read generically); furthermore, ordinations are under diocesan authority, and a diocese could proceed to act in this matter on its own. His arguments were unavailing, but he himself determined to move ahead, as did several of the women deacons across the country.

In January, 1974, Bishop DeWitt resigned as diocesan bishop, having served the Diocese of Pennsylvania for ten years, which he felt was long enough. His resignation actually freed him to work more effectively for the ordination of women; and in our catholic tradition he remained very much a bishop, retaining the authority to ordain. The new diocesan bishop was Lyman C. Ogilby, whose installation took place at a great service at the Advocate on February 2, 1974. Lyman Ogilby strongly favored the ordination of women but just as strongly believed that it would be best to wait—hoping for and working for a favorable vote at the next General Convention.

Things came to a head in the month of June. On June 15, 1974, the Very Rev. Edward Harris, dean of the Philadelphia Divinity School, preached at the annual diocesan service of ordination of deacons. In his sermon he issued a call for immediate ordinations of women priests. Earlier that month, in Syracuse, New York, Charles Willie, a black educator who as chairman of the House of Deputies of General Convention was the highest-ranking layperson in the Episcopal Church, had made a similar call, asking any bishops willing to ordain women to do so without delay. Deacon Suzanne Hiatt was emboldened by all this.

Immediately following the service, Sue called Bishop DeWitt,

Ed Harris, and me together. She confronted us. She spoke quietly but her words were like thunder: "Ed, in your sermon you called for the immediate ordination of women. Why don't you do it?" In response, we committed ourselves to work toward fulfilling what we all knew to be the will of God.

Not long after, I received a chilling call from Ed. "Paul, you are invited to attend a meeting at Sue Hiatt's house to plan a service of ordination of women to the priesthood. If you come to this meeting, be prepared to discuss the Advocate as a possible place for this service. You will not receive another call in reference to this meeting." That was it, period. Goodbye. "Behold, we are going to Jerusalem" (Matthew 17:31).

I attended the meeting of "conspirators." Sue had been on the job, phoning women deacons who would be willing to be presented for ordination. That meeting was followed by another in Ambler, Pennsylvania, at the home of Bishop DeWitt on July 10, 1974. Five bishops, seven priests, six deacons, and four lay people attended. We all appeared to be of one mind and one accord. We decided that the date would be July 29, the Feast of Sts. Mary and Martha. We felt reasonably sure (wrongly, as it turned out) that among the ordaining bishops there would be, in addition to three retired bishops, at least one or two active diocesan bishops. We fully understood that such ordinations would be "irregular" because they would not be done in accordance with all the applicable canons of the church. But we all believed they would be "valid" nonetheless, since carried out by bishops of the church who would be ordaining as priests deacons whose only impediment to ordination was the fact that they were women.

Then came the question, Where? Someone mentioned a Presbyterian church in New York. Even Bishop DeWitt's tennis court was mentioned. Suggestions like these met with total disapproval. Then Bishop Edward Welles spoke. The retired bishop of West Missouri, Welles was the father of Katrina Swanson, one of the women to be ordained. I remember his strong and animated voice as he proposed, "I'd like to hear what Father Washington has to say about having it at the Church of the Advocate."

The living room was crowded. I recall that some were standing.

I was seated on the floor directly in front of my bishop, Lyman Ogilby. I responded: "I don't know what the consequences will be for what I am about to propose, but that is not the question. The question is 'Where shall this event take place?' I would like to offer the Church of the Advocate for the service." There was applause and laughter. Soon thereafter we dealt with some of the details. It was decided that all inquiries from the press or elsewhere were to be referred to me and that all contributions to help defray expenses would be sent to me.

The only person present opposed to going ahead with the plan was Bishop Lyman Ogilby, who, of course, would have to deal with the inevitable divisions in his own diocese of Pennsylvania. Also he would have to deal with Sue and me, since we were both under his canonical jurisdiction.

How the word got to the press I will never know, but my office phone during the day and my home phone in the evening began ringing incessantly, with calls not only from the press across the United States but also from Europe and as far away as Australia. These calls escalated after both Presiding Bishop John Allin and Bishop Ogilby requested the three retired bishops not to ordain the women as intended. My only response to the callers was that the ordination would take place as planned. I refused to answer questions about the statements by Bishops Allin and Ogilby.

At the next Sunday service at the Advocate following the July 10 meeting, I asked the congregation for their support for the commitment I had made. That was the very first time that I had ever asked the congregation to concur with a decision I had made regarding the Advocate's ministry. In this historic, revolutionary act, I wanted them to be participants in the decision and the action to follow. It was a momentous decision and the consequences for the Advocate could have been disastrous.

They gave their support wholeheartedly and without dissent. Because Sue Hiatt was our own candidate, there was special pleasure that her ordination could take place here. As her pastor, I would be her clergy presenter on the day. Sue asked a faithful member of the congregation, Ann Robb Smith, to be her lay presenter. Ann Robb Smith's growth in the faith had led her in a very personal way to July 29, and her struggles in the church show how issues of racial justice and justice for women were coming together for many of us. The fact that Ann, years later, would herself be ordained a priest and come to serve as assistant to Isaac Miller, my successor at the Advocate, adds a special interest to her story.

Ann was white and well-to-do, the wife of a prominent physician living in the wealthy suburb of Bryn Mawr, where she had once attended the Episcopal Church of the Redeemer, a pillar of financial support for the whole diocese. When Sue Hiatt had served Bishop DeWitt as his suburban missioner in the late 1960s, Ann was one of the group of women who met with Sue to discuss what they could do about segregated housing and other problems of race and poverty. With Sue's coaching, these suburban women took on sexism as well, challenging the male leadership of their parish and deanery on issues of women's representation on decision-making bodies of the church. They won some important battles, including a charter change at the Church of the Redeemer that allowed women to serve on the vestry, previously an all-male club. As Ann tells it, the men of the vestry met for dinner in one another's homes and made decisions for the church over brandy and cigars.

In the fight against sexism, Ann could measure some progress, but the racism in the white suburbs seemed intractable. She saw so much evidence of racist feelings and acts among even her closest neighbors and friends—and this at a time when her own consciousness was being rapidly raised—that she experienced great stress and came near to an emotional breakdown. Marjorie Thomas, who with her husband, Ned, had previously left the Church of the Redeemer to join the Advocate, advised Ann to come to see me. It was a day in March, 1970, that she did so. I remember that we had a heartfelt talk, which lasted perhaps only forty-five minutes, but at the end of it Ann said that now she could carry on; she felt she was not bearing her burden alone.

Then began a period of dual citizenship, urban-suburban, during which she tried to fulfill her duties at the Church of the Redeemer, where she was president of the Episcopal Church Women, while coming to the Advocate for her spiritual needs. On a typical Sunday morning, Ann would go to the 9:15 service at Redeemer, then get in her car and drive the ten miles or so to 18th and Diamond, arriving late for the 11:00 service.

In 1971 Ann was chosen to be president of the Episcopal Church Women of the Diocese of Pennsylvania. She took this as her cue to formally join the Church of the Advocate. That certainly solved her Sunday morning identity problem, but her identity as a member of the Episcopal Church was now in question. While giving strong leadership to the women of the whole diocese, she felt disgust for the manner in which the Episcopal Church nationally was responding to the movement for the ordination of women. She told me that it was only her respect for our bishop and her connection with us at the Advocate that had kept her in the church during those years. So it was with real joy that Ann joined the other members of the parish in their hurried preparations for July 29.

The women of the parish made a frontal for the altar that proclaimed, based on Galatians 3:28: "There is neither Jew nor Greek, black nor white, male nor female; we are one in Christ." We were on course at the Advocate, theologically, emotionally, and every other way. But I knew that others were faltering.

Great efforts were being made to dissuade the bishops from going forward with the service of ordination, and several of the participants became fearful that some of the opponents would move beyond attempts at persuasion to disruptive acts or confrontations. I simply trusted God for a good outcome, but Sue Hiatt, who, for all her virtues, is something of a Cassandra, was imagining the worst possible scenarios.

"What shall we do if there are bomb threats?" she wanted to know. There was nothing I could offer to deal with those fears except my long experience of doing risky things at the Advocate and coming through in one piece by the grace of God. Some things we could plan for and did. David Gracie was put in charge of security and soon found he had an abundance of women volunteers—activists in the women's movement, some of whom had been trained in crowd control and karate. They would serve as ushers on the day. Buckets of water would be placed around the church in case of stink bombs. We even figured out an easy escape route to the church basement in case of a major disruption, so that the ordinations could go forward.

The father of one of the women to be ordained envisioned a crowd of agitated white clergy acting out at a much-respected black community church. He thought that was a recipe for trouble, so he alerted the Philadelphia police to the service. They would show up in busloads on the 29th, but agreed to stay out of sight several blocks away except for the plainclothes civil disobedience squad members, some of whom knew their way around the Advocate well enough.

At one point a member of the planning group fearful of disruptions suggested that the ordination of the women take place before the 11 A.M. announced time for the service (now being reported by news media around the world), and that at 11 A.M. there be a concelebration of the Holy Communion by the women priests. When Bishop DeWitt mentioned this possibility to me, I told him to count me out if there was any such change in our plans. The bishop said to me: "Paul, stay with us. The church at this moment is very small."

The pressure on the three bishops was intense. Bishop Ogilby had sent a mailing to all diocesan clergy informing them of the planned ordination and his opposition to it. Presiding Bishop John Allin had telegraphed his admonitions to the women deacons. Other bishops added threats and warnings. A court injunction had been sought, but John Ballard, the attorney representing the women, explained to us that the judge had declined to hear arguments because he felt that the church should handle this issue in its usual manner—"at the stake." The mass media were picking up on the events with great enthusiasm, enjoying the sight of church members at odds with one another, and (one hoped) recognizing the significance of the issue within the church and beyond.

Came the morning of July 29, "the great gittin' up morning" as we have come to call it, and the church was filled to overflowing. It is estimated that two hundred representatives of the media from around the world were present. Protesters had arrived in some numbers (mostly white, male clergy in black clerical attire), but the great majority were there because they believed that the fullness of time had come. They wanted to be present at a historic event in the life of their church and in the movement for the equality of women. I welcomed the great throng.

"Good Christian people: In response to and in obedience to God the Holy Spirit, we the Church—baptized, confirmed, ordained, and consecrated members of Christ's Body—have come together from all over this land and beyond, to ordain to the sacred order of the priesthood persons commended by you, admitted to the order of deacons, and found qualified to be ordained priests by the bishops who will ordain them.

"Our actions today are untimely, but the dilemma is, what is one to do when the democratic process, the political dynamics, and the legal guidelines are out of step with the imperative which says: Now is the time!

"What is a mother to do when the doctor says, 'Your baby will be born on August 10th,' when on July 29th she has reached the last stages of labor and the water sack has ruptured?"

I concluded by saying: "May we see in this day which is upon us a day which the Lord has made. May we rejoice and be glad in it. May we accept the rightness of this action as a call above its timing. May we accept the justice in this action as a call outweighing technicalities. May we accept the spirit as life, knowing that the letter killeth. May we praise the Lord for those this day who act in obedience to God, as we love and respect those this day whom we cannot obey."

When my remarks were followed by the opening hymn, which happened to be "Come, Labor On," the 2,000 people gathered for the service erupted in laughter.

Barbara Harris had flown back to Philadelphia from Sun Oil business in California to be the crucifer who led the procession.

She said it felt like Pentecost as she carried the cross toward the chancel during the singing of that hymn and the laughter. Because of the concern for security and for the safety of all, it had been decided not to process outdoors and to take the shortest route inside to the chancel and choir. Barbara wished it could be otherwise, as recorded in her description of her feelings and the sight of the ordinands on that day.

"As crucifer, I was tempted to throw caution to the wind, and stride forth like Joshua and lead that courageous band 'seven times around the walls.' But remembering that the church, like any other place, has its share of crazies, my better judgment prevailed and I accepted the discipline. But, my God, it would have been like walking about in Zion.

"Faces from that day remain indelibly etched upon my memory. Tears streaming down the cheeks of Jeannette Piccard's son . . . pride shining in the eyes of Bishop Edward Welles, father of ordinand Katrina Swanson . . . the madonna-like quality of Alison Cheek's countenance . . . the rugged-jaw 'cool' of my rector, Paul Washington, and the ever watchful, ever alert visage of our Cassandra, Sue Hiatt, expecting the worst. Another hymn came to mind, 'I sing a song of the saints of God, patient and brave and true . . . and there's not any reason, no not the least, why I shouldn't be one, too.' Perhaps the stirrings in my heart that day marked the unrecognized beginning of my own response to call and my journey to ordination."[1]

Barbara led on, but the procession was slowed by people embracing the participants. There was applause and cheering when the bishops emerged. Bishop Welles, who was the tallest and who wore an old-fashioned red mitre, drew the loudest applause. Said Ann Robb Smith to Sue Hiatt when the bishops emerged: "They're going to do it, Sue. They're really going to do it. The Holy Spirit has grabbed them by whatever hair they have left and they're actually going to do it."

The level of joy and excitement remained high throughout the three-hour service, nor was it dampened by expressions of opposition. Those who had come to protest made their statements at the time allowed in a service of ordination for any objections to be made. The Rev. George Rutler, who later left the Episcopal Church to become a Roman Catholic priest, took the microphone to say that he could no longer recognize the bishops in charge as bishops of the church; they were "raising the sight and sound and smell of perversion." Fr. Rutler went on to say he could smell sulfur in the air. His statements evoked jeers and boos from the congregation. I stepped forward after he had spoken to remind the congregation that the prayer book provides for objections to be raised and that they should be received with respect. After he had concluded his intemperate statements, George Rutler led those who were joining him in protest out of the church in a very orderly fashion, accompanied by Gracie and the volunteer ushers.

Charles Willie, the preacher for the service, was cheered during his sermon when he spoke of justice delayed being justice denied and then connected what was happening that day with the historic achievements of the civil rights movement. "As blacks refused to participate in their own oppression by going to the back of the bus in 1955 in Montgomery, women are refusing to cooperate in their own oppression by remaining on the periphery of full participation in the church in 1974 in Philadelphia." When seventy-nine-year-old Jeannette Piccard was ordained first of the eleven, one hundred clergy pressed as close as they could around the Rt. Rev. Daniel Corrigan, her ordaining bishop, reaching out their hands, too, to place upon her head. Barbara Harris, standing in the midst to hold the only portable microphone in the church, was convinced that at that moment she heard, as on the Day of Pentecost, "the rush of a mighty wind."

And so Jeannette Piccard, Betty Schiess, Ala Bozarth-Campbell, Merrill Bittner, Carter Heyward, Emily Hewitt, Marie Moorefield, Katrina Swanson, Suzanne Hiatt, Alison Cheek, and Nancy Wittig were ordained priests in the church of God, the first women so ordained in the Episcopal Church.

The day after that Pentecost, that "great gittin' up morning," brought a quite different mood for me. We had experienced heavenly light breaking into the darkness of history; but now that it was over, a darkness descended upon me as I faced up to the full dimensions of what had been done in my church.

I thought of the letter that had been sent to the clergy and congregations of the diocese by Bishop Ogilby: "I have not given consent or approval." Recent headlines in the *Philadelphia Inquirer* flashed before me: "Bishops are warned on women priests," "Don't ordain 11 women, Episcopal leader [the presiding bishop] urges," "Three bishops defy pressure, will ordain 11 women."

After the event I had time to stop and realize what I had gotten myself into. In obeying God in heaven, I had disobeyed the principal powers in the church. Furthermore, I was the most vulnerable of all the main participants. The three bishops were retired, pensioned, and socially secure. *If* the church ruled that the ordinations were invalid, the eleven women could perhaps be ordained at a later date. But I was a bishop's appointee in an aided congregation, and I had disobeyed the bishop whom I was now relying on not to unfrock me, and not to withhold continued support from the church where the congregation had approved the action. On top of this, what we had done met with the disapproval of the presiding bishop, the leader of the Episcopal Church, U.S.A.

I had been in threatening and frightening situations in the past, but this one threatened my life itself. I was born for a ministry such as this. The Advocate was where I found the suffering and risen Lord. This was life to me. Would I be kicked out of the church? Today, so many years later, one might say, "Your fears were exaggerated. You should have known that such would not have happened." But at that time I knew only one thing: A black priest in an aided parish had disobeyed his bishop, the presiding bishop, and the General Convention in an action that was broadcast to the world. I was in trouble.

Beyond that, in August I was to go to Uganda for a Partners in Mission consultation. Would the presiding bishop call and tell me that the Province of the Church in America could not be represented by a person who had done violence to the church he was supposed to represent? This was truly the lowest and perhaps the loneliest moment of my life.

When Bishop Ogilby's secretary phoned one day to say that the bishop wanted me to call him at his home, and that he was at that moment leaving the office, I figured that in forty-five minutes I would know my fate. I called when I thought he might be entering his house. His wife Ruth said, "I'm sorry, Paul, Lyman has just sat down to eat. Call back in about a half hour." That would be thirty more minutes to judgment day. I called exactly 180 seconds later.

"Hello, Bishop, this is Paul."

"Oh, yes, Paul, I have something that I have to tell you."

"Is that right?"

"Well, you know you violated the Constitution of the Church."

"No, I didn't know that. I read the Constitution and Canons and others have also. We have not violated them."

"Yes, you violated Article VIII of the Constitution, the declaration of conformity to the doctrine, discipline, and worship of the Episcopal Church. I'm going to have to admonish you."

"All right, Bishop. I have no choice but to accept your admonition. Thank you."

Admonishment! Only a verbal and then a written admonition stating that I had done something wrong. This was the least possible disciplinary action the bishop could have chosen. I felt that I had been redeemed once again by the one who said to us, "Take my yoke upon you and learn of me, for I am gentle and lowly of heart, and you will find rest for your souls. For my yoke is easy and my burden is light" (Matthew 11:29). But I could not have known how light that burden would be until I had accepted his yoke. Along with the yoke of Christ, like the cross, we are to expect suffering, but how beautiful and fulfilling it is to endure a suffering that is life-giving and redemptive.

After returning from Uganda (I also revisited Liberia's Cuttington College, where I had worked for six and a half years), I called Jackie Wallace, the bishop's secretary, and asked her to give me an appointment to see him. "Not fifteen minutes or half an hour. I want an hour." I walked into his office at two o'clock on September 17. He had absolutely no idea of why I wanted to see him. Was it to ask him why he was not one of the ordaining bishops? As I knew that he had always stood for the ordination of women, would I ask why had he publicly warned the clergy of the diocese not to participate? As I grasped his hand in greeting, I said to him, "Lyman, I am here out of my concern for you. You have gotten it from both sides. Some condemn you because you were not a participant and others because you permitted it to take place in your diocese. You must have been going through a living hell." (He had. He had lost considerable weight.) We talked together for an hour. I assured him that I understood the position he had taken and he assured me that he understood my position.

When this event of love, respect, and understanding ended, we stood, held each other's hands, prayed, and embraced each other. I left realizing that bishops are chief pastors in the church of God in an ecclesiastical institution fraught with all the political dimensions of this world. But I also left him realizing that bishops respect and thank God for the prophets. He was glad and relieved that women were finally ordained—and in his diocese; but he was deeply pained that he was not one of the ordaining bishops.

Bishop Ogilby would display his own courage in many ways during his tenure as diocesan bishop. I was happy to be with him on March 1 of the year following the first ordination of women, and only a little more than one year after his own installation as our diocesan bishop, when he ordained as a deacon in the church a man serving a sentence for murder in Graterford state prison. He had not participated in the historic event of ordaining the first women as priests, but he made history when he ordained Vaughn Booker a deacon in the church of God in that prison chapel.

In the sermon, I said, "We know God forgives. Here the church forgives." And I went on to express the hope that in our day the church in so many ways was "breaking out of its own prison."

15. MOVE

Where does the tragic story of MOVE belong? How can I describe this "family" of revolutionaries? They were recognizable on the streets of Philadelphia in the 1970s by their dreadlocks (the Rastafarian hairstyle), their profane outbursts against "the system," and their disruption of public events, including Board of Education meetings and meetings of peace groups and other organizations. They demonstrated at the Philadelphia Zoo, protesting the caging of animals there. In the neighborhood in West Philadelphia where they first took up residence, they were known by their children, who wore little clothing, by the fifty or sixty dogs they kept, by the smell that came from their backyard because garbage was left in the open. The logic behind this behavior had to do with a notion of returning to ways that were in harmony with nature. Their revolutionary logic led to repeated, intensifying encounters with authority, especially the authority of police, courts, and prisons. The criminal justice system had so delegitimized itself over the years by tolerating abuse of black and poor citizens that MOVE could gain a measure of sympathy and support from some who did not subscribe to their general philosophy of life at all.

Others have attempted to tell their story in detail. I will simply relate my interactions with them, which began in 1975, when I reached out to them to try to understand who they were, and led eventually to my serving in 1985 on a city commission investigat-

ing the causes of the destruction by the police and fire depart-
ments of a MOVE residence, and the resulting deaths of eleven
members of the MOVE family. This event sent shock waves
around the world because it involved the dropping of a bomb on a
home in a residential neighborhood. The conflagration that followed destroyed not only the MOVE house and its occupants,
including five children, but also burned down sixty-one homes of
250 neighbors.

Of the different strands that came together to form the MOVE
family in the late 1960s and early 1970s, one was certainly the
frustration of young black men and women who had identified
with earlier movements for justice that they thought of as revolutionary. I tried to understand MOVE members in the context of
those other movements I had known so well. Louise James's description of her attraction to MOVE in testimony presented to the
commission investigating the 1985 events shows this side of the
group's appeal. (Louise was the sister of John Africa, founder of
MOVE. Her brother and her son were destroyed in the May 13,
1985, fire.)

"Before I came to the MOVE organization, I am the type of
person who has always looked for something that would help me
to find justice. I have never liked the injustice, the prejudice, the
oppression of this system. However, I have never thought of myself as a leader, but I felt that I could be a good follower. And
because I felt that way, I was constantly seeking out people to
follow. Prior to MOVE, for example, I followed and supported
the Black Panther Party. I followed Angela Davis; I was mes-
merized by that woman. I thought she had it all together. I
thought she was just brave, courageous, and a black woman with
a purpose. I felt she had been misused and abused. I followed . . .
George Jackson. As I continued to see nothing working in this
political system for me, I continued to search. When I came across
the teachings of John Africa, my search ended."[1]

Another MOVE member said: "The Black Panthers never
brought forth the true communist society they preached about. I
read the book [the writings of John Africa] and saw that you must

start with a personal revolution." Bennie Swans of Philadelphia's Crisis Intervention Network has commented, as an objective observer: "MOVE had grown out of the revolutionary period of blacks in this country. It talked about a different value system. It was concerned about the caging of animals and the desire to free themselves both in mind and spirit from the system. Group living became a vehicle."[2]

When I first heard about MOVE I felt I could identify with the group's motivation, no matter how bizarre their behavior might seem. It was Christine who first called MOVE to my attention. She had been watching the public television broadcasts of Philadelphia Board of Education meetings, where she saw young people in dreadlocks, who all used the surname Africa, charging the school board with miseducating the children of Philadelphia.

The school board meetings carried on public television were open to public input in an exemplary way. This was especially important during a period when other city government bodies lacked a similar openness. Because the meetings of the school board were so open and democratic, they could easily be used as a forum by a group like MOVE, which thereby made its presence known to the many TV viewers. The MOVE members had impressed Christine because of the merit of some of their criticisms.

I found that they had a telephone, rang them up, and arranged for a meeting at my office. I wanted to begin a dialogue, but when eleven MOVE members arrived at the appointed time I found that they gave me little opportunity to ask questions. They had come to acquaint me with the teachings of John Africa, which they presented, as I remember it, under the following headings:

1. "Education" is not education, but training to serve "the system" (It was this conviction that led them to begin by attacking the Board of Education.)
2. "Justice" is not justice, since many are prejudged and never receive fair treatment.
3. Canned and processed foods are carcinogenic. Therefore, we eat raw, unprocessed foods.

4. We intend to keep our children from being contaminated by the system.

5. We use profanity on purpose to show how people can be revolted by profane language but not by a profane society that does such violence to so many.

6. Animals should be treated as humans.

I found myself in complete disagreement only with the last point. There was enough truth in the other assertions the group was making that I decided I wanted to stay in touch with them. I was prepared to make myself available to them as I had to other "outsiders" who were trying to bring about change. MOVE members did stay in close touch with me and asked for my help in different ways.

They asked for my accompaniment to the House of Correction to visit imprisoned members. This I was quite willing to do, so I often went with Robert Africa to the jail. I also went to court when requested so the group could show me their style of defending themselves, a style that showed their contempt for the "justice" system. When they asked me to write a letter to school board president Arthur Thomas protesting their treatment at school board meetings, I did that, too. I would say that I was one of the closest clergy sympathizers, defenders, and supporters of the group at that time.

I soon learned how very demanding MOVE members were of anyone who offered them support. If one of their members was in hospital after having been beaten (according to their account) by the police, I or anyone else who had ever spoken out against police brutality would be expected to drop everything and accompany other MOVE members to the hospital to see that proper treatment was being offered. On one occasion when I received a phone call requesting my presence and said that I was sorry but this time I could not come, I heard another voice on the line from the MOVE residence saying, "Forget this son of a bitch; he's just like all the rest of them."

I could absorb that kind of insult and still maintain the relationship, but that attitude did cause me to back off a bit and more carefully evaluate the reasons for my involvement on their behalf. I decided that whenever I felt the city or the police were violating the rights of MOVE members, I would be in their corner; yet I realized that many of those situations were provoked by MOVE.

My most difficult intervention was called for on May 20, 1977, when I received a phone call from a neighbor of the MOVE house in Powelton Village, West Philadelphia, telling me that hundreds of people were on the street as a result of an altercation between a MOVE member and the police. Residents of the MOVE house had heard that Chuck Africa had been arrested and brutally beaten by the police. Enraged, they were parading up and down on their porch with guns in their hands.

I immediately went to West Philadelphia and found that the police had solidly blocked access to the MOVE house. I walked through their line. No one attempted to stop me, so I went right in to talk to Delbert Africa to attempt to negotiate a settlement. I said to them, "They want your guns." They responded, "We'll surrender our guns if they bring Chuckie and show us that he's not bloody and broken."

Going outside, I spoke with Police Commissioner Joseph O'Neill, who agreed to bring Chuckie for everybody to see that he had not been brutalized by the police. I went back to Delbert and said, "We have a deal. They will bring Chuckie to show that he hasn't been worked over." To which Delbert responded, "We don't just want to see him. We want him released." Not only did I feel chagrined, I felt like a fool, betrayed. The commissioner chuckled and said to me: "You see, Reverend, you don't know these people." Let it be noted that for a police commissioner to be willing to bring a prisoner from jail for the MOVE members and the public to inspect was quite unheard of and represented a real readiness on his part to compromise.

In spite of this double dealing, I was able to play something of a peacekeeping role that night, for Clarence Farmer of the Human Relations Commission and I were able to talk MOVE and the police into stepping back a bit from the dangerous confrontation.

Two hundred uniformed police were withdrawn and replaced by one hundred plainclothes officers who began round-the-clock surveillance. My frustrated attempt to negotiate a more meaningful peace than that led me to conclude that for MOVE the system was not an entity with which they could negotiate. They would never make peace with what they saw as oppression.

This rigidity revealed a more basic flaw, which I tried to point out to MOVE members in ongoing conversations with them. I said that in many ways John Africa could be a prophetic voice in society but unfortunately he would not be heard in that way, because true prophets must display deep love and compassion for the people. True prophets may scold, chide, warn, and pronounce judgment on the people, but they do it out of love, concern, and compassion. I said that in no way could people feel that MOVE had that kind of compassion. Their message came through more as contempt for anyone who would not accept the teachings of John Africa.

The crisis continued in Powelton for months as the city pressed MOVE members to leave their house, turn over their weapons, and submit for prosecution those members who had displayed guns on May 20, 1977. A series of would-be mediators attempted but failed to find any middle ground. After a judge ordered MOVE's eviction, word got around that the city planned to blockade the house and starve the MOVE family (men, women, and children) into submission. People who were shocked by the idea of this tactic came to the house and passed food, clothing, and other survival items over the tall wooden barricade MOVE members had erected. I personally delivered six cases of canned food.

During the long siege that then set in, beginning March 16, 1978, when hundreds of police sealed off a four-block area, I was permitted through police lines to talk to MOVE members whenever I chose to do so. Two other mediators, Msgr. Charles Devlin of the Cardinal's Commission on Human Relations and the Rev. Rufus Cornelson of the Metropolitan Christian Council of Philadelphia, talked at length with Delbert Africa and carried messages to the office of the city manager, but to no avail.

A Citywide Community Coalition for Human Rights came into being, made up of black religious, political, and community leaders who wanted to pressure both sides to find a solution that would avoid bloodshed. I worked with the coalition, which offered itself as guarantor of any agreement MOVE might reach with the city, recognizing MOVE's complete distrust of the city administration.

Walter Palmer, formerly of the Black People's Unity Movement, helped the coalition to organize a demonstration of thousands of people, who temporarily blockaded City Hall to register their protest of the police blockade of the MOVE house. Palmer and Attorney Oscar Gaskins were working with MOVE members to hammer out some kind of agreement, but they experienced the same difficulty that I had the year previous. Walt Palmer said: "Many times I had to scream and holler at them because they said yes to one thing, and would later say that is not what they said." Walt kept on hollering until an agreement was reached and signed by city officials and MOVE on May 5, only to fall apart in the weeks that followed.

On August 8 in the early morning, the long siege ended when Mayor Rizzo ordered the police to attack the house. It was a massive assault, which began when an armored bulldozer knocked down the heavy fence and a cherry picker knocked out the windows of the house. Tear gas grenades and water from fire hoses were alternately used to force the surrender of the MOVE members, who had taken shelter in the basement. But the surrender did not come until after an exchange of gunfire in which police officer James Ramp was killed and Officer William Krause seriously wounded.

When Delbert Africa emerged from the flooded basement he was seized and viciously beaten by uniformed police, an act of brutality and revenge that was photographed by a *Daily News* photographer and given wide exposure. Immediately after the evacuation of the MOVE members, the Philadelphia city attorney ordered the complete destruction of the house by bulldozers.

A 4 P.M. press conference called that same day by Mayor Frank

Rizzo set the emotional stage for the next round of the ongoing conflict between the city and MOVE. "Put them in the electric chair and I'll throw the switch myself," he said of those he believed to be responsible for the death of Officer Ramp. After a difficult trial lasting twenty-one months, nine MOVE members were convicted of third degree murder and conspiracy and sentenced to prison for terms of thirty to one hundred years. A tenth was later sentenced to ten to twenty years. Three police charged with beating Delbert Africa were found innocent in a directed verdict by a judge who said he was taking it upon himself to stop Philadelphia from "bleeding to death" because of the MOVE tragedy.

MOVE dropped from public view for a time, but their new cause became the release from prison of the members of their family they believed had been unjustly convicted. It had never been proved who fired the bullet that killed Officer Ramp, nor had intent been established. MOVE members' outbursts in court as they tried to conduct their own defense and the public emotion that had been aroused because of Officer Ramp's death produced an emotional field in which it was difficult to apply reason and rule of law. "MOVE 1, Police 0" was a graffito reportedly seen soon after the shootout. Both sides still had a score to settle, it seemed.

Over the next few years I was not in direct contact with MOVE members. Like other Philadelphia citizens, I became aware that there was a new MOVE house in the city when in 1981 members of the dispersed family began to move into the rowhouse owned by Louise James on Osage Avenue in Southwest Philadelphia, in a middle-class black neighborhood. The neighbors there soon began to complain of the garbage, dogs, cats, and rats. A fight took place between a neighbor and a MOVE member. But the city administration did nothing. The year 1983 was an election year and all eyes were on W. Wilson Goode, who ran a successful campaign for mayor and raised hopes among many, especially in the black community, that a period of civic unity would begin.

MOVE nursed its own anger and was not at all impressed

when the city elected its first black mayor. By Christmas Day, 1983, MOVE was ready to begin its campaign for the release of the imprisoned brothers and sisters. The group intended to make life so difficult for the neighbors that they would complain to City Hall, thereby gaining some bargaining leverage for MOVE. A loudspeaker was set up on the MOVE house and a voice was heard on Christmas morning. "Motherfucker Santa Claus," it said. The neighbors were treated to an eight-hour barrage of profanity and protest on that Christmas Day.

The events leading up to the second siege and shootout have been well recorded elsewhere, and I was not directly involved in any of them, apart from a brief conversation with Mayor Goode at a memorial service for a mutual friend in early May, 1985. He asked me if I had had any dealings recently with MOVE members. I told him no. The mayor said that he was going to have to do something about the house on Osage Avenue but wanted to be sure we did not have another unfortunate occurrence like that in 1978 in Powelton Village.

By that time, however, the house had been heavily fortified, with a bunker on the roof, and it was believed MOVE had an assortment of weapons. As the second armed confrontation drew nearer, MOVE began to boast of having wired the whole block with explosives (this was a bluff) and threatened to kill the mayor and any police who tried to enter their house.

The mayor had decided that negotiations would not work. MOVE was demanding the release of convicted criminals. How could he satisfy such a demand? Attorney Oscar Gaskins thought something could be done. At least one MOVE member had already served a minimum sentence of seven years, and the convictions of 1981 were questionable in themselves. But the prevailing thought in the community, in which I shared, was that the demand was unattainable. MOVE was on a suicide trip and had chosen a collision course.

The mayor defined the problem as a matter for the district attorney, who prepared warrants for the arrest of certain residents of the MOVE house on misdemeanor charges, and for the police, who prepared an armory of assault weapons. That there were children in the house did not seem to affect the military-style planning that was underway.

May 13, 1985, is a day that will never be erased from the memory of Philadelphians. After creating a free-fire zone by evacuating all the neighbors for blocks around, the massive police assault fired 10,000 rounds of ammunition in a three-hour period. Machine guns and automatic weapons were employed. Finally, in an incredibly foolish and desperate move to dislodge the bunker on top of the house, a police helicopter flew over the house and dropped a bomb on the roof. The house burned down and sixty-one other houses near it. "Let the bunker burn," said the police commissioner to the fire commissioner when he first wanted to take action to put out the fire. Six adults and five children burned to death within the house; only one woman, Ramona Africa, and one child, Michael Ward (then called Birdie Africa), escaped with their lives.

The whole city watched it happen in daylong television coverage from the scene. I was at home when the bomb was dropped, but immediately upon seeing it dropped and the instant conflagration of everything around it on the roof, I got into my car and drove to the scene. I walked to the spot where Harvey Clark of CBS, channel 10, was standing, describing the events for the television audience, blow by blow, hour by hour, as he had from early morning to this incredible moment. He spotted me in the crowd and immediately beckoned me to join him in the broadcast.

I declined. This situation was entirely too complex and controversial to accommodate any statement that could be helpful. I knew the complexity well. I knew that the MOVE members had wanted to precipitate a crisis that would force what they believed would be the just release of the members of the MOVE family sentenced to thirty to one hundred years in jail, even though there had been no direct proof that any one of them was responsible for the death of Officer Ramp. I also understood the neighbors who had demanded that something be done to give them peace from the deliberate disturbances of the peace by the residents of 6221 Osage Avenue. While understanding both sides, I saw no possible solution to the problem, nor did I see any sign of compromise coming from MOVE, the city, or the state. Finally, I had talked with the mayor and sensed the tremendous pressure he was under to resolve the problem. He felt it was imperative to do something, hoping and praying that it would not end in disaster. But that was what was happening.

Harvey Clark again asked me to join him. When he insisted, I very reluctantly agreed. The first question he asked me was whether I felt it might have been possible to reach a negotiated settlement of the issues. I responded, No. I saw no possibility of a negotiated settlement.

During the interview there were additional questions and responses, but among my responses I made one statement that should have provoked thousands to ask me, "What did you mean by that?" Over the years no one has ever confronted me with a question about it. What I said was: "It was a successful operation, but the patient died." I was trying to compare what was happening to radical surgery, whereby a surgeon in removing an object from the body destroys the body in the process. This was not the moment for such a statement.

A few moments later I heard gunfire in such rapid succession that it had to have been an automatic weapon. The police rushed into the crowd and bellowed: "Get back, get back; they're coming out!" No one at that moment knew that eleven human beings had been destroyed, either by gunfire, fire, dynamite, or the bomb. No one knew that the only two who would escape would be Ramona and little Birdie. Nor at that time could any realize the irreparable damage that would be suffered by us all, by all of humanity, in the events of that day. The operation was indeed a success: the occupants of 6221 Osage were evicted. But on that day *we died*.

A member of MOVE said to me in the aftermath that John Africa knew that people were capable of doing exactly what they had done. "This is what he was trying to tell us about the system, but we just don't want to believe it." I believe it. Philadelphia poet Lamont Steptoe would later capture the feeling of many in the city with these words from his poem "The Fire Burns."

> gone-gone-gone-gone
> and now this city lies
> under heaven its aura
> stained with blood
> its people
> shocked to silence
> or secrecy of rejoicing
> none
> can look
> each other in the eye
> all
> are guilty of something
> the mark of Cain
> is everywhere[3]

I felt the mark of Cain; and if that mark was on us all, it was certainly on the mayor of the city, not only as a symbolic representative of the rest of the citizens but as the one who, according to the testimony of Managing Director Leo Brooks, had himself authorized the bombing. The situation was intolerable for many of us who had put our hopes in Wilson Goode and had seen his election as the beginning of black political power that would be exercised for the benefit of all. Many of the leading black clergy of Philadelphia, Goode's strongest supporters in the race for mayor, felt the need to rally to his support. To this end they organized an outdoor prayer vigil, held in the neighborhood near the ruins of the homes. I did not take part; I was not called to participate.

Just two days after the fire, Mayor Goode announced that he was creating the Philadelphia Special Investigation Commission (it would become known as the MOVE Commission) to look into the events of May 13. His move was greeted with widespread skepticism. Should the mayor, whose own actions needed to be judged, be the one to appoint an investigating commission? Was this simply an attempt to dodge responsibility? The skepticism abated somewhat when the names of the commissioners were announced. They were persons of integrity, like the commission chairman, William H. Brown III, former chairman of the U.S. Equal Opportunity Commission; Henry Ruth, an attorney who had been one of the chief Watergate prosecutors; and Charles Bowser, former deputy mayor of Philadelphia. Three members of the clergy were also appointed, and I was one of them.

Paid investigators went to work almost immediately, but the public hearings of the commission did not begin until October, 1985. They ran for five weeks, four days a week, six hours a day, and were broadcast live over public television. In all, we had at least twenty-three meetings. I found the staff to be top-notch. No question was too sensitive to pursue, no personality was above criticism, and nothing would be left unsaid that needed to be said. Fears of a whitewash proved to be unfounded.

We heard testimony from the mayor and his appointees, from firefighters and police who had been on the scene, from residents of Osage Avenue, former MOVE members, and others. The drama of the hearings centered at one point on the testimony of police officer James Berghaier, who had rescued the child, Birdie Africa, from the back alley at risk to himself. The testimony of the "Big Four," Police Commissioner Gregore Sambor, Fire Commissioner William Richmond, Managing Director Leo Brooks, and the mayor, captured the attention of the city for days. Each day at least 1 million television viewers were observing the hearings.

During the examination of the Big Four, I asked one question of each of them: "Were the members of MOVE terrorists?" Each had difficulty in answering the question. They readily agreed with the findings of the Investigation Commission, that "MOVE had evolved into an authoritarian, violence-threatening cult"; but it was clear that in the minds of these four men the group had crossed the line between being a "violence-threatening cult" and had actually become terrorists.

The commission members needed the month of January and

most of February, 1986, to work through the transcripts and make our findings. We would conclude that the mayor had been grossly negligent for not calling off the operation on May 12 when he knew there were children in the house; that the managing director and police commissioner were grossly negligent for risking the children's lives by failing to take steps to detain them; that the plan to bomb the house was reckless; that the decision by the police commissioner and fire commissioner to use the fire as a tactical weapon was unconscionable. We further concluded that the mayor had abdicated his responsibilities as a leader by turning so many decisions over to his police commissioner.

While we agreed without much difficulty in assigning this level of blame to the Big Four, we were not able to agree easily on the question of whether to call for their resignations. The police commissioner had already resigned—under pressure from the mayor, he said. The internal debate in the commission centered on whether the mayor or the fire Commissioner, or both of them, should be asked to step down. Some of us presented a position that the others were able to accept: The commission should put forth its criticism of the administration, but leave final judgment in the hands of the voters. "Our findings are harsh," we said. "They speak loudly for themselves. In the light of these findings the electorate can reach its own conclusions." This became our stance, but we also recommended that the Philadelphia district attorney convene a grand jury to determine whether criminal indictments should be returned.

As it turned out, neither the grand jury nor the electorate would take any punitive action. District Attorney Ron Castille reported in May, 1988, that the grand jury had found that while the decisions to drop the bomb were "morally reprehensible," they were not criminal. A federal grand jury concluded its investigation in September, 1988, and likewise recommended no indictments. In November, 1987, the voters reelected Mayor W. Wilson Goode, although by a very slim margin. His opponent was none other than former police commissioner and mayor Frank Rizzo, who was running this time as a Republican. In the campaign, Rizzo proudly compared his handling of the 1978 MOVE raid with Goode's performance in 1985. "Bomber Goode," he called him.

After Goode's reelection and the grand jury findings, many if not most Philadelphians decided to forget. One group in the city decided otherwise. The Lessons of the Move Tragedy Committee came into being under the leadership of William Meek, a senior statesman in the Philadelphia black community and veteran of many community struggles. Bill Meek worked with the support of the Community Relations Division of the American Friends Service Committee to organize memorial services and panel discussions, held each year around the anniversary of the MOVE fire. I have been actively involved with the Lessons of the Move Tragedy Committee in pressuring the city administration to reorganize its response to neighborhood crises, so that what happened on May 13, 1985, can never happen again.

Among the committee's other early concerns was the denial of parole to Ramona Africa, the woman who escaped with her life along with Birdie. Incredibly, she, a survivor of the inferno, was imprisoned as a result of the events of May 13. When Ramona was found guilty of riot and conspiracy charges, I wrote a letter to the court requesting that she be sentenced only to "time served." I said that she had "suffered enough," and that I did not see that any purpose could be served by extending her incarceration. Nevertheless, she received a seven-year maximum sentence. Ramona could have been released much earlier if she had promised not to associate with any other members of the MOVE family. This condition of parole she adamantly and unconditionally rejected. She would do her seven years' time and be free to associate with whom she chose.

I was overjoyed to be in the white stretch limousine rented by community activist Novella Williams to pick up Ramona Africa upon her release from Muncey State Prison at 3:30 A.M., May 13, 1992. We were in a caravan of ten cars that went up to greet her and bring her home. We have also actively sought, but failed to achieve, a review of the sentences of the MOVE members imprisoned because of the events of 1978. The MOVE story is not over. As Lamont Steptoe says, The fire still burns. But in whose human fabric is that fire still burning?

Certainly Ramona and Birdie can never forget that flaming inferno from which they escaped. Not only their bodies will forever bear the scars of that fire; so will their minds and their psyches. To this day, they remember John Africa, Frank, Raymond, Rhonda, Theresa, and Conrad. They remember the children, Tomaso, Tree, Phil, Melissa, and Netta. The fire burns for Louise James, who watched 6221 being incinerated, her younger brother and only son inside. It burns for the mothers, fathers, sisters, and brothers of the others whose lives were destroyed.

It burns for nine members of MOVE sentenced to thirty to one hundred years in prison for killing Officer Ramp, while the sentencing judge stated publicly that he didn't know who had killed Ramp. It burns for many who saw the system that John Africa condemned do exactly what John said it would do. "The system," whatever its character, will destroy those who challenge its sovereignty. The fire burns because many of us place law and order above justice, and we condone and support that system in oppressing those who are victims of injustice and rebel against it. The fire still burns.

But for police stakeout officer Jimmy Berghaier, too, the fire still burns. In his memory not only does he see the fire, but a woman and a child trying to escape. The child stumbles and falls. He won't make it! Berghaier runs into the alley, grabs the child, and brings him to safety. The trauma of that experience, humane and heroic, precipitated discord with fellow officers, psychiatric therapy, and the loss of job and family, in this fickle world where things are just not what they ought to be.

And the fire still burns in the soul of W. Wilson Goode, a man whom I have known for more than thirty years, seeing him first at work at a desk at the Philadelphia Council for Community Advancement, of which I was a board member. I voted for him as executive director, then president, and worked with him closely when I became chairman of the board. He worked as though possessed, never stopping. As chairman of the Deacons' Board at his

Baptist church, he invited me to be a guest preacher. Soon he was called by Governor Milton Shapp to serve on the state utility commission; then it was back to Philadelphia to be city managing director under Mayor Green. Finally, he became mayor himself.

He was a man for all seasons, and a role model for all, trudging from the mud of a North Carolina farm to the office of mayor of the nation's fourth largest city. Yet I found myself, as a member of the MOVE Commission, concurring with its findings and conclusions, which faulted the mayor for "gross negligence," "failure to perform responsibly," "not actively participating in the preparation, review and oversight of the plan" for May 13—a plan of action that was "unconscionable." And I heard Wilson Goode taunted as "the mad bomber." May 13 had to have been for him a descent into hell.

My judgment of W. Wilson Goode, however, is determined not by his actions and behavior of one day, May 13, 1985, but by thirty years of experiences. During that period of time, I have known him to be conscientious, considerate, responsible, hardworking, and of good character. To have been elected twice mayor of the City of Philadelphia, he must have been seen by others as I saw him.

Let us all pray that a lifetime of character building is not destroyed by one wretched, tragic day. Yet I know that while I over the years have been seen as a man of character, one single day or a single moment of infamy could eclipse my totality for the rest of my life. The fire still burns; but, for God's sake, why don't they put it out?

I was a participant in a colloquium with Ramona Africa at Temple University on March 10, 1993, on the theme: "Why MOVE?" On that night, someone asked Ramona, "Do you blame Wilson Goode for what happened on May 13?" She responded, "Oh, I don't know. I think there is enough blame to go around." I was both arrested and surprised by her answer; and I am still wondering who is included among those to blame and those who are blameless.

16. Honors and Dishonor

It was late 1970 or early 1971 when I received a letter from the Diocese of Washington, D.C., informing me that I had been nominated for the office of suffragan bishop in that diocese. Instead of being delighted at this honor, I was deeply disturbed. As a bishop of the Episcopal Church, how could I identify with, and agitate with, the activists who were fighting for justice? In 1968 I had hosted the convention sponsored by the advocates of Black Power. In 1970 I had hosted the convention sponsored by the Black Panthers. I had been arrested, photographed, and fingerprinted. I was indeed an Episcopal priest, accorded all the courtesies and respect given to that class, but deep down inside I was still an American Negro, harboring all the pain, the indignities, resentments and, at times, the rage of Dred Scott. I could certainly function in the Episcopal Church, but I could not function as a part of its establishment.

No other establishment in our society can perpetuate racial discrimination as does the church. The Commonwealth of Virginia can elect an African American as governor, but white congregations consistently refuse to elect African Americans to be rectors of their parishes; and bishops, with the power to appoint, to this day will not appoint an African American priest to be vicar of a white diocesan mission—although they will appoint white priests as vicars of black congregations.

When the Rev. James Woodruff, executive director of the Union of Black Clergy and Laity, returned to Philadelphia after a visit to Washington, D.C., he phoned, almost breathlessly, to give me what had to be good news. "Paul. I just got back from Washington, and the brothers say that you are going to make it. They have been telling all the white boys that you are their man." At this point I made up my mind. I would not do it. If I became a member of the House of Bishops, I would be like "a house divided against itself."

The next day I sent a telegram to the person who had written me and said simply: "Please remove my name from the nominees for the office of Suffragan Bishop of the Diocese of Washington." St. Paul once wrote to Timothy: "This is a true saying. If a man desire the office of a bishop, he desires a good work (Timothy 3:1). But I did not desire the office of a bishop.

In 1973, in my own diocese, I was nominated for the office of bishop coadjutor (that is, the bishop to succeed Robert DeWitt). This time I did not withdraw my name. Pennsylvania knew me and I knew Pennsylvania. If by any miracle I was elected, they all knew what they would be getting. But, unlike the prospects in Washington, D.C., I knew that my chance of being elected was that of a snowball in hell. Although Pennsylvania was the diocese of the first African American priest in the Episcopal Church (Absalom Jones, 1818), it would lag twenty-six years behind the Diocese of Massachusetts and seventeen years behind the Diocese of Washington, D.C., in electing an African American bishop (Suffragan Bishop Franklin Turner, 1988).

I was prepared to leave my chances in Pennsylvania at the point of simply not withdrawing my name, but Barbara Harris decided to make something of my candidacy. Her professional instincts took over, and she suddenly became my campaign manager. She drafted a letter that she mailed at her own expense to all of the clergy and lay delegates to the electing convention. In part she wrote: "The church has to make a decision as to whether it is to maintain a chaplaincy to the oppressor or exercise a ministry to the oppressed. If it is the latter, then elect Paul Washington as the next bishop of the Diocese of Pennsylvania."

Not expecting significant support for my candidacy, I was quite surprised that of the four priests of our diocese who had been nominated I received the strongest support in the clergy order. Bishop Lyman Ogilby, former bishop of the Philippines, then serving as assistant to Bishop DeWitt in our diocese, drew stronger support than any of the rest of us. But we saw that someone from outside the diocese, whom none of us wanted to be elected, was getting stronger and stronger on each ballot. One of the candidates called a quick caucus between ballots, and we four priests agreed that we would all withdraw our names before the next ballot.

Charles Long: "I withdraw." Jack Hardwick: "I withdraw." Tom Edwards: "I withdraw." Paul Washington: "I withdraw." On the very next ballot, Lyman Ogilby, whom we had hoped would be the new bishop, was elected. The *Philadelphia Tribune*, the Negro biweekly, carried a headline: "Father Washington withdraws from race. His supporters lead to victory for Lyman Ogilby."

In 1976 I received a letter from Bishop Paul Moore of the Diocese of New York. He wished to talk with me about a position on his staff as archdeacon of Manhattan. (An archdeacon is in charge of an area within a diocese, working directly for the bishop.) I went to New York City and we talked. I had a lot of questions. What were the needs and problems of the Manhattan congregations? What were the clergy like who served there? What aid was the diocese able to give where there was a clear need for financial subsidies? But, most important, what did he expect of the archdeacon and how seriously would the archdeacon's recommendations be taken? What would my salary be, and what was the cost of living in New York? On and on I questioned. Bishop Moore recommended that I speak next with the Manhattan clergy, which I did on another visit. I found that they were unanimously enthusiastic about the possibility of my coming to New York.

When a letter arrived from Bishop Moore offering me the position, I decided I would accept the appointment. I explained my decision to Christine and the children, who were not happy about it but accepted it. It was a case of the male head of the family having the right to make decisions for the family—an old way of thinking that dies hard.

The call came at a time when I had begun to ask how long one was supposed to stay in one position. At that time there was floating around in our profession a kind of unwritten law that clergy should move on after ten years. Then, too, I had friends who were beginning to ask me how long I was going to stay at the Advocate. They asked if I had had no invitations for other positions. Some suggested that I was afraid to leave and accept new challenges.

So obsessed was I with these questions that I invited some of the people closest to me to give me their counsel and advice. I asked Barbara Harris, my close friends Fr. Van Bird and his wife, Eva, and (of course) Christine to have dinner with me to talk this all out. We met in a center-city restaurant and discussed every aspect of my questions; but I was left with a whole smorgasbord to choose from, and I finally realized it was up to me alone to decide. I had really hoped that there might be a consensus among my friends and counselors either that I should remain in North Philadelphia or that I should go to New York. Since they would not tell me what to do, I decided to talk to Jesus. He caused me to realize that I was thinking only of myself and my own ministry. He led to me to think about Christine's ministry.

She had moved from being wife and mother to becoming one of the most effective and productive housing developers in Philadelphia. Could she continue this ministry in New York? I answered that question with an emphatic no. Was my ministry more important than hers simply because I was a man and a priest? Again, no. Had I not just risked my professional life in taking a stand for the right of women to be priests in the church? Was it more important for women to become priests than it was for Christine to be a housing developer? For what reason and by what right could I disrupt and perhaps destroy my wife's ministry?

And, finally, what about the notion that there should be a set period of years for a clergyperson to serve in a given place? I concluded that it was not the quantity of years but the quality of one's work that mattered. Did I not still have a challenging, needful, and perhaps unique ministry in Philadelphia? The church for too long had been concerned only about its dues-paying members and its pew warmers, and not about the "other sheep not of this fold." I was definitely a shepherd to the "other sheep," who accepted me as their shepherd; and I believed I was setting an example, even to other ministers, that as Jesus came to "the world," our ministry had to be directed to the world, especially to the worldly.

I wrote to Bishop Moore. I thanked him for the belief in me that had led him to invite me to head the very vital and needed ministry in New York City. But I told him I would decline his offer, principally because if I accepted I would be destroying the life and ministry of another—my wife.

Little did I expect, however, when declining the invitation of Bishop Moore to become a member of his staff, that within a couple of months I would be appointed by Bishop Ogilby as urban missioner on his staff. Fr. Van Bird, who was then a member of the bishop's staff, had spoken up in a staff meeting during the month when I was in conversation with Bishop Moore. He said that in our diocese there was a priest with a city-wide ministry whom we took for granted, but whom the bishop of New York City was calling to come to his diocese. It was just when I had made up my mind not to go to New York that Bishop Ogilby learned of this. He invited me to his office and said, "I heard you have been thinking about going to New York. We need you here, and I want you to be on my staff even while you continue to serve at the Advocate. I will not write out any job description for you. Just keep on doing what you are doing and attend our weekly staff meetings."

Van Bird, priest and professor of sociology at LaSalle University, has been to me educator, adviser, counselor, critic, and one of my dearest friends. I once wrote a note to him and his wife Eva, saying that since I had no living mother, father, sister, or brother, I was conscripting them to be my sister and brother. Van has paid a price for being my brother. I call him constantly to enlighten me on confusing and controversial social issues.

With the decision about New York behind me and with new responsibilities in the diocese of Pennsylvania, 1976 was almost like my second call to Christ's ministry. But it came only after a struggle. It might have been like Jacob's wrestling with that angel at the ford of Jabbok. He refused to let go of the angel until he had been blessed. I held on to the Advocate until I felt God's blessing upon me and Christine at this place. At least for the present there was still much for us to do here. But it was not until an encounter with members of a search committee from a parish in Rochester, New York, that I was forced to really think through the particular task that I was to perform in building the Kingdom of God.

In the Episcopal Church, vestries form search committees to identify candidates for the rectorship of their parish. The local congregation, with the guidance of the bishop, is responsible for calling their own minister. The members of the Rochester search committee introduced themselves to me, with a touch of pride as well as chagrin, by saying: "We are not from the Hertz congregation in our diocese. We are the Avis congregation. We try harder."

They arrived in Philadelphia on a Saturday. We had dinner together at a first-class restaurant and talked at length. They attended worship service on Sunday morning. Later some members of the committee came to Philadelphia a second time to talk with Christine and me. They informed me that they would strongly recommend to the whole committee that I be called as their next rector.

At that point, I began to raise some very serious and penetrating questions with myself. The main question was, How could I labor and struggle for my own people, still oppressed, "despised and rejected," as the rector of a white parish? It would be like immigrants to America trying to fight for the liberation of brothers and sisters somewhere across the ocean, thousands of miles away. At that point, I saw clearly again where I belonged. I could help best by being in the midst of the struggle, staying with my people. I prepared to write a letter to Rochester to say that I wanted to be removed from consideration as their next rector.

But before I got to my typewriter, I received a call from a member of the Rochester committee. "We feel strongly that you have much to give to our congregation, but if you were here with us, we would stifle you. We would all but destroy your spirit." Once again, it was a matter of *race*, the line that revealed to them not just how destructive it would be to me, but beyond that, that *they would be the destroyers*. They did not realize, however, that they would not have been able to destroy me, nor that I might have been a channel of grace for them.

Up to this point in my ministry, I had made some decisions to which I had given only cursory thought. Van Bird once said to me, "The heart has its reasons, which the mind knows not of." It was time now for my mind to see and understand why I said no sometimes when it would seem that my answer should be yes.

First, I had to think about that American dilemma, race, and how it has affected us all. If I really believed that race is a barrier that cannot be overcome, then I would have to agree with Nietzsche that God is dead and the only power is not that of the omnipotent God, but man's own will to power. But, thanks be to God, I have seen that barrier overcome, and I know that Christ is reconciling the world unto himself. In him we are one. I know children of God who have risen to the fullness of the stature to which we are called; they possess a maturity that has outgrown the race, color, class, nationality, and gender with which they identify. The truth is that we are one, and when we diminish others we diminish ourselves.

Second, I asked whether an "elevation" is always a greater opportunity for service and fulfillment. Elevations in our society are usually measured in cultural values that are far from Christian values. And, tragically, there are many who are elevated beyond their capacity to serve most effectively. The Peter Principle operates in a way that punctures inflated egos. We should not be conformed to the values of this world, which are vain and fickle.

Third, I thought about whether an "advancement" always

meant that one was getting closer to the goal. Advancements can be transplants from a corner in the backyard where we flourished to the front lawn, where we might indeed stand out and be seen, but where we might also be located beyond the perimeter of those whom we are to serve and nurture and who serve and nurture us.

None of this is to say that we are to shun "going up higher," nor that advancement always means unfruitfulness. (Today I do not know how morally to define "higher" or "advancement.") I do mean to say that we must know who it is we are serving— God, man, or ourselves, remembering that Jesus emptied himself of his glory. I am convinced, in looking back on my life and what might have been, that the ghetto, the vineyard of North Philadelphia, was where my life could be most fruitful.

The year of my personal decisions, 1976, was the bicentennial year of the U.S.A. Many groups that had struggled for justice over the decades in this land decided not to participate in the official ceremonies but instead to have a "people's bicentennial," to remind America that for millions this was still not a land of "liberty and justice for all." On Sunday afternoon, July 4, about 25,000 people from far and wide marched through the streets of Philadelphia and rallied in Fairmount Park. Milton Street, a folk hero, who had risen from street vendor to member of the Pennsylvania senate, and I were the two main speakers on this occasion. I am sure I was chosen to speak because the Church of the Advocate and I had become symbols of the struggles and the striving of poor and oppressed people in this country.

A few years later I would be chosen again to play this representative role in a mission that would take me far from home in Philadelphia. In June of 1980, at the height of the hostage crisis, I found myself, along with former U.S. attorney general Ramsey Clark and eight others, participating in the "Crimes of America Conference" in Tehran. The crimes to be examined had to do with U.S. support for the Shah of Iran and his brutal reign over his people. Clark felt it important at this moment of extreme tension between the American people and the Iranian people that some Americans publicly acknowledge the evil role our government had

played, through the CIA, in the overthrow of a previous government and the installation of the shah, with his terrible torture
chambers. Only if we were honest about this history could we
hope to win a hearing for the release of the American hostages.

At the conference, the U.S. delegation decided that one of us
should make a direct appeal for the hostages to the 325 delegates
assembled, who had come from many Arab nations, Canada, the
United Kingdom, and other European countries. They decided
that a black delegate should do this, and they chose me. I made an
impassioned appeal to the Iranian president, which was telecast in
England and Germany, as I learned later from Philadelphians who
were visiting those countries at the time. But it was *not* broadcast
in America.

Our trip itself did draw U.S. media attention when President
Carter said that we could face penalties of up to ten years in jail
and fines of $50,000 for going to Iran, and speaking out as we
had. Upon our return to New York, when I saw attorney William
Kunstler among the welcoming party I realized that we could be in
very serious trouble. Bill spoke to us before we were questioned by
the CIA. He made it clear to us that our passports could not be
revoked and that we were not to surrender them under any circumstances. Never would I have expected to see my wife, Christine, as soon as we got off the plane, but Bill Kunstler recognized
her in the crowd, took her hand, and steered her through the reporters, customs officers, and perhaps a hundred others who were
there just to see us and hear what we had to say. I am happy to
say we never faced prosecution for our trip.

Over the years, in spite of all the controversy, I accumulated same
honorary degrees: a doctorate of divinity from Ursinus College
and from three Episcopal seminaries: Philadelphia, Berkeley (at
Yale), and General (in New York City). Then there was a doctorate of public service from neighboring Temple University. In
1985 and 1986 there were two overwhelming tributes from the
citizens of Philadelphia, which made me realize that my decision
to stay in Philadelphia was indeed the right one.

On February 21, 1985, at the Bellevue Hotel, 1,200 people attended a banquet called "Tribute to the Man," where one after another of my friends, neighbors and colleagues from across the city rose to speak of what the Advocate and our ministry there had meant to them. When the mayor of the city, W. Wilson Goode, presented me with the traditional city gift, the Philadelphia bowl, he left me in tears when he said: "No matter what I have accomplished, if I could be anyone in the world, Father Washington, I want to be like you."

Just three months after that tribute, the infamous raid on the MOVE house on Osage Avenue took place. So, in the following year, on April 15, 1986, it was in the context of a city struggling to recover its moral balance that I was given the city's highest honor, the Philadelphia Award, which included a prize of $25,000. A close friend tells me he thinks that Philadelphians needed to feel good about themselves again after the shameful conduct of May 13, 1985, so they chose me for the award, hoping that by identifying with the ministry of the Advocate to the poor and the outcast they could show that Philadelphia was a city that still had a heart. Who knows? He may be right.

In my acceptance speech, I tried to be as honest as I could about myself. I confessed that there is anger inside me—resentment and bitterness that sometimes borders on hatred. I'm sure some people don't know it is there. I explained that I had prayed that God would cleanse me of these feelings, but that he said to me: "I can make pure what is corrupt, and hatred is but corrupted love." He told me he would not take away the negative feelings, but he would show me how to use them by making me sensitive to injustice wherever I saw it.

Had I elaborated that evening I might have referred to Christ's words to Peter (Luke 22:31), which I hear as though spoken to me: "Peter, Satan has desired to have you, that he may sift you as wheat, but I have prayed for you that your faith fail not; and when you are converted, strengthen your brethren." Incredibly enough, I recall addressing an all-white group on the Main Line back in the 1960s and telling them how as a child growing up in

South Carolina, every time I heard of a Negro being lynched I felt like getting a machine gun and shooting up all white people. Some sympathized, some empathized, and almost all understood. It was said in compassion; it was real.

The City of Philadelphia had honored me very highly, but life on the streets of the city kept me from thinking more highly of myself than I ought to think, no matter how many honorary degrees or awards I had received. Let me tell just two stories of sidewalk encounters that reduced me to being just another frustrated citizen.

One rainy day driving north near Diamond Street, I was passing a bar when I saw a woman being pushed out the door. I stopped the car and got out to help her since she had literally fallen into the gutter. As I reached for her hand, a man came out and angrily demanded: "What the hell do you think you're doing?"

"The woman fell. I am just helping her up."

"Yeah, she's on the ground because I knocked her there. Now you get the f—— on!"

Something welled up in me. I was not going to be ordered to move; so I stood there, not moving an inch. Within those few moments ten to fifteen people had come out of the bar into the street. They all heard the hostile order.

When he ordered me a second time to get the hell on about my business, I still didn't move. When he raised his fist I thought to myself, Surely one of those guys will come to my rescue, or at least say: "Leave the man alone; don't you know that's Father Washington?" But no one said a word. Let it be understood that had he begun to attack me, I was going to fight back. I felt I had a right to stand up on a city street.

The woman, seeing what was about to happen, hastily left the crowd and started running down the street. She saved us both. The man did not strike me, but feeling compelled to do something, he shoved me before he ran down the street to try to catch his woman.

Some time later, when I sat somewhere talking to Father Ed

Rodman, I told him the story. He asked me why I had acted as I did. I told him I thought that if Jesus had seen the woman knocked to the ground and lying in the gutter, he would have helped her. Ed asked me, "Have you ever seen Jesus help a person who did not first ask for help?" I have thought about his question many times, and he and I have discussed the matter further. Ed said that Jesus indeed gave us the parable of the Good Samaritan, but Jesus himself gave to those who sought his help. I am still asking myself what Jesus would have done outside the bar, but I am also wondering why no one came to my rescue. At least half a dozen of the men who stood watching knew me, some had even been helped by me; but no one said a word to defend me. From that day to this, I have determined that if I feel I ought to help someone in trouble, I will do it; but I won't expect help from anyone else if my efforts get me in trouble.

The other story concerns the one time I was mugged. Neither my clerical collar nor my reputation was able to save me from being stalked by a would-be thief one day as I was leaving the State Store at 22d and Diamond with a bottle of wine. I was heading for my parked car when I sensed someone behind me. I put the bottle on the ground and turned to face him. He lunged at me, locking his arms about my body, but I also grabbed him. We tussled and tumbled to the concrete. I shifted my weight and managed to land on top of him. He struggled desperately and got up, trying to get hold of my head to pound it on the concrete. Once again I immobilized him in a bear hug.

When he realized that this preacher was not quite ready to turn the other cheek, he managed to break my armhold around his torso, then got up and ran away. The fellows who are always congregated around the State Store were watching all this and having a good laugh. Some of them knew me, but, once more, not a soul said a word to save the preacher. The mugger, no thanks to them, did not get my wine. He was about twenty-five; I was sixty.

Rejection on the sidewalk was one thing, but rejection on the public stage is something else again. Along with the public recognition had come memberships on some prominent boards and committees: the Harrison Foundation, the William Penn Foundation, the American Civil Liberties Union, to name a few. These positions reflected a great deal of trust by people in positions of power. Of course, I was also used to being in close, trusting conversation with many groups of powerless people struggling for their rights. On September 19, 1983, I came to realize how tenuous those relationships were. It was a rare day in which I experienced rejection by both the powerful and the powerless.

I had been invited to Harrisburg, the state capital, for a ceremonial function in the governor's reception room. On the same day some welfare groups and their supporters were staging a live-in at the capitol building to protest Governor Richard Thornburgh's vicious welfare cutbacks. The governor was determined to drop tens of thousands of "able-bodied" people from the General Assistance rolls, regardless of whether they had any other means of subsistence. My heart was with the demonstrators, including Roxanne Jones and her group, Philadelphia Citizens in Action, but on that day I had come to Harrisburg at the governor's invitation for something quite unrelated to the protest—or so I thought.

When I arrived at the capitol building, my friends in Citizens in Action greeted me, thinking I had come to join them. I explained where I was going and proceeded to the reception room. That clued the demonstrators to where the governor would be. It seems that they had been looking for him for days.

The guests at the governor's reception were carefully screened and the doors to the second-floor reception room were locked before the ceremonies commenced. But my friends, shut out, began hammering on the doors; they shouted and banged away violently. I was made nervous by the commotion and the strange position I found myself in. I decided I must speak to the governor directly, so I went over to him and asked, "Do you know what those sounds are and who is making them?"

He had smiled when I approached him, but his countenance and manner of speech quickly changed. "I do not talk to rabble," he said. Sensing how he had tensed up, the governor's bodyguards immediately surrounded the two of us. I said to the governor, answering my own question: "They are Pennsylvanians, your people. They are suffering and are calling to you for help." He said once more: "I don't speak to rabble."

The bodyguards then pressed close around me and moved me to the door. Instead of a proper, privileged Pennsylvanian I had suddenly become a rejected member of the rabble, numbered once again "with the transgressors."

The group outside cheered me, applauded me, and demanded that I speak. I told them that I had spoken to the governor and told him why they were there. I had told him the sounds he heard were the sounds of the suffering and the downtrodden. They applauded. They cheered. And then I added something they obviously did not want to hear.

I said that many of us had been in Washington just the month before when thousands celebrated the twentieth anniversary of that demonstration that will be forever remembered in our land. We could never forget the "I have a dream" speech of our apostle of nonviolence. Remembering what he stood for, we should try to conduct ourselves as he would teach us—peacefully and quietly.

Suddenly all hell broke loose, and I knew why. I had tried to say to them, obliquely and inconspicuously, I thought, that they should conduct themselves with more dignity and a little less noise, but they would not hear it. In the booing and catcalls at me, I heard anger, rejection, and hostility. Roxanne Jones spoke to the demonstrators: "You should know better than that. You know that we all should respect Father Washington." But to me she added "Father, you should have known better than to come outside and tell us to be quiet."

In the midst of this terrible confrontation, I became aware of two women beside me. Each locked an arm into my arms and starting moving me ever so slowly toward the semi-circular steps that lead from the second floor of the capitol to the first. Something strange began to happen. The noise abated and the crowd followed, almost as though hypnotized. Slowly, ever so slowly, we reached the main floor, directly in the midst of the rotunda, in dead silence. The two women then left me and I stood alone.

A young man came up and confronted me: "Father Washington, did the governor send you outside to tell us to be quiet?"

I responded softly, "No."

"All right. We'll believe you. I started that stuff upstairs because I thought the governor sent you out to tell us to be quiet."

I said nothing, and with that it was finished. I moved around, chatting, laughing, embracing, and then left Harrisburg for home. But I kept remembering those two women. Who were they? From whence did they come? How had they perceived that their action would quiet that storm? When I think of them today, I refer to them as "the two angels."

I could have used my angels on another occasion of controversy in 1983, when I was invited to speak at a center-city church on the occasion of the tenth anniversary of the Supreme Court decision *Roe v. Wade.* Abortion rights is an issue where I have taken a stand, although I cannot say within myself that those on one side are totally right and the others totally wrong. I have chosen to be a practical realist.

My ministry among people who live in poverty is the factor that tilted me in favor of supporting the right of a woman to abort a fetus. I have seen too many children bearing children, bringing them into a world where the poor and the children of the poor are dealt with inhumanely, often with contempt and cruelty. But as a result of my stand on this issue, I have been subjected to bitterness and hatred as in no other experience in my ministry.

When I spoke at the tenth anniversary gathering, I mentioned that I had assisted a family to get the money for an abortion. My remarks were reported in the media, and shortly thereafter I received a letter from a Roman Catholic priest who had invited me to speak to the men of his parish. His letter mentioned that we had marched and demonstrated together many times, and he had appreciated our participation in those causes together, but he could not have a man who was "anti-life" speaking to the men of his church.

Then I was invited to participate in a debate at LaSalle College with a woman who was the chief spokesperson for the "pro-life" movement in the Philadelphia area. I spoke first, pointing out that for me to be debating a "pro-life" person practically denoted that I am "anti-life," which is not the case. I then gave my reasons for being "pro-choice." Her rebuttal was devastating. She attacked me personally, calling me a murderer, a traitor to my vocation, and a menace to society. Most of the students present also attacked me viciously.

In my final statement, I also became personal. I told the audience they were a bunch of hypocrites. They shed crocodile tears for the unborn but had no compassion for those born into poverty. None of them would support a bill for aid to dependent children, and when such children got in trouble, they would say, "Put them in jail." Furthermore, they probably were all in favor of capital punishment. I concluded by saying that I would favor "pro-life" in the womb when they favored "pro-life" for those outside the womb. Then I left.

At a later time, I was to participate in a press conference on Good Friday morning at the Planned Parenthood Center on Locust Street. When I arrived at the center, it was completely surrounded by "pro-lifers." I walked up to the crowd, indicating that I wanted to enter. A man came from the crowd and shoved me. "You're not going in there," he said. "Nobody is going into this place that murders children." I exploded: "Get your hands off me! Don't touch me!" His venomous demeanor had evoked a response from me that was identical in character. I then went to a policeman and told him I wanted to enter the center. He responded: "You can't get in there now. Go over there and wait until these people leave." As I left, while driving home, I asked myself, But what would they have done to me if I had been a woman or a doctor?

The Bible says: "Beware when all men speak well of you." That is one warning I will not have occasion to heed.

17. Church Repairs and Church Renewal

I was troubled by the thought of retiring, but I knew that the time was coming. I was in my sixties and had had unbroken job commitments for all but ten of my years. I knew I would stay active until I died, but as the 1980s wore on, I had to think about leaving the Advocate. I wanted to leave it in as good a shape as I possibly could, and that meant not only tending to the community ministry, but also to the building itself, and the spirit that I hoped could be carried into the future.

The 1980s, the Reagan years, would spell hunger for many people, as the so-called safety net developed great gaps because of decisions made in Washington and in Harrisburg. "Thornfare," Governor Thornburgh's welfare cutback, denying general assistance to many thousands in the state, was just one dramatic example of the trend. If more people were going to be hungry and homeless, we resolved that we must try to feed them. Providentially, the Rev. Franklin Turner, then director of Black Ministries for the national church, gave us a grant of $7,000 to begin a ministry of feeding people. For this I was grateful, but I asked myself how far $7,000 would go toward feeding perhaps a hundred or more people a day. Nevertheless, we started, and the people came—slowly at first, but soon in the hundreds. The newspapers and TV stations put out the word that at the Advocate there were signs that the Depression had returned: "Soup lines are here again." The $7,000 continued to multiply as people began mailing in checks to feed the hungry.

Now, sixteen years later, the Advocate serves more than 2,000 meals a week, more than 140,000 a year. I am reminded that Jesus fed 5,000 people with five barley loaves and two small fishes (John 6:9). The many volunteer hands needed to feed up to three hundred people a day these are provided by members of the parish, regular helpers from other parishes, and students from Temple University.

In the 1980s, my preaching also changed. Throughout all my years, both at the Advocate and at St. Cyprian's before the Advocate, my preaching was intended to move people to action. But I realized that Americans had become immune and insensitive to marches, confrontations, civil disobedience, and arrests. Both Reagan and Thornburgh had openly and brazenly said by their actions that the plight of the poor and oppressed was not on their agenda; but, even beyond that, they projected that the poor were responsible for their own state of impoverishment and should have been like the hardworking, motivated, determined people who were "making it."

I began preaching that we were facing difficult days, that then, more than ever, we had to understand what is meant by "redemptive suffering." More than ever, we had to face Good Friday, knowing that Good Friday was the road to the Resurrection, the defeat of the grave.

In 1983 the church building itself began to fall apart. We had never had the money to properly maintain our French Gothic cathedral, so it is no wonder that the stones began to fall—large, granite stones weighing sixty to a hundred pounds. The first that fell flattened my wife's Volkswagen Beetle, which was parked between the rectory and the chapel. Thank God there was no one in or near the car at the time.

The chapel building would have to be demolished at once. We

brought in contractors to look at the whole complex of five buildings. The steeple on the main sanctuary had to come down, the roof had to be replaced, the stones pointed, stained glass windows repaired and covered. The total cost was estimated to be $2 million, of which $50,000 would come from the trustees of the Advocate for the chapel demolition. The next priority was a new roof for the church proper: $680,000. Where would the money come from? All I knew was that I could not walk away leaving my successor to be faced immediately with the task of raising over half a million dollars for this imperative need.

I got the word out that the Advocate was in desperate need of repairs and had to be saved if we were to continue our ministry. The response to this announcement was immediate. A good friend of many years, Bernard Watson, the chief executive officer of the William Penn Foundation, came through for us. Bernie, who had always respected, supported, and affirmed our work, told me that he would give us the first grant, $200,000, to broadcast to all that the William Penn Foundation believed the Advocate should be helped. The Pew Charitable Trust then gave us a grant of $250,000, and the Diocese of Pennsylvania, $50,000.

The media, which for years had gotten news from the Advocate, informed the community of our need. I was invited to speak on all the TV and radio stations, and Cody Anderson of radio station WDAS conducted a Saturday "radiothon" for us that netted thousands of dollars. Richard Tyler, director of the Philadelphia Historical Commission, worked very closely with me, emphasizing especially the fact that the Advocate was one of the most beautiful historical structures in Philadelphia and had to be saved.

In addition to the ancient beauty of the church building and its classic stained glass windows, more recent works of art had been installed around the walls of the sanctuary. Over the three year period 1973–76, two outstanding African American artists from Philadelphia, Walter Edmonds and Richard Watson, had painted a series of fourteen murals on large canvases for permanent display in the church. The two largest canvases measure twenty by twenty-five feet. Their size and vivid colors compel anyone entering the church to deal with their theme: the history of Black Americans placed alongside the Biblical stories of the deliverance from slavery of the Hebrew people. Beginning with our creation by God, the panels highlight the acts of Nat Turner, Elijah Muhammed, Malcolm, Martin, and others. On one canvas, Frederick Douglass appears as our Moses, his body emerging from a mountaintop with arms outstretched as he proclaims liberty to the captives.[1]

The artists had donated their services, the church supplied the materials, and I discussed with the artists the Biblical stories. The resulting murals powerfully reflect the spirit of the struggles for black power and liberation that have been so close to the heart of our church since the 1960s. Some of them are violent, but when I suggested to one of the artists that they might be too much so, he said to me calmly, "Do you expect me to paint this violent history to look pretty?" The murals are there—offensive to some, but uplifting to others. To the latter they say, *we* participated in our liberation. These paintings, too, had become part of the Advocate heritage we had to try to preserve.

"Save the Advocate" buttons were sold in shopping malls and on street corners as part of our fund-raising appeal to individuals. Hundreds of letters came in from all over, saying, "Dear Reverend, Here is $5 (or $10 or $25) to save your church." Contributions came from churches of all denominations, including $5,000 from Bryn Mawr Presbyterian Church. Even with all that support, I had to return to the William Penn Foundation three times, and each time they came through.

I continued to raise money for a year after I retired in June, 1987, exactly twenty-five years after I had come to the Advocate. The main task had been accomplished, a new roof and other vital repairs, at a cost of $680,000. (But the Advocate still needs at least $2 million worth of work.)

Part of the excitement of fixing up the Advocate was the removal of the angel Gabriel from his high post above the church for cleaning and restoration. People commonly spoke of the Advocate as the church with the angel on top. Unfortunately, we would lose the steeple, which would have cost $200,000 to repair; but Gabriel would have to be saved—it meant something to be watched over by an angel.

With financial help from the William Penn Foundation, we contracted with the firm that had just worked on the Statue of Liberty. They brought Gabriel down to earth and hauled him away to Washington, D.C., where they would restore him to be reperched atop the church for another hundred years. Never in all my life would I have believed that so many people would be upset because "the angel was gone." I was asked almost daily by people of the community if we were going to put the angel up again. I assured them that we would.

Finally, after almost a year, Gabriel was returned and anchored on a platform in back of the church until he could be raised to the top again. Everybody who came into church had to touch him. A couple chose to be married under Gabriel. And then the day came to elevate him once again to his place to watch over us.

The crane came to hoist the angel, and the Philadelphia Fire Department brought its cherry picker to hoist the workmen to put him in place. I got into the basket along with a newspaper photographer and the workmen. I wanted to see the last bolt that would be tightened, but I also wanted to see that over which Gabriel watched. It was not only North Philadelphia, it was over all of Philadelphia that he kept watch. By this time I was no longer rector of the Church of the Advocate, but I felt that my work there would not be finished until Gabriel was back in his place to say that the Advocate is still here keeping watch over us all. Once he was aloft, my work at the Advocate was finished.

I rejoiced to know that the Advocate congregation, still small but incredibly faithful, would carry on the work with or without me. Each member of that congregation was important to me, and at the close of each Sunday Eucharist I enjoyed very much the sharing of happiness and troubles, victories large and small, when we formed a circle of prayer together. All were important, but one member would gain historic importance in the life of the Episcopal Church and the Anglican Communion: Barbara Harris.

Barbara's decision to seek ordination as deacon and then priest is best told in her own words:

"It was some time after the Philadelphia ordination [July 29, 1974] when I decided to pursue ordination. At first I was not fully convinced that this was what I was called to do. I wrestled with it for a long time, all that time trying to test this with Paul Washington. I think initially Paul was not convinced either. We went back and forth on this for a year or more.

"Finally one evening we had a marathon conversation. It began at 7:15 in the evening and at ten minutes past 3:00 we stood up to pray together in my den. In this conversation I think we explored every possible area of strengths and weaknesses, vocation, call rightness. . . . When we finished praying, Paul said to me: 'When shall we go to the bishop?' "[2]

Barbara was ordained to the diaconate on September 29, 1979, and on October 18, 1980, to the priesthood, both services taking place at the Advocate. Shortly before she was ordained priest, Barbara and I shared an experience that neither of us will ever forget and that provided a lesson, if either of us needed it, about the tensions built into the peculiar ministry of the Advocate. The lesson was punctuated with a gunshot.

On August 28, 1980, while I was on vacation in Cape May, New Jersey, and Deacon Barbara was taking services at the Advocate, a Philadelphia policeman shot and killed a young black man named William Green. Those who had seen the killing were outraged; to them it was murder. It was the hottest time of the year, and the August heat further heightened the tempers in the black community. Wilson Goode, then serving as managing director in the administration of Mayor William Green, feared a violent reaction in the city streets.

Wilson called me in Cape May and said simply, "We might have some trouble in the city, and I want you here. I can send a car to get you if you want." I said that I would return to the city immediately. When I got home I found that Barbara had already given permission to a group to hold a mass meeting at the church. This fit well with what I had in mind. Sound trucks were already out on the streets, calling for people to come to the church that evening.

Without touching bases with those who had called the meeting, I proceeded to phone certain people who might be able to command the attention of the crowd and pour water on a fuse already lit, before it could get to the dynamite. Sister Falaka Fattah and Clarence Farmer were two of those I invited. Seeing my actions as taking over a meeting that I had not called, the organizers were livid.

When the meeting began, they took over from me. I responded by cutting off the amplifier. Meanwhile, people were screaming: "It was murder, murder!" Then someone in the back of the church fired a gun. I saw the flash and actually thought I heard the bullet going by. Then all hell broke loose. It was like an erupting volcano, with people in flight, some trampled, and pews being overturned in the mad rush to get out.

I was frozen, petrified. I did not move a step until I turned to look for Barbara. She was gone! I went into the sacristy and called, "Barb, where are you?" She came halfway down the stairs from my second-floor office. "Paul," she said, "are you all right?" I told her I was, and asked how she got upstairs so quickly. She responded dryly: "How do you think I got up here? I flew!" When she came down, I said, "Girl, when that gun was fired I actually heard the bullet as it whizzed past my face." Barbara said, "That wasn't no bullet; that was me."

There were only two acts of violence that evening. Some fellows jumped the guy who fired the gun and took it from him, and a reporter who was trying to interview the mother of the slain youth was beaten and his camera smashed. The police had surrounded the church to a saturation point; so those who might have intended further violence knew that "there was no hiding place" out there.

When all had quieted down, I lay in bed next door in the rectory, thinking about the happenings of the past few hours. I concluded that the fever had broken. The firing of the gun in the Advocate (which has a seven-second echo), the fear, the flight, and the violent stampeding from the church had been a vicarious explosion of the emotions that had been waiting to erupt.

I called Wilson Goode the next morning and told him that I thought we had passed through the crisis. I turned things over to Barbara at the church and headed back to Cape May. Of course, the officer's action was later determined to have been justified.

With all her training at the Advocate, it seemed right some years later that Barbara Harris should be asked to serve as interim priest there after I retired. But three members of the vestry stood in the way of that, and they persuaded the other members to seek another priest. Their objection to Barbara was really a continuation of their objection to the outreach ministry of the Advocate during my tenure. They didn't want more of Fr. Washington after he had gone. The priest who was selected lasted only a few months, having decided that the Advocate was not for him. After that experience, and at the insistence of many in the congregation, the vestry called Barbara to serve and she accepted. Soon the Advocate was as people believed it should be. It was while serving as interim at the Advocate that Barbara Harris was elected suffragan bishop of the Diocese of Massachusetts, on September 24, 1988—the first woman chosen bishop in the entire history of the Anglican Communion.

That she chose me to preach at her consecration service was the crowning glory of my Advocate ministry. "Get your sermon ready, Paul," she said when she called me on the day of her election. But this assignment was also a cause of great trepidation. I would be standing before 8,500 people in the Hynes Auditorium in Boston, with how many more listening on radio and watching on TV? That sermon I knew would become a part of history; I also felt a keen personal obligation not to disappoint Barbara on the greatest day of her life.

When Christine and I were registering at the hotel desk in Boston the night before the great day of Barbara's consecration, a young, recently ordained bishop came up to me, genuflected, and said: "May I kiss the hem of your garment?" Others who knew me came up and said: "Paul, we are waiting for the Word tomorrow." By the time I was preparing for bed I was really "beside myself," wondering who the person was beside me who was to be tomorrow's preacher.

As I knelt to pray that night, I remembered Herman, the man from my hometown of Charleston to whom I had ministered at Eastern State Penitentiary as he awaited execution for a double murder. Herman had been dead for a long time, but I remembered his promise to me, that as soon as he got to heaven he would begin watching over me, and that if I ever needed him to talk to "God and Jesus" for me, I should just call on him.

I was convinced that I needed a special intercessor right then and there, so I called out: "Herman, I need you tonight. I need you to talk to God and Jesus and tell them that I am lost and can't find myself. Tell them that I have to preach the Word tomorrow, but that I am in the way and I might end up preaching myself instead of them. Tell them to give me their Spirit so that I can preach the gospel."

I awoke on the morning of February 11, 1989, with a great feeling of peace; but when the service began a very lonely feeling overtook me. I joined the great procession, including sixty-five bishops of the church, many clergy, choirs, and acolytes. Barbara entered the great hall to an explosion of sounds of joy. The service began, and, as on July 29, 1974, some came forward to state their objections. The presiding bishop, Edmund Browning, listened to them and then announced to all that we would proceed. Again the house exploded. Finally, it was sermon time.

I could still hear, "Paul, we are waiting for the Word." The lonely feeling persisted until I got to the following words in the ninth draft of my prepared manuscript: "This day was inherent in eternity." At this, there was applause. I looked over at Barbara and my old friend Ed Rodman. They were smiling and nodding their heads approvingly. From that moment on, I forgot myself and left the rest to the Holy Spirit. Herman had gotten through!

"Although for us, finite creatures of time, this day reveals an event never before beheld by the eyes of humankind, that which is happening for us today was inherent in eternity. Long ago, when God said, Let there be light, the light which we see at this moment began its journey, before the beginning of time. That light moved at the speed of light, at times challenged by the awful gravity of black holes from which even light cannot escape, yet that darkness could not prevail, and today we behold its beauty, its warmth, its energy and the new life which it holds as a light of the world."

In the course of an hour, with much spontaneous response from the congregation, both laughter and tears, I spoke of Barbara's call from God to serve this church as bishop. I told of her phone call to me on September 24 of the previous year, bringing the news of her election. "I can't believe it," I had said. Barbara said, "I can't believe it either. How could I have been elected to be a bishop in this church?" I compared the news she had received with the news that Mary had received 2,000 years ago, and her incredulity as she asked, "How can this be, seeing I know not a man?"

I recalled July 29, 1974, a time when the church had been shaken to its very foundations by the ordination of the first women to the priesthood. "Barbara," I said, "you were in California that morning, you jumped on a plane and came to your church and you led the procession. You did not know when you led that procession that God was preparing you to lead another procession."

And I was led to tie together in my sermon the two strands in Barbara's life and ministry that she can never untie, since she is black and a woman. This was a day of victory for women and for all black people in our church, which is still a church that has to be challenged to end its racist and sexist ways.

We cannot, and we must not, overlook the fact that this woman who is being consecrated today is not just an American woman. She is a black woman. Called at one time a Negro. Called at one time colored. "Stony the road you've trod. / Bitter the chastening rod / felt in the days when hope unborn had died. / Yet with a steady beat, / have not our weary feet / come to this place for which our fathers sighed?" However, while our church will have consecrated seventeen persons of African descent to the office of a bishop, including one woman, to this date only seven black priests have ever been elected to be priests or rectors in white congregations. The camel has gotten through the eye of the needle.

As bishop, Barbara would serve many parishes, white and black, Hispanic and Asian, within the Diocese of Massachusetts. She would inspire men and women around the world, as she already had just by her election as bishop. I rejoiced to think that this expanding ministry would be rooted in our experience of feeding the hungry, praying for the sick, housing the homeless, and visiting those in prison at the Church of the Advocate in North Philadelphia.

18. "One Fold, One Shepherd"

It was in the late 1960s that I received a call from a bishop of our church who was on official business in New York City and who wanted to spend some time talking with me. He came to Philadelphia the same day.

The bishop was interested in having congregations in his diocese reach out to minister to the powerless, the poor, and the oppressed. But he had a concern: It seemed that somehow the ministers who engaged in such "outreach" ministries always ended things by breaking up their congregations.

One sentence from the pages of history has helped me to understand why this happens. Back in the late eighteenth century, Absalom Jones and Richard Allen worked as one to help the Negroes of Philadelphia, forming the Free African Society in 1787. Because of the rude racial segregation in the worship at St. George's Methodist church, to which they belonged, they realized that Negroes needed to worship the God who liberates and redeems his people in a church of their own. They were divided, however, on the question of religious denomination. In one brief history of their conflict, I read this line: "And Allen departed from them." Allen became bishop over the African Methodist Episcopal Church, with nearly 7,000 members, while Absalom Jones became the leader of the congregation of St. Thomas African Episcopal Church, "which attracted the more prosperous blacks, [and] remained small."

Today, two hundred years later, although African Americans are viewed by white America as a monolith, we find within our racial family a similar division. Some, with a "prosperous mentality," prefer to be identified with a white, Anglo-Saxon, Protestant denomination, like the Episcopal Church; others cannot live in peace organically connected to people who refuse to accept the theology of the oneness of all of God's children. We must not forget that it took sixty-nine years, from 1787 to 1863, for St. Thomas African Episcopal Church to be admitted as a voting member of the convention of the Episcopal Diocese of Pennsylvania.

The bishop who made the trip from New York City to seek my advice was disturbed that congregations that reached out to the "unprosperous" so often shattered. I wish I could have helped him to look back in history to that tragic moment two hundred years ago, when "Allen departed from them." Those who went along with Jones into the Episcopal Church were the "prosperous." I know that such a split is not just a phenomenon of the Episcopal Church, which has historically been seen as a "class church." I have found that religious people generally are class-conscious so that, regardless of the denomination, church members may disdain those who look or behave differently from them. But it is in the Episcopal Church that I have had to work to overcome this dividing line, so I draw my lessons from my experience there.

In my twenty five-years at the Advocate, the more I tried to reunite us as one people, engaged in one struggle, the more the historic division revisited us. As word got out about meetings of the "unprosperous" taking place in our church, many became uncomfortable and disturbed. I tried to preach that this is the church's mission: saving and redeeming was what Jesus was all about. I instituted home meetings where ten to twelve church members would gather to learn, not only about our "pilot project" of ministering to the people around us but, more important, about the meaning of the ministry of Jesus. The meetings helped very little. Those who already understood were supportive; those who would not understand remained opposed.

The two medical doctors in the Advocate congregation "departed from us." All the teachers, except Dorothy Lovell, left. (We later named an ACDC twenty-five-unit apartment for the homeless the Dorothy Lovell Gardens.) Slowly, but painfully and noticeably, longstanding members left the church, which had lost the character with which they wished to be identified. Vestry meetings became battlegrounds: "Fire John Chuchville, that Black Muslim!" (John, my gang worker, was in fact not a black Muslim.) "Send the money back to the foundation that underwrote his salary. The Church of Jesus Christ cannot be racist! It cannot preach black unity and black power. After all, we still have white members."

Walter Morris, church treasurer of many years, a distinguished gentleman recognized as epitomizing the character of the Advocate, complained to the trustees of the Advocate (the white, male body that handled the endowment) and to Bishop DeWitt about my open-door ministry. When neither of them made any move to restrain me, he stopped paying the church bills and refused to fill out the financial portion of the annual report, which by canon law had to be submitted to the diocese.

But, by God's grace, my treasurer and I grew to accept each other. When I told him that I felt as though I could love him as a father, he was embarrassed but he said that he could see me as a son. Nevertheless, he was discomforted by what had happened to his church. For Walter, the church was intended to be a refuge from conflict, not at the center and forefront of conflict.

Bill Farmer was a faithful parishioner who loved me, and I him; but, like Walter Morris, he would say to me on occasion: "Father, when I get up in the morning, I always read the papers while eating breakfast. I don't need to come to church to hear about what is happening in the world." Bill and I are great friends. I ministered to him at the deaths of two wives. But Bill taught me a lesson that afterward caused me to violate a canon of the church. The woman who was to become Bill's second wife, Madeline, had been divorced, and I told him that before I could officiate at their marriage, I had to present her divorce papers to the bishop and get his approval for the ceremony. Bill reacted with indignation: "You have to ask the bishop if you can marry us?" He and Madeline went to Delaware and were married there.

Now that I can no longer be disciplined for violating canons, I will admit that after that experience, I never again took divorce papers to the bishop for his approval. I examined them myself, counseled the man and woman, and, if I was satisfied, I officiated at their marriage. (When, sadly, Madeline died, I said to myself that Bill and Eleanor, another faithful member of the congregation, would be married. Bill and Eleanor never cease to wonder how I knew this, even before they did.)

If we took attendance at church, Clarence Brogden would have a 98 percent record. How he has stayed at the Church of the Advocate, I find it hard to understand. He timed my sermons, and I always preached too long. He was never in agreement with my political positions, and when Barbara Harris preached, he did not agree with her. But rarely does he miss a Sunday.

Jean Mack, now deceased, was a very reserved, dignified woman, a person of grace and tasteful sophistication. A retired schoolteacher, she was a good friend of Walter Morris and one of the bridge players of the church. When I visited her to explain the character of my ministry, she told me, "You do not have to explain anything to me. I understand, and I agree with you." Her acceptance and affirmation of the church's mission as I saw it was most gratifying.

Of my first confirmation class at the Advocate, Becky, Lois, and Joe remain. Becky Chamberlain left us for a season when she found the "notoriety" of her church not only disturbing, but, in her own words, "frightening." Eventually she returned, but then at first she was quite critical of the people who were coming to eat at our soup kitchen. Some of them were young and able-bodied. They should be working, she thought. Today she is the strongest supporter of this ministry. She looks with understanding and compassion upon those who are given to us, and she "blames" me for having changed her attitude.

Lois Peeples never faltered. She is full of energy and uses it up working in the church. When our family moved from the rectory to the house where we would live following my retirement, she came straight to our house after work to help us fix it up. She is carpenter, painter, interior decorator, and "boss." She gives much and expects nothing in return.

Joe Overton is the other member of my first confirmation class who is still with us. For a while Joe left, too, but he felt drawn back to the life of the parish. He is one of those who works for a living, but seems to find his life fulfilled in the church. Joe has a magnificent baritone voice. His whole family is gifted, and their choral group, "The Overton Family," is well known and in great demand.

Of the few white people who transferred to the Advocate during my tenure, Marge Thomas was the first. She came to us from the Church of the Redeemer, Bryn Mawr, and was later joined at the Advocate by her husband, Ned. Marge and I met during the 1960s when I was speaking on the Main Line on race relations. She shared with me the trials and tribulations of her son Mort, who had been arrested in Mississippi while engaging in voter registration work. Ned, a trust officer at a Philadelphia bank, eventually became a member of the Advocate vestry and the parish treasurer. The Thomases' daughter, Elizabeth, was a counselor in our summer day camp, where she met William McMullen, another counselor. Their relationship during that summer led to courtship and marriage in 1971.

Because of their different races and backgrounds—Elizabeth reared on the affluent Main Line and William in North Philadelphia—I counseled them in depth and at length. During one of our counseling sessions I asked Elizabeth, "Is your father giving you away?" To which she responded, "My father is not giving me to William. I am giving myself to William." William was one of seven children, nurtured in a household of one parent, his mother Margaret, a most remarkable woman. In spite or their material poverty, the principles, values, and faith of the McMullens can only be described in superlatives. Margaret McMullen was recently honored by the members of the Advocate for being "Margaret McMullen." William, a Ph.D. in psychology, and Elizabeth have two brilliant sons. This pair who met in our summer day camp over twenty years ago still love, honor, and cherish each other. Christ can overcome culture.

I cannot write about each member of the Church of the Advocate, but it must be clearly understood that these regulars provide the home for "the other sheep." They are the people who are counted and accountable, according to the canons of the church, as the Church of the Advocate. Today most of the members of the Advocate actually feel fulfilled to have the "other sheep" coming into the home that they support, nurture, and sustain. They are not class-conscious. They are people-conscious. To round out that picture, I must mention a few more.

Georgia Thomas was and is an anomaly. She feels that the Advocate belongs to her, and that everything and everybody should satisfy her. She attends every event that goes on at the church, being present daily to distribute clothing from the clothes closet and to dictate to the people running the soup kitchen. She has brought more people into the church than anyone else. As the Advocate's oldest member, in age as well as in membership, Georgia feels that her credentials entitle her to the most authoritative voice in the church—even above the rector's. She has been known to challenge anyone who acts contrary to her judgments. During the 1960s and 1970s, when the Advocate was opening its doors to those "who did not belong," she was asked how she felt about Black Power meetings at the church. She replied that she was adamantly opposed to them; when told that Black Power advocates were not going away but would meet somewhere in any case, she said: "If they are going to meet and cannot be stopped, then I guess the Advocate is the best place." She was able to accept the new, but never without putting up a good fight to conserve the old.

Miss Hattie Williams came to the Advocate twenty years ago. One of the first black persons to buy a house on Diamond Street, forty years ago, she is a strong woman and a good leader, whose organization makes more money for the church than any other. The women in Club 6 say that she is a slavedriver, but they love, respect, and follow her. At a testimonial for Hattie, I told her that I had always feared she would leave us. I wondered how she could worship with us Anglo-Saxonized Episcopalians, who don't even want to cough in church. When Hattie Williams feels the Spirit during worship, she will call out at the top of her voice, "Tell it like it is!" or "Preach, Barbara!" or "Yes, Lord, you're so good! . . . Thank you, Jesus!" She may be the only voice in the wilderness, but she would not care if she "couldn't hear nobody [else] pray."

Bill Harling means more to me and to the Advocate than many will ever realize. When I hired him to be our sexton, he was a heroin addict; but he realized that this privileged job at the church was so important that he could not allow his addiction to destroy it. He was faithful, and, unlike so many addicts, he did not steal from the church. Eventually he got into a methadone program to break his addiction. A product of North Philadelphia, whenever Bill faced conflict he used to react in the way some North Philadelphians do, with violence. But he told me that he had watched how I handled conflicts. He admired my calmness and my gentle approach to hot situations. He began trying this tactic, and found that he could make it work. In recent years, Bill's life has been devoted to taking care of his ailing mother and the Advocate. I have told him that he is as much a minister of this church as I was, and he feels that way.

The quality of the music at the Advocate was and is superb. Edward Collins-Hughes is an accomplished musician and an excellent choir director. He chose the music that belonged in a cathedral and could not accept my wanting music that was sung from the souls of black people. I am not particularly a lover of gospel music, but I am of the Negro spiritual. To me, the spiritual is to the Negro what the Psalms are to the Jewish people. Even though, canonically, the rector has the responsibility for selecting the music for worship, Ed argued that he was the minister of music, and should have as much right to exercise his ministry as I had to exercise mine. But beyond that, most of the choir members felt that Ed chose the kind of music that was right for the Advocate. I eventually accepted the scripture: "The letter kills, but the spirit gives life." I had the letter of the law on my side, but if I acted by the letter, I would kill the spirit that existed among Ed and the choir. Ed became organist and choir director of the Advocate the Sunday before I became rector, June 15, 1962. He is still organist and choir director today, thirty-one years later. A circle does not have opposing ends; it is an unending continuum.

Jim Rhinehart is a diamond in the rough. He is thoroughly charming, but disconcerting when he uses "improper" words for emphasis. When he wears socks, shirt, and tie, I have to ask him: "What's the special occasion?" He loves and enjoys people, and everyone responds easily to him. He can disagree with you without being disagreeable. Jim is a relative latecomer to the Advocate, but as he is one who needs to be involved, it did not take long for him to be elected to the vestry, eventually becoming senior warden, chairman of the soup kitchen committee, active in the men's club, and anywhere else he could be of help.

Occasionally, Peter McGurdy would come to church with Jim. Although Peter was Roman Catholic, he finally decided to be received into membership in the Episcopal Church. Peter and Jim have been companions for over twenty-five years, and their relationship has opened the eyes, the hearts, and the minds of the Advocate family. Many in America say this or that about the Jims and Peters of this world, but in the Advocate they are just two beautiful people who love and respect one another. They live in our midst and we behold their love.

The Advocate is unpredictable, moving from one extreme to another. The Eucharistic liturgy can be unfolding with the magnificence characteristic of the Episcopal Church when Essie McFadden enters, sees Barbara preaching in the pulpit, and bellows out: "Barbara, I'm from South Carolina and I saved my money and I'm going home for a visit." Barbara stops and says "That's fine, Essie. Now why don't you just sit and worship with us for a while?"

This is the church where, with great ceremony, two bishops have been installed in office; but it also hosted the convention of the Black Panthers, when everyone had to be patted down before entering the premises. This is the church that gave to the Anglican

Communion its first woman bishop, a black woman; but its rector precipitated a crisis at a special convention of the Episcopal Church by calling for "all black people" to leave a meeting. The Advocate is where eleven white women were (irregularly but validly) ordained as the first women priests in the Episcopal Church; it was also the site of a Black Power Conference, and of a Black Unity Rally in 1966, where we said that whites were not welcomed, as blacks began their movement toward black empowerment, pride, and identity. It is a church whose membership defies definition, being made up of black and white, poor and affluent, professionals and domestic workers, graduates of Ivy League colleges and some who are barely literate.

This is not the church of "the comfortable pew." In fact, the Advocate, like its Lord, has been "numbered among the transgressors." I quote from the May 26, 1968 memo to the director of the FBI: "The Rev. Paul M. Washington, Rector of the Church of the Advocate, has made his church's facilities available to Negro extremists and has associated with them at his church. He has also been quoted in the Negro press as being against the Vietnam War, and desirous that the funds being expended on that conflict be used to solve the problems of the ghetto.

"Rev. Washington is the rector of a ghetto church and involved in the problems of the Negro. His expressed views and the type of meetings that he has permitted in his church would indicate he is a Black Nationalist sympathizer, but he is not an advocate of violence."

That the church and its rector should have been under FBI surveillance represents the eternal tension that must always exist between Christ and Caesar, and between the church and the establishment. My unique role as rector of the Advocate was pretty well summed up by attorney Charles Bowser, former deputy mayor of the City of Philadelphia, in his book *Let the Bunker Burn*. He said that I was "a member of the anti-establishment, who was understood and trusted by the establishment."[1]

The trust that matters most, and the love that sustains one, even in a ministry as complex and full of tensions as mine has been, comes from the family. I have increasingly come to recognize that in this work to which my mother committed me, the character people see in me is my father's. As I wrote in the first chapter of my story: "If I could be like anybody, I want to be like my daddy." The words from the *Book of Common Prayer* that the bishop spoke to me when I was ordained a priest, "You are to love and serve the people among whom you work, caring alike for young and old, strong and weak, rich and poor," are words illustrated and modeled in my father's life.

The sustaining love, through all my ministry, has been that of my own family. Miss Jackson, who consented to be the wife of Father Washington on August 23, 1947, one year after her graduation from high school, has been from the beginning all I could pray for. I at first wondered if a person Christine's age would be willing and able to leave family, friends, and all that was dear to her, to go to Africa, of all places. She did it as though it was simply advancing from high school to college.

Marc and Kemah, born in Africa, and Michael and Donya, born in such different surroundings, when we lived among the flowers and vegetable gardens and unpaved streets of Eastwick, all rose to the challenge of family life in North Philadelphia. Our children went to the public schools, and their friends were of the neighborhood. They lived among the gangs, but never joined. And, thank God, although drugs abounded, our family life was pleasurable and fulfilling enough that drugs would have detracted from their pleasure rather than enhancing it.

Our children became members of the Church of the Advocate without being persuaded. Having been exposed to the many meetings, demonstrations, and great thinkers of the movement, they became writers and interpreters of the movement themselves. As a youngster, each one, from Marc, the eldest, to Donya, the youngest, was a prolific writer (or scribbler), on anything that was available. Christine, who knew the value of these writings, saved and compiled all that she could find, and presented in booklet form to our children one Christmas Day their own musings and analysis of their intimate and sometimes confused experiences of the movement.

Michael now works with Christine in ACDC; he seems headed for a career in housing development. Kemah, employed by Boeing-Vertol Company for fifteen years, is married to a beautiful young schoolteacher named Santissa. They are parents of three sons—Kemah, Akeem, and Kareem. (Kemah the father was born in May when I was thirty years old, little Kemah also in May when his father was thirty, and Santissa was born in May on her husband's birthday.)

Marc, our oldest son, is living in Budapest with his wife, Agnes. When Agnes came to America from Hungary and attended Marc's English class at International House in New York City, she was not conscious of the fact that she was white and Marc was black. She saw only a member of the human family, a man who fulfilled her heart's desire. They married seven months after meeting each other. Marc operates an English language school in Budapest, and Agnes is a schoolteacher there. They have a daughter, Christina.

Donya, our fourth child (also born in May), is a therapist in a mental health–mental retardation center in Philadelphia. She earned her bachelor's degree at Temple University. Donya is now packing up to leave our duplex in the Strawberry Mansion area of Philadelphia for an apartment in Germantown. It is a sobering experience to have our last child moving away from us.

With children grown and the years of parish ministry behind me, what comes next? I am often asked the question, "What are you doing in retirement, Paul?" I faced the question long before June 15, 1987, and at first I was truly afraid. Having worked from the age of ten, could I say, Thank God, now I am free to do some of the things I always wanted to do? But I have always done what I wanted to do. As I look at my appointment book today, I have no fears. I know the unique ministry of the Advocate is being carried forward by my able successor, the Rev. Isaac Miller, and I am personally still engaged in the work I love.

God still calls me, and he still speaks through the voices of people who are afflicted and those who struggle for justice. One day it is a homeless group asking me to participate in their action on the streets of Philadelphia. (In one such demonstration I was arrested for the second time in my life, in the good company of homeless advocates Chris Sprowal and Sister Mary Scullion.) Another time it may be Rita Adessa calling about a demonstration for gay and lesbian rights. Barbara Smith of Jobs with Peace. Leona Smith of the Employment Project. The Philadelphia Anti-Apartheid Committee, raising money for voter education in South Africa. The group working to commute the sentence of Mumia Abu Jamal, now sitting in prison on death row. Ramona Africa, still demanding justice for her brothers and sisters serving thirty- to one-hundred-year sentences in jail.

God called me just today from Media, Pennsylvania, through the pleading voice of a Mexican farm worker, asking if I would join in the mushroom workers' march as they strike for better working conditions, higher pay, and health care. God called me to Israel to join thousands of people from around the world in saying, It's time for peace; and to Russia for an international leadership conference. He still calls me to serve the diocese, in which I have had two interim rectorships of three years or more; and I am still invited many places to preach.

Retirement? As another Philadelphia priest used to say, "I am not retired; I am retreaded." For me, retirement is different only in that I now live on a pension and no longer have the responsibilities of a full-time parish priest. But I have always known that I was especially called to the "other sheep not of this fold." In the many calls, I hear Jesus saying: "Them also I must bring, and they shall hear my voice, and there shall be one fold and one shepherd." That will happen when God's love for all is manifested— not when everyone belongs to one church, but when everyone shares in God's justice.

Afterword | The Rt. Rev. Barbara C. Harris
Suffragan Bishop, Diocese of Massachusetts

Needless to say, I was flattered when Paul and David asked me to offer this Afterword to Paul's compelling autobiographical account of his ministry at the Church of the Advocate. I feel both humble and proud to have been a participant and an observer in so many of the situations that Paul describes with modest understatement and a thorough commitment to honesty. I feel humble, naturally, about those portions of the story that involve me personally. Proud, because the rigorous example set by Paul must have had some impact on my own spiritual formation. This is not to say that other influences and individuals have not been significant in my own spiritual journey, but without question it was in the crucible of service to our Master at the Church of the Advocate during the rectorship of Paul Washington that my own sense of mission and ministry was tested and refined.

The coincidence of person and place that is recounted in Paul's autobiography is truly a testimony to God's grace in action, putting the right man in the right place at the right time. Paul observes early in the story that the byword of the Advocate is "This Church Lives the Gospel," and the truth is documented in Paul's narrative. There is a great temptation for me in these few pages to elaborate on some of Paul's stories so as to indicate just how formidable his presence really was. But that would be unfair to Paul and to the integrity of his story, and would also diminish the importance of the small community of faith that surrounded and supported him through trials and tribulations. Indeed, any of us who were there during his ministry can take pride in the faithfulness that Paul's leadership called forth from us. His narrative often refers to having made "unilateral" decisions, but what those of us who were there saw more often than not was a man of faith following his Lord fearlessly. I would be untruthful if I did not acknowledge, as he himself recognizes, that on occasion some of us may have thought that this time he had gone too far, but I can honestly say that in most instances our initial concern was a result of our lack of vision, our inability to see God's hand at work in the world about us.

Under Paul's guidance, the Advocate became a haven for people with no place else to go. Too often those who were not directly involved in or knowledgeable about the incredible pastoral ministry that took place at the Advocate failed to see the connection between the loving concern for individual persons in trouble or pain or need and the search for justice. In responding to legitimate needs, the inevitable and logical movement from charity to justice took place. All authentic prophetic action flows from a genuine pastoral concern. My only real criticism of Paul's story of this full Gospel ministry is that he had neither the time nor the space to explore the many steps that he and others had to take in developing the faith and courage to discern the action that was needed. The result was always to translate God's loving concern for people into love distributed to the whole community.

The various momentous decisions so often criticized as controversial in the media or in church circles were merely the last step in an inevitable journey that began when we began to care and had the audacity to believe that the Advocate could make a difference. I believe that Paul and the ministry of the Advocate must ultimately be judged on faithfulness to the Gospel, not as a model for political astuteness or correctness. The fact that the ministry was controversial in many instances is merely testimony to the righteousness of the stand.

In much of what Paul writes, one gets a sense of what I observed first-hand, that the depth of his own spirituality had the capacity to evoke the best from even the worst of people. Such loving concern in action leads directly to the growth of community and it is, therefore, not surprising that so many of the controversial actions associated with Paul's ministry at the Advocate involved the hosting of community gatherings. The Black Power Conference, the efforts to unite the gangs, the 1974 ordination of women—each in its own way was a community gathering in the name of justice and reconciliation. This style of ministry extended its reach further and further beyond the geographic bounds of the parish, into the life of the city, the church, and ultimately the world. Think globally and act locally: to me this is what authentic ministry is all about.

Never has an architectural gem dedicated to God been so transformed, in its use and in the perception of it, as the Church of the Advocate, an incarnation of God's presence among us. Needless to say, this was not achieved without internal rancor and struggle, and it is to Paul's credit that this autobiography makes no attempt to put some of his local critics in their place. On more than one occasion I confronted some of them outside Paul's earshot, and in less than spiritual terms explained to them why we were doing such and such a thing in such and such a way, and what they could do if they didn't like it. I suspect Paul would have been appalled at the directness of my approach, but as a person trained in communications, I understood that appeals to a person's higher nature are not always the most effective means of making a point. I can assure you that the full range of human discourse transpired not only with those we sought to serve, but also among ourselves when our reluctance to serve would get in the way. It was particularly galling to me that so many of these occasions had to do with the use of property rather than with the treatment of people.

Two other observations are in order. One is that Paul had the remarkable quality of becoming personally engaged in any cause or situation he espoused. While many who were not close to him at the Advocate were often amazed at his cool demeanor and flawless aplomb, those of us who knew him well also knew when that internal struggle of decision making was at work. His faith in the correctness of the path he had chosen could inspire a remarkable calm, once a commitment was made to move forward. I am delighted that Paul chose to share some of his internal struggles and self-doubts with the reader, so that his humanity shows forth with the same power as his faith. While most folk begin to mellow as they approach retirement, Paul has remained steadfast in his activism and his commitments. His honesty, which embodies the twin virtues of social criticism and self-criticism, remains an inspiration to many. For me, there was no question as to who should preach to me at my consecration.

The second observation is that in some ways the most compelling part of Paul's personal journey, as he recounts it and as I and others experienced it, was his own personal growth in understanding the emerging role of women and the horrendous burden of sexism. I believe it is true that no other parish in the country has produced more women priests than the Church of the Advocate, nor has any church been as affirming of women's ministries, whether lay or ordained. The fact that the Advocate was the site of the historic service for the ordination of women to the priesthood was but a natural outgrowth of Paul's and the community's progress in understanding this vital issue. The Advocate's commitment preceded the service and has remained consistent to the present time.

The authentication I was given by Paul and the community has given me the strength to take on the burden of being the first woman bishop, in the full realization of all that it would entail. Many make much of my professional experience as having prepared me for the role, but I can assure you that it was my spiritual formation in the ministry of service at the Advocate with Paul Washington that made the real difference.

Paul's ministry certainly taught us the reality of Ephesians 6:12: "For we do not wrestle against flesh and blood, but against principalities, against powers, against the rulers of the darkness of this age, against spiritual hosts of wickedness in the heavenly places." Paul stands as a witness to God's grace in action and to the power of faith working through community to bring about justice, peace, and reconciliation. The work of the Advocate wasn't always tidy. It was never wrapped up in a neat ribbon and pronounced well done. And most important, it was never lost. In responding to the needs of people first, the Advocate truly became a house of prayer for all people, with Paul Washington as pastor, prophet, and priest. Thank God for Paul and the Church of the Advocate, and for this book.

Sources

General

Assefa, Hizkias, and Paul Wahrhaftig. *The MOVE Crisis in Philadelphia: Extremist Groups and Conflict Resolution* (University of Pittsburgh Press, 1990).

Booty, John. *The Episcopal Church in Crisis* (Cowley, 1988).

Boyette, Michael, with Randi Boyette. *"Let It Burn!": The Philadelphia Tragedy* (Contemporary Books, 1989).

Church Society for College Work. "Issues at Notre Dame: A Running Account of Events and Issues at Notre Dame, August 30–September 5, 1969, Special General Convention II" (1969).

Cluster, Dick, ed. *They Should Have Served That Cup of Coffee: 7 Radicals Remember the 60's* (South End Press, 1979).

DuBois, W. E. B. *The Philadelphia Negro: A Social Study* (1899; Schocken, 1967).

The Episcopalian (the newspaper of the Episcopal Church, U.S.A.).

FBI files on Fr. Paul Washington, 1966–68 (made available through the Freedom of Information Act.)

Hiatt, Suzanne R. "How We Brought the Good News from Graymoor to Minneapolis: An Episcopal Paradigm." *Journal of Ecumenical Studies* 20 (Fall 1983): 4.

Marable, Manning. *Race, Reform, and Rebellion: The Second Reconstruction in Black America, 1945–1982* (University Press of Mississippi, 1984).

Philadelphia Evening Bulletin, 1955–82. Urban Archives, Paley Library, Temple University, Philadelphia.

Philadelphia Inquirer, 1955–93. Urban Archives, Paley Library, Temple University, Philadelphia.

Philadelphia Tribune, 1955–93.

Report of the Philadelphia Special Investigation Commission (MOVE Commission), March, 1986.

Weigley, Russell F., ed. *Philadelphia: A 300-Year History* (Norton, 1982).

The Witness (monthly magazine published by the Episcopal Church Publishing Company).

Introduction

1. Neal R. Peirce and Jerry Hagstrom, *The Book of America: Inside 50 States* (Norton, 1983), p. 110.
2. Du Bois, *Philadelphia Negro*, p. 397.
3. W. E. Burghardt Du Bois, *The Souls of Black Folk* (1903; Fawcett, 1961), p. 17.
4. DuBois, *The Souls*, p. 17.
5. From an interview with Thomas Paine Cronin by David Gracie, 1992.
6. Jane Power, "How the Eighties Went Out in Jerusalem," in *Bringing the Lessons Home* (Palestine Aid Society of America, 1990), p. 29.

Chapter 4

1. Robert L. DeWitt, "1964–1974: Decade of Crises in a Stormy See," *The Witness* (July, 1984): 6.

Chapter 8

1. The quotations from J. Edgar Hoover and Harold Cruse are from Marable, *Race, Reform and Rebellion*. We rely on Marable for information about the first Black Power Conference in Newark and about preparations for the conference in Philadelphia.
2. In Marable, *Race, Reform and Rebellion*, p. 110.
3. James H. Cone, *Martin & Malcolm in America* (Orbis, 1991), p. 110.

Chapter 9

1. Booty, *Episcopal Church in Crisis*, p. 61.
2. DeWitt, "Decade of Crisis," p. 7.
3. Booty, pp. 61–62.

Chapter 10

1. "A Way to Fight Back: The Black Panther Party—An Interview with Reggie Schell," in Cluster, ed., *They Should Have Served*, pp. 47, 63.

2. Martin Luther King, Jr., *Why We Can't Wait* (Harper and Row, 1963).
3. "Reggie Schell," in Cluster, ed., p. 65.
4. Ibid., p. 61.

Chapter 11

1. From an interview with Barbara Harris by David McI. Gracie, 1991.

Chapter 14

1. Barbara C. Harris, "Pentecost Revisited," *The Witness*, special issue; 10th Anniversary of Episcopal Women Priests, 1984, pp. 10–12.

Chapter 15

1. Assefa and Wahrhaftig, *The MOVE Crisis*, p. 12. This book is the source of some of the other direct quotes and background information in this chapter.
2. Ibid., p. 143.
3. Lamont Steptoe, "Osage," in *American Morning/Mourning* (Whirlwind Press, 1990).

Chapter 17

1. For more information about the murals, see "The People's Art: Black Murals, 1967–1978," an illustrated booklet from The African American Historical and Cultural Museum, Philadelphia, 1986; also, Penny Balkin Bach, *Public Art in Philadelphia* (Temple University Press, 1992), p. 240.
2. Jeanie Wylie-Kellermann, "Learning self-discipline: an interview with Barbara Harris," *The Witness*, April, 1992, pp. 14–15.

Chapter 18

1. Charles Bowser, *Let the Bunker Burn* (Camino Books, 1989), p. 91.

Index